Medicine, Health and Risk

Sociology of Health and Illness Monograph Series

Edited by Jonathan Gabe
Department of Social Policy and Social Sciences
Royal Holloway
University of London

Current and forthcoming titles:

Medicine, Health and Risk
Edited by Jonathan Gabe

Health and the Sociology of Emotion
Edited by Veronica James and Jonathan Gabe

The Sociology of Medical Science
Edited by Mary Ann Elfton

Medicine, Health and Risk

Sociological Approaches

Edited by Jonathan Gabe

Blackwell Publishers/Editorial Board

Copyright © Blackwell Publishers Ltd/Editorial Board 1995

ISBN 0–631–19484–3

First published in 1995

Blackwell Publishers Ltd
108 Cowley Road, Oxford OX4 1JF, UK
and
238 Main Street,
Cambridge, MA 02142, USA

British Library Cataloguing in Publication Data

A CIP catalogue record for this book is available from the British Library

Library of Congress Cataloging-in-Publication Data

Medicine, Health and Risk: Sociological Approaches /
edited by Jonathan Gabe
(Sociology of Health & Illness monograph series; 1)
p. cm.—
Includes bibliographical references and index.
ISBN 0–631–19484–3
1. Health risk assessment—Great Britain.
2. Medical Policy—Great Britain.
I. Gabe, Jonathan. II. Series. RA427.3.M43   1995
306.4′61′0941—dc20

Printed in Great Britain by Page Bros, Norwich, Norfolk.
This book is printed on acid-free paper.

Editorial Note

The Editorial Board of *Sociology of Health and Illness*, in association with Blackwell, has decided to publish a monograph alongside the journal with the aim of identifying and contributing to new areas of debate and research in the sub-discipline. *Medicine, Health and Risk* has been selected as the first in the series on the basis that the sociology of risk has only recently started to influence work in the area of health, illness and medicine and has considerable potential. Future volumes will consider *Health and the Sociology of Emotions* and *The Sociology of Medical Science*. Subsequent topics have yet to be decided and colleagues with ideas for further volumes in the series are invited to contact the series editor, Jonathan Gabe.

A number of people have helped with the present volume and the editor is indebted to them. The co-editors of the journal, especially Mike Bury, have been extremely supportive and helped to keep the project 'on the road'. All the chapters were read and commented on by anonymous referees and their observations and suggestions have helped the contributors enormously. Judy Clayton has helped with the copy editing and Liz Gabe with the proof reading, and their efforts are much appreciated. Finally, the staff at Blackwell must be thanked for helping to keep things moving along without too many hiccups.

Jonathan Gabe
Royal Holloway, University of London

Contents

Health, medicine and risk: the need for a sociological approach

Jonathan Gabe

In May 1994 Britain was gripped by a panic about a deadly, quick spreading gangrene known as necrotising fasciitis. The media, particularly the tabloid press, were full of horror stories about 'the killer bug', linked with the streptococcus group A bacterium, with new victims being identified with each day that passed. Of the 15 cases that had come to light by the end of the month 11 had died. While one expert, a professor of bacteriology, claimed that he had evidence that the bacterium was becoming more virulent, thereby heightening public concern, another, the Director of the Public Health Laboratory Service, which monitors diseases and provides advice about the control of infection, tried to assuage this concern by stating that reported cases were within expected annual figures. The Service's response was also echoed by the Government which refused to make the infection a notifiable illness, requiring doctors to report it, as it felt that no new information would be gained.

Eventually the tabloid press lost interest in the story and broadsheet leader writers were left to reflect on the significance of this latest health scare and why the nation's psyche had been gripped by it. One response was that it highlighted a 'mixed-up perception of risk' in modern society, with people in reality experiencing far greater risk from driving at speed on a motorway, smoking and lack of exercise than from diseases such as necrotising fasciitis (*Guardian* 1994). Another was that public concern reflected a realisation that science and technology were as baffled and helpless in the face of this disease as ordinary people (*Observer* 1994).

This episode encapsulates nicely the way in which 'risk' is now a major issue for lay people and experts, journalists and government. The risk of 'rogue' micro organisms is, of course, only one of a number of threats to health. The risks to personal health from poverty and an unhealthy life style are also important, and are paralleled by public risks from industrial, agricultural and technological processes.

The risk industry

The term risk is not new of course. It is derived from the French word risque, and first appeared in its anglicised form in England in the early

2   Jonathan Gabe

nineteenth century (Moore 1983). Originally employed in a neutral
fashion as a wager made by individuals after taking account of the probability of losses and gains (Dake 1992), it has come to refer in more recent times
only to negative outcomes (Douglas 1990, cf. Carter, this volume); to the
likelihood of some adverse effect of a hazard (Short 1984).

Over the last three decades a veritable industry has developed concerned with risk and, in particular, risk assessment, drawing primarily on
disciplines such as engineering, toxicology, biostatistics and actuarial science, and institutionalised in the *Society for Risk Analysis* and the journal
Risk Analysis (Golding 1992, Hayes 1992). Perceiving risk assessment to
be essentially a technical matter to be resolved by developing more accurate scientific information, physical and life scientists and government
agencies have sought to develop 'rational' means to make decisions about
health risks. Emphasis has thus been placed on developing quantitative
measures which can facilitate comparing the risks of different choices,
calculating their costs and benefits (often in monetary terms) and communicating these to the public and to government (Nelkin 1989). The aim of
such exercises is to find out what the risks really are on the assumption
that all risks are discoverable and measurable and can be controlled with
the requisite skill and expertise (Thompson 1989). Such optimism is in
marked contrast to earlier times when attitudes towards risk were usually
fatalistic, and danger and uncertainty were managed primarily through
prayer, sacrifices and other rituals (Herzlich and Pierret 1987).

The current 'rational' approach to risk has become particularly popular
with industrial managers and developers who have recognised the need to
employ risk analysts to assess (and legitimise) the environmental risks of
new technologies, in the face of legislation and mounting public concern
about industrial hazards following a series of disasters. Accidents such as
that of Seveso in Italy, Three Mile Island in the United States and
Chernobyl in the Ukraine have illustrated the limitations of recent technological developments and the enormous health costs when things go
wrong (Brown 1989). Faced with such public concern risk communication
strategies have been developed, aimed at bridging the gap between public
and expert perceptions of acceptable risks (Golding 1992). Despite such
developments lay opposition to technologies such as waste incinerators
and nuclear waste repositories grow ever more vocal, especially in the
USA (Cvetkovich and Earle 1992) which is now faced by what has been
called 'technological gridlock' (Irwin 1995).

Assessing risk has also become a major issue in the health field. In
curative medicine much effort is now expended calculating the risk of
various medical procedures and technologies and techniques have been
developed to reduce the risk of iatrogenic diseases. Risk management,
monitoring devices and systematic surveillance of perioperative complications have all been introduced in health care systems in industrialised

countries in an attempt to reduce risks and control costs (Skolbekken 1995). This has been particularly the case in insurance based systems where the increase in premiums is of major concern (Brown 1979).

Assessing risk has also become a key element of public health as the account of 'the killer bug' panic described above illustrates. Epidemiologists calculate the 'relative risk' or numerical odds of a population developing an illness when exposed to a 'risk factor', compared with a similar population which has not suffered such exposure (Frankenberg 1994). It is on the basis of such risk assessments that governments have conducted health education campaigns to warn the public about the dangers of certain activities, presuming that 'risky behaviour' will be reduced as a result of the information transmitted.

According to Lupton (1993) public health discourse about risk can be divided into two kinds. The first concentrates on the environmental level and considers the risks to particular populations from nuclear waste, pollution and other hazards. The emphasis here is thus on the by-products of economic and social activity and the need for health promotion policies to maintain the purity of the natural environment (Armstrong 1993). While dangers are everywhere, they are seen as external to and outside the control of individuals. An environmentally friendly, ecological response based on legislative action is therefore advocated as the main way of reducing risk and achieving a healthy environment (Beattie 1991).

The second form of discourse, by comparison, constructs risk as the consequence of the 'lifestyle' choices made by individuals, and emphasises the need for self control. To this end health persuasion strategies are designed and transmitted through convenient media to warn people about health risks (Beattie 1991), on the assumption that knowledge about the dangers of certain lifestyle activities will result in their avoidance (Lupton 1994).

This second public health approach is clearly illustrated in the AIDS field where gay men have been identified as having a higher risk of getting AIDS compared with heterosexual men because of gay 'life style' practices such as anal intercourse and multiple sexual partners. In this case risk has been calculated on the questionable assumption that all gay men ascribe to a single set of cultural practices and values (Glick Schiller et al 1994). These assumptions have, in turn, underpinned government health education materials about AIDS, encouraging the 'general population' to perceive HIV infection as a problem which concerns gay men rather than heterosexual men and women (Glick Schiller et al 1994).

Psychological risk analysis

While engineers, epidemiologists and actuarial scientists have developed assessments of risk based on measures of mortality and morbidity, psychologists have attempted to incorporate public perceptions of risk in risk analysis. Their involvement was stimulated by the realisation that lay people perceived the riskiness of technology differently from expert risk analysts (Brown 1989).

Although focusing on perceptions of risk rather than impersonal factors, the approach adopted by psychologists has much in common with technical risk assessment (Douglas 1990). In particular, the aim is to be as objective as possible and use a comparable quantitative methodology.

Early work in the late 1960s and early 1970s by Starr (1969), for example, adopted a behaviourist approach in order to establish objectively acceptable levels of risk which might facilitate decision making about hazardous technologies. Defining acceptable risk on the basis of existing social behaviour, he claimed that such behaviour revealed people's preferences and trade-offs between the risks and benefits of a hazard. To illustrate his approach he focused on how voluntary/involuntary exposure to hazards influenced people's perception of risk. He claimed to show through an analysis of accident data that 'voluntary' risks such as smoking or car driving were more acceptable than risks imposed on people such as air quality standards. Subsequent research however questioned the application of this voluntary/involuntary dimension, independent of particular social contexts (Otaway and Cohen 1975). It also challenged the assumption that failure to protest about the level of a particular risk necessarily implies its acceptance (ibid).

In the late 1970s and 1980s behaviourism was displaced by cognitive psychology as the dominant research paradigm on risk perception. The leaders of this latter approach, Slovic, Fischoff and colleagues in Oregon, have employed questionnaires and psychometric scaling techniques in order to identify the criteria lay people use to access the amount of risk from certain dangers, compared with experts' judgements. Their research showed that lay people and experts differed in their risk assessments. Lay people reported global catastrophes such as nuclear accidents as particularly risky because of the perceived horror of the potential results if such an event occurred (Slovic and Fischoff 1980). For them this fear or 'dread factor', along with other risk attributes such as whether the risk was involuntary, uncertain or unfamiliar, were the most difficult to accept. In contrast, experts' perceptions of risk were not closely related to any of these risk factors, and were instead highly correlated with estimates of annual mortality (Slovic 1992).

Another important finding from this work is that people tend to view current risk levels as unacceptably high for non medical chemicals and radioactive materials but as acceptable for many prescribed medicines. For instance recent survey research in Canada and Sweden suggests that people in these countries see nuclear power, pesticides, cigarettes and food additives as being of very low benefit and high risk whereas diagnostic X-rays, prescription drugs, antibiotics, vaccines and vitamins are seen as being of high benefit and low risk (Slovic *et al* 1989, Slovic 1992). The favourable perception of prescribed medicines was attributed to the recognition of direct benefits and trust in the managers of technology, in this case the medical and pharmaceutical professions (Slovic 1992).

This cognitive psychological approach has been extremely influential and has helped to clarify the sorts of properties which people include in their perceptions and reactions to risky activities. However it has been criticised, like behaviourism before it, for assuming that risks have an independent objective existence, separate from the more complex social, cultural and institutional contexts in which people experience them (Nelkin 1989, Turner and Wynne 1992). While those adopting this perspective have considered aggregate attitudes to particular risks, the insights gained have been limited by the assumption that such attitudes depend mainly on the characteristics of the risk itself rather than on individuals' membership of particular social groups or involvement in particular cultural milieu (Nelkin 1985).

However, some social psychological approaches have been developed which concentrate on the individual as the source of behaviour rather than on particular risk attributes and consider the ways in which these individuals' perceptions of risky activities are related to broader beliefs and value systems (Turner and Wynne 1992). From this standpoint risk perception can not be understood without giving due consideration both to these beliefs and values and the extent to which individuals differ in their allegiance to them.

Within the health field one example of this approach is the Health Beliefs Model, first developed in the 1960s, which examines factors which might predict health behaviour. Readiness to embark on risky behaviour is seen as being based on one's perceived susceptibility to a health threat and upon the perceived seriousness of that threat (Scambler and Scambler 1984, Kronenfeld 1988). In addition, the model recognises that certain triggers are necessary for a course of action to be embarked upon. External events are seen as cues which are perceived and appraised by the individual in an interactive way prior to deciding upon a course of risk behaviour or risk avoidance (Ogden 1995).

Like other psychological approaches the model has been criticised for treating individuals as free agents in terms of their response to risk and ignoring social factors which constrain choice (Denscombe 1993). Despite this and other limitations it still remains an important stimulus for psychological research on risk perception and behaviour.

Cultural theories of risk

While psychologists, like engineers, actuarial scientists and epidemiologists, have generally treated risk as an objective phenomena to be measured and explained, anthropologists and sociologists have argued that risk can best be understood as a social construct.

No one has argued this more cogently than the anthropologist Mary Douglas. Over the last three decades she has produced a series of influential books (Douglas 1966, 1970, 1986, 1992, Douglas and Wildavsky 1982) in which the ontological status of risk as an objective measure has been questioned and redefined as socially constructed within particular historical and cultural contexts. Her approach developed from her work on ritual in tribal societies in which she focused on cultural 'pollution', including uncleanliness, food taboos and risky behaviour (Douglas 1966). She argued that many classes of risk avoidance in tribal societies could be explained in terms of their role in creating order out of contradictory experiences and moral confusion. Beliefs about defilement, animal taboos and forbidden food helped to maintain a sense of order (Krimsky 1992).

The importance of Douglas's work lies in the bridge it provides between classical anthropology and the cultures of late modern societies. On the basis of her earlier work she, and those who have been influenced by her, have addressed the key question of why different cultures have selected particular risks for attention and in turn proscribed certain practices as part of their belief system (Krimsky 1992)? To this extent her approach shares with that of psychology the assumption that people attempt to create cognitive consistency between their experiences in different contexts (Turner and Wynne 1992).

Douglas first addressed this question in detail in relation to contemporary society in the early 1980s, when she focused on the environmental controversies then gripping the United States (Douglas and Wildavsky 1982). For her what was of interest was that groups of people identified different risk attributes and even different types of risk as a result of their particular form of social organisation and the nature of their interaction in the wider political culture.

This approach illustrates Douglas' concern with groups and institutions rather than individuals (Bellaby 1990), and with the way in which such collectivities' response to risk is functional for the maintenance of a chosen form of social organisation. The argument was formalised in an analytic scheme which has come to be known as the grid/group analysis, a typology of social structures and perceptions of risk first systematised a decade earlier in *Natural Symbols* (Douglas 1970). According to Douglas and Wildavsky:

> [Grid/group analysis] is a way of checking characteristics of social organisation with features of the beliefs and values of the people who are keeping the form of organisation alive. *Group* means the outside boundary that people have erected between themselves and the outside world. *Grid* means all the other social distinctions and delegations of

authority that they use to limit how people behave to one another (1982:138).

By linking grid and group four distinct world views or 'cultural biases' were identified which justified different ways of behaving towards a hazard. Douglas and Wildavsky named these hierarchist (high grid/high group), egalitarian (low grid/high group), fatalist (high grid/low group) and individualist (low grid/low group). In practice this meant that hierarchists, for example, were said to be well integrated (group axis) and accepting of externally imposed expert risk assessments (grid axis) whereas egalitarians, whilst also being well integrated, challenged the dictum that 'experts know best' on the grounds that these experts' calculations threatened their group's way of life (grid axis).

As the Royal Society Study Group (1992:112) has pointed out, the implications of this approach for risk assessment and perception are that 'people select certain risks for attention to defend their preferred life styles and as a forensic resource to place blame on other groups'. When people feel that they are 'at risk' they focus on external sources such as stereotyped minorities and blame them, rather than concentrate on the dangers afforded to their community by their own members.

Although highly influential at a theoretical level there have been few attempts to apply Douglas' cultural approach empirically (Rayner 1992). In the field of health and medicine the two best known examples are Rayner's (1986) study of occupational differences in response to radiation hazards in an American hospital, and Bellaby's (1990) research on perceived health risks amongst managers and workers in the pottery industry, and amongst motorcyclists and car drivers. The latter author is also one of the few to evaluate Douglas's approach empirically (although see Bloor, this volume). In Bellaby's opinion the data indicate the viability of the grid/group approach and also its limitations. In particular it is said to be too static a model and fails to explain how organisations and individuals may change their risk perceptions over time. Others have criticised the approach for oversimplyfing more complex shades of social difference (Royal Society 1992) and for encouraging the exclusion of risks which are inconsistent with the characteristics of each social type (Turner and Wynne 1992). Even so the approach does offer the opportunity to explore how conflicts over risk can be understood in terms of plural social constructions of meaning which are culturally framed.

Social theories of risk

Until relatively recently sociologists have paid little attention to risk analysis (Kronenfeld and Glick 1991). Those that have, like anthropologists, have taken as their starting point that risks are socially constructed or framed and collectively perceived. Where they have differed has been in their concern with material constraints and social interests as well as cultural factors in shaping risk perceptions and their management. Much of this work has been theoretical in orientation but there has recently been an increasing interest in undertaking empirical research in this area, especially amongst medical sociologists.

Social analyses of risk as they relate to health can be divided into those micro level studies which concentrate primarily on what C. Wright Mills (1959) famously called 'personal troubles of milieu' (concerning the individual's self and those limited areas of social life of which she or he is directly or personally aware) and more macro level work concerned with 'public issues of social structure'. The latter refers to things which transcend the individual's local environment and the range of his or her inner life and are seen by the public as threatening some cherished value. I shall briefly consider each of these approaches in turn.

Micro level studies in the health field have been concerned with the meanings of risk and the ways in which these are used to achieve practical results. Those taking this interpretive approach have tended to concentrate on two broad areas: perceptions of risk and risk behaviour; and the relationship between lay and expert knowledge of risk. In the former area attention has focused on how people interpret risk rationally and instrumentally within the circumstances and constraints which impinge on their daily lives. For example, Becker and Nachtigall (1994) have examined how the quest for pregnancy affects the construction of risk by couples going through infertility treatment. They show how such perceptions are shaped by biography (the women's deep rooted desire to have children) and bodily knowledge, their ongoing experience as patients in the health care system and by cultural values about fertility (conceptive technology mobilises and reinforces faith in 'persistence' as a way of achieving ones goal).

The role of contextual factors in risk perception also feature in Parsons and Atkinson's (1992, 1993) work on lay construction of genetic risk. They show how women live with the risk of Duchenne Muscular Dystrophy and how awareness of being 'at risk', is related to critical junctures in the life course, such as the beginning of courtship or being in a stable relationship and wanting to have children. Perceptions of risk were also shown to influence whether the women were risk takers or risk refusers, although other biographical factors such as prior reproductive desire and the structuring of genetic information in personal stocks of knowledge were also found to be important.

The second and related area of interest for micro sociology has been the relationship between lay and expert perceptions of risk. One example of this in the health field is the work of Davison et al. (1991). In their study of lay beliefs about the risk of coronary heart disease (CHD) in

South Wales they found evidence that both mirrored and diverged from expert opinion. While those interviewed agreed with the health promotion experts that they should accept some responsibility for their health and could minimise the risks of CHD by reducing smoking and altering their diet, they also drew on other ideas which differed from and to some extent conflicted with official thinking. In particular, they referred to the social circumstances surrounding the occurrence of CHD and drew on more fatalistic ideas when either personalistic or social types of explanation seemed inadequate. Thus they demonstrated lay people's willingness to assess rationally official information on the risk of CHD and apply it to their lived experience on an ongoing basis.

A similar concern with comparing lay and professional views has been demonstrated by Roberts et al (1992, 1993) in their study of the risks of childhood accidents in Glasgow, Scotland. They too found some common ground between the two groups – in this case parents on a local housing estate and professionals with some occupational responsibility for the estate – but also considerable differences. For instance, while both groups saw parents as responsible for the safety of their children, the parents had considerably more knowledge of local hazards and risks, were much more likely to identify specific administrative bodies as responsible for these hazards (rather than talk in terms of generalised social responsibility), and advocated a wide range of structural improvements and a greater sharing of local resources (instead of relying on education) in order to prevent accidents. The Glasgow respondents however differed from those in South Wales in that they were not fatalistic or complacent and stated that they routinely took measures to minimise the risk of accidents.

In addition to this interpretive research on group risk perceptions and behaviour there has been some more macro level work on the role of social institutions and structures in the framing of risk. As noted earlier in the example of necrotising fasciitis, the mass media play an important role in public perception of risk. They serve as filters through which both lay people and experts – both policy officials and health professionals – receive news and interpret events (Nelkin 1989). Through the selection and coverage of particular health stories they set the agenda of public discourse and affect the priorities which guide individual's risk behaviour.

Surprisingly given the importance of the media in risk communication (Nelkin 1989), there have been relatively few attempts by sociologists to analyse its role in the perception of health risks. With the exception of a few studies concerned with press coverage of occupational health issues (Raymond 1985) and road safety (Stallings 1990), most of this small body of work has been concentrated on the content and reception of AIDS coverage. For example, Nelkin (1991) has discussed what shapes the content of press and popular magazine coverage of AIDS in the US and the way such coverage is received. She shows how the constraints of news-work, and the need to rely on external sources to explain complex techni-cal information about which there was some uncertainty, shaped coverage of AIDS. In addition, she suggests these media messages have been influ-ential in making AIDS visible to lay people and turning it into a public issue which required a regulatory response, if only to protect the agencies' public image. In Britain similar work on the production, content and reception of AIDS messages has been undertaken by the Glasgow University Media Group (Miller and Williams 1993, Beharrell 1993, Kitzinger 1993).

One of the external sources of information journalists turn to about particular risks are social movements. These campaigning groups make claims about the risk status of what they perceive to be environmental, technological or medical developments, and in the process help construct such dangers as social problems worthy of public attention (Short 1984).

Again there has been relatively little research on the role of social movements in defining health and medical risks as public issues. One exception is Elston's (1994) study of the anti-vivisectionist movement in the UK. She shows how the contemporary animal rights movement has deployed arguments about the risks and limitations of modern medicine from within academic social science and medicine to provide an 'external' critique of the utility of medicine.

In addition, there have been a limited number of studies of community based protest movements and their attempts to turn local environmental health hazards into a public issue. For example, Williams and Popay (1994) have documented how local residents in Camelford, North Cornwall, chal-lenged two government-backed reports by an expert group on the health effects of the poisoning of their water supply. The case was taken to show how 'popular epidemiology' – the synthesis of political activism and lay knowledge – was used to challenge scientific criteria for assessing risk and experts' claims to technical knowledge. Other studies with a similar focus include Brown's (1992) ground breaking work on the identification of and response to a leukaemia cluster amongst children by residents in Woburn, Massachusetts and Phillimore and Moffatt's (1994) research in Teeside and Tyneside on the role of local knowledge in explaining the link between industrial air pollution and the health of people living nearby.

The focus of these studies on the relationship between lay and expert knowledge in turn reflect a more broad based theoretical concern amongst social theorists about the declining trust in expert authority in late modern societies. According to Giddens (1990) we are living in a period in which the judgements of experts are constantly open to scrutiny or 'chronically contested', and are either accepted or rejected by lay peo-ple on the basis of pragmatic calculations about the risks involved. In such circumstances even the most cherished beliefs underpinning expert systems are open to revision and regularly altered, and the dominant source of authoritative interpretation is undermined (Giddens 1991).

The depth of ambivalence or alienation which people feel towards experts and risk management institutions in turn relates to a recognition that we now live in a 'risk society' (Beck 1992a, 1992b); that is, one that is increasingly vulnerable to major socio-technical dislocation and growing interdependency. Social and economic processes have created global nuclear, chemical, genetic and ecological hazards for which there is no satisfactory aftercare. These structural features reinforce the need for trust in expert authority at the very time that increasing reflexivity and a growing recognition in the indeterminate status of knowledge about risk work to undermine it. In a 'destabilised' and 'runaway' world the landmarks of a more certain era are displaced by the 'politics of anxiety' (Turner 1991).

Faced with such anxiety the role of the medical sociologist is perhaps to attempt to help further develop an alternative to the existing technical approach to risk assessment by revealing the socially constructed or framed nature of health risks and the various plural rationalities involved (Thompson 1989). The following questions may provide the focus for such work:

- what role do social, cultural and institutional processes play in the perception of health risks?
- how are the processes of defining health risks related to cultural attributes of blame and responsibility?
- to what extent do calculations about the probability of health risks influence decisions and actions of specific social groups?
- how do expert and lay frames of reference with regard to particular risks differ?
- how are public health risks constructed and legitimated by scientists, the mass media, government agencies and social movements?
- what are the constraints and opportunities for social movements to challenge expert assessments of public health risks?
- to what extent is trust in experts' assessment of risk being undermined in late modern societies and with what consequences?
- how do expert discourses on health risks throw light on key elements of social order and cultural change?

These are the questions which variously underpin the chapters of the contributors to this monograph. The book is divided into four sections. The first two focus on more micro concerns about the perceptions of health risks and their management, and the risk acceptability of medical interventions. In the latter two sections emphasis is on macro level issues concerning social movements, public health risks and the policy process, and the social construction of health risks and their regulation.

In the first chapter Michael Bloor presents an overview of three contrasting approaches to theorising risk perception and risk management; psycho-social models exemplified by the Health Beliefs Model, a 'situated rationality' approach and the 'Culture of risk' approach, associated with the name of Mary Douglas. Possible deficiencies in these approaches are identified with reference to data from an ethnographic study of HIV-related risk behaviour of male prostitutes. An alternative conceptualisation is identified with heuristic merits, based on Alfred Schutz's phenomenology.

The next chapter, by Anne Grinyer, addresses the risk from occupational injury, and in particular from HIV infection, as it is constructed by management and perceived by the workforce. Based on fieldwork amongst policy makers and workers in two health authorities, the author shows that policy makers and management frequently have little understanding of the prevailing conditions under which many health service workers carry out their jobs. As a result safety regulations are based on an ideal model which appears to bear scant resemblance to the reality of working life in a busy hospital.

In the third chapter Karen Lane considers how the medical model of the body legitimates the use of a limited set of criteria to assess risk in childbirth. By assigning risk to the individual rather than to structural and social causes it is argued that the medical profession effectively acts as a force for social control. It also plays an important role in the construction of moral communities, conceals the iatrogenic causes of intervention and morbidity and constricts debates about childbirth to the risk of mortality. However, Beck's (1992a) thesis that medical science has remained impenetrable to external critique is not sustained in relation to consumer criticism of medicalised birth.

The next chapter, by Anne Rogers and David Pilgrim, considers the risk acceptability of mass childhood immunisation (MCI). MCI enjoys the support of government health agencies internationally. However, non-compliant parents sometimes challenge and undermine the rationale and practice of the policy. The authors examine the perspectives of four groups (health promoters, medical scientists, primary care workers and dissenting parents) about the benefits and risks of immunisation and place their views in a social context. The understandings of different groups about the nature of risk of infection are then contrasted, and a shifting moral discourse about the threat of contagion is outlined.

In the fifth chapter Phil Brown examines lay-professional perspectives on environmental health hazards. He argues that hazard detection and solution seeking activities in Woburn, Massachusetts, and other communities are examples of *popular epidemiology*: the process by which lay persons gather data and marshal the knowledge and resources of experts in order to understand the epidemiology of disease, treat existing and prevent future disease and remove the responsible environmental contaminants. Based on different health needs, goals and methods, lay people and professionals have conflicting perspectives on how to investigate and interpret environmental and health data. Brown argues that citizens facing actual and potential hazards frequently view many professionals as allied with corporate polluters and with government secrecy and information control. This has generated an extensive social movement in the United States, composed of largely working class and lower middle class people, extensively made up of and led by women, and more recently involving large numbers of minority populations.

Chapter Six, by Gareth Williams, Jennie Popay and Paul Bissell examines the way in which public health risks are perceived and responded to by lay people, and the implications of this for health policy. In particular, it looks at the relationship between public health risks and social movements in the context of changing relationships between experts and the public. Much of the literature on both social movements and risk perception emphasises the importance of cultural values and perceptions underlying the mobilisation of communities against health hazards. However, by way of a small-scale study of people's perceptions of health risks in an inner city area of Salford, England, the authors argue that even where the awareness of risks and knowledge about their causes is highly developed, the weight of structural and material factors can prevent these lay perspectives entering the public sphere in debate and action.

The next chapter, by Simon Carter, analyses the technological culture of risk assessment. He argues that while there is a large 'scientific' literature on the application of the concept 'risk' to investigations of health, 'lifestyle' and medical treatments, along with a social literature on the ways in which danger and uncertainty are culturally negotiated, there have been few attempts to examine critically the place that scientific ideas about risk increasingly hold in late modern culture. As a contribution to this broader project of rethinking the way that risk has become a defining mentality in late modernity this chapter attempts a preliminary examination of the sociology of scientific risk knowledge. Of particular interest is the way in which expert knowledge about public health risks can serve as a form of social control and boundary production that constructs particular 'others' as dangerous. However, Carter argues that this process does not operate as a simple exclusion of the dangerous 'other' but more as a process of 'colonisation'. As a result the risky 'other' is employed to achieve 'expert' control of transgressions or connections between those sites defined as dangerous and those defined as safe.

In the concluding chapter Sue Scott and Richard Freeman set out to show that contemporary discourses of illness prevention, rather than being a solution to external and specific problems of risk, are themselves both a consequence of, and a problem for, late modernity. Using HIV and AIDS as an example the authors begin by considering public policy relating to this disease. They set this policy against the wider social and historical background of the production and governance of risk, delineating liberal and authoritarian patterns of response. They go on to explore the liberal discourse of prevention, pointing to tensions inherent both in its expression in public policy and in its administration by 'expert systems'. These internal contradictions result in the increased individualisation of risk management, much of which, in the context of HIV and AIDS, is left to be negotiated in the sphere of the intimate. Recent attempts to theorise risk are then evaluated in relation to the negotiation of safer sex.

These contributions, which cover the gamut from micro processes to macro issues of social order and social change, hopefully illustrate the ways in which medical sociologists can make an important contribution to the debate about the private risks which people face and the ways in which public dangers are managed at the end of the twentieth century. The issues raised are too important to be left to the 'risk industry' alone.

Acknowlegements

I should like to thank Mike Bury for his comments on an earlier draft of this chapter.

References

Armstrong, D. (1993) Public health spaces and the fabrication of identity, *Sociology*, 27, 393–410.

Beattie, A. (1991) Knowledge and control in health promotion: a test case for social policy and social theory. In Gabe, J., Calnan, M. and Bury, M. (eds) *The Sociology of the Health Service*. London: Routledge.

Beck, U (1992a) *Risk Society: Towards a New Modernity*. London: Sage.

Beck, U. (1992b) From industrial society to the risk society: questions of survival, social structure and ecological enlightenment, *Theory, Culture and Society*, 9, 97–123.

Becker, G. and Nachtigall, R. D. (1994) 'Born to be a mother': the cultural construction of risk in infertility treatment in the US, *Social Science and Medicine*, 39, 507–18.

Beharrell, P. (1993) AIDS and the British press. In Eldridge, J. (ed) *Getting the Message*. London: Routledge.

Bellaby, P. (1990) To risk or not to risk? Uses and limitations of Mary Douglas on risk acceptability for understanding health and safety at work and road accidents, *The Sociological Review*, 38, 465–83.

Brown, B. L. (1979) *Risk Management for Hospitals: A Practical Approach*. Rockville: Aspen Systems Corporation.

Health, medicine and risk: the need for a sociological approach 15

Brown, J. (1989) Introduction: approaches, tools and perceptions. In Brown, J. (ed) *Environmental Threats: Perception, Analysis and Management*. London: Belhaven Press.

Brown, P. (1992) Popular epidemiology and toxic waste contamination: lay and professional ways of knowing, *Journal of Health and Social Behaviour*, 33, 267–81.

Cvetkovich, G. and Earle, T. C. (1992) Environmental hazards and the public, *Journal of Social Issues*, 48, 1–20.

Dake, K. (1992) Myths of nature: culture and the social construction of risk, *Journal of Social Issues*, 48, 21–37.

Davison, C., Davey Smith, G. and Frankel, S. (1991) Lay epidemiology and the prevention paradox, *Sociology of Health and Illness*, 13, 1–19.

Denscombe, M. (1993) Personal health and the social psychology of risk taking, *Health Education Research*, 8, 505–17.

Douglas, M. (1966) *Purity and Danger: An Analysis of Concepts of Pollution and Taboo*. London: Routledge and Kegan Paul.

Douglas, M. (1970) *Natural Symbols. Explorations in Cosmology*. Harmondsworth: Penguin.

Douglas, M. (1986) *Risk Acceptability According to the Social Sciences*. London: Routledge and Kegan Paul.

Douglas, M. (1990) Risk as a forensic resource, *Daedalus*, 119, 1–16.

Douglas, M. (1992) *Risk and Blame: Essays in Cultural Theory*. London: Routledge.

Douglas, M. and Wildavsky, A. (1982) *Risk and Culture: An Essay on the Selection of Technological and Environmental Dangers*. Berkeley: University of California Press.

Elston, M.A. (1994) The anti-vivisectionist movement and the science of medicine. In Gabe, J., Kelleher, D. and Williams, G. (eds) *Challenging Medicine*. London: Routledge.

Frankenberg, R. (1994) The impact of HIV/AIDS on concepts relating to risk and culture within British community epidemiology: candidates or targets for prevention? *Social Science and Medicine*, 38, 1325–35.

Giddens, A. (1990) *The Consequences of Modernity*. Cambridge: Polity Press.

Giddens, A. (1991) *Modernity and Self Identity*. Cambridge: Polity Press.

Glick Schiller, N., Crystal, S. and Lewellen, D. (1994) Risky business: the cultural construction of AIDS risk groups, *Social Science and Medicine*, 38, 1337–46.

Golding, D. (1992) A social and programmatic history of risk research. In Krimsky, S. and Golding, D. (eds) *Social Theories of Risk*. Westport, Connecticut: Praeger.

The Guardian (1994) A bug and a context. Editorial, 25 May.

Hayes, M. V. (1992) On the epistemology of risk: language, logic and social science, *Social Science and Medicine*, 35, 401–7.

Herzlich, C. and Pierret, J. (1987) *Illness and Self in Society*. Baltimore: John Hopkins University Press.

Irwin, A. (1995) Reasons to be fearful, *The Times Higher*, 24 March, 17–18.

Kitzinger, J. (1993) Understanding AIDS: researching audience perceptions of Acquired Immune Deficiency Syndrome. In Eldridge, J. (ed) *Getting the Message*. London: Routledge.

16   Jonathan Gabe

Krimsky, S. (1992) The role of theory in risk studies. In Krimsky, S. and Golding, D. (eds) *Social Theories of Risk*. Westport, Connecticut: Praeger.

Kronenfeld, J.J. (1988) Models of preventive health behaviour change and roles for sociologists, *Research in the Sociology of Health Care*, 7, 303–28.

Kronenfeld, J.J.and Glick, D.C. (1991) Perceptions of risk: its applicability in medical sociological research, *Research in the Sociology of Health Care*, 9, 307–34.

Lupton, D. (1993) Risk as moral danger: the social and political functions of risk discourse in public health, *International Journal of Health Services*, 23, 425–35.

Lupton, D. (1994) *Medicine as Culture. Illness, Disease and the Body in Western Societies*. London: Sage.

Miller, D. and Williams, K. (1993) Negotiating HIV/AIDS information: agendas, media strategies and the news. In Eldridge, J. (ed) *Getting the Message*. London: Routledge.

Mills, C. Wright (1959) *The Sociological Imagination*. Oxford: Oxford University Press.

Moore, P.G. (1983) *The Business of Risk*. Cambridge: Cambridge University Press.

Nelkin, D. (1985) Introduction: analyzing risk. In Nelkin, D. (ed) *The Language of Risk. Conflicting Perspectives on Occupational Health*. Beverley Hills: Sage Publications.

Nelkin, D. (1989) Communicating technological risk: the social construction of risk perception, *Annual Review of Public Health*, 10, 95–113.

Nelkin, D. (1991) AIDS and the news media, *The Milbank Quarterly*, 69, 293–307.

The Observer (1994) Folly, facts and the killer bug. Editorial, 29 May.

Ogden, J. (1995) Psychosocial theory and the creation of the risky self, *Social Science and Medicine*, 40, 409–15.

Otway, H.J. and Cohen, J.J. (1975) Revealed preferences: comments on the Starr benefit-risk relationship, *International Institute for Applied Systems Analysis Research Memorandum*, 76–80.

Parsons, E. and Atkinson, P. (1992) Lay constructions of genetic risk, *Sociology of Health and Illness*, 14, 437–55.

Parsons, E. and Atkinson, P. (1993) Genetic risk and reproduction, *The Sociological Review*, 41, 679–706.

Phillimore, P. and Moffatt, S. (1994) Discounted knowledge: local experience, environmental pollution and health. In Popay, J. and Williams, G. (eds) *Researching the People's Health*. London: Routledge.

Raymond, C.A. (1985) Risk in the press: conflicting journalistic ideologies. In Nelkin, D. (ed) *The Language of Risk*. Beverley Hills: Sage.

Rayner, G. (1986) Management of radiation hazards in hospitals: plural rationalities in a single institution, *Social Studies of Science*, 16, 573–91.

Rayner, G. (1992) Cultural theory and risk analysis. In Krimsky, S. and Golding, D. (eds) *Social Theories of Risk*. Westport, Connecticut: Praeger.

Roberts, H., Smith, S. and Lloyd, M. (1992) Safety as a social value: a community approach. In Scott, S., Williams, G., Platt, S. and Thomas, H. (eds) *Private Risks and Public Dangers*. Aldershot: Avebury.

Roberts, H., Smith, S. and Bryce, C. (1993) Prevention is better . . ., *Sociology of Health and Illness*, 15, 447–63.

Royal Society Study Group (1992) *Risk Analysis, Perception and Management.* London: Royal Society.

Scambler, G. and Scambler, A. (1984) The illness iceberg and aspects of consulting behaviour. In Fitzpatrick, R., Hinton, J., Newman, S., Scambler, G. and Thompson, J. *The Experience of Illness.* London: Tavistock Publications.

Short, J. (1984) The social fabric at risk: toward the social transformation of risk analysis, *American Sociological Review*, 49, 711–25.

Skolbekken, J-A (1995) The risk epidemic in medical journals. *Social Science and Medicine*, 40, 291–305.

Slovic, P. (1992) Perception of risk: reflections on the psychometric paradigm. In Krimsky, S. and Golding, D. (eds) *Social Theories of Risk.* Westport, Connecticut: Praeger.

Slovic, P. and Fischoff, B. (1980) Perceived risk. In Schwing, R. and Albers, W. (eds) *Societal Risk Assessment: How Safe is Safe Enough?* New York: Plenum Press.

Slovic, P., Kraus, N., Lappe, H., Letzel, H. and Malmfors, T. (1989) Risk perception of prescription drugs: report on a survey in Sweden, *Pharmaceutical Medicine*, 4, 43–65.

Stallings, R. (1990) Media discourse and the social construction of risk, *Social Problems*, 37, 80–95.

Starr, C. (1969) Social benefit versus technological risk, *Science*, 165, 1232–8.

Thompson, M. (1989) Engineering and anthropology: is there a difference? In Brown, J. (ed) *Environmental Threats: Perception, Analysis and Management.* London: Belhaven Press.

Turner, B.S. (1991) Recent developments in the theory of the body. In Featherstone, M., Hepworth, M. and Turner, B.S. (eds) *The Body: Social Processes and Cultural Theory.* London: Sage.

Turner, G. and Wynne, B. (1992) Risk communication. In Durant, J. (ed) *Biotechnology in Public. A Review of Recent Research.* London: Science Museum for the European Federation of Biotechnology.

Williams, G. and Popay, J. (1994) Lay knowledge and the privilege of experience. In Gabe, J., Kelleher, D. and Williams, G. (eds) *Challenging Medicine.* London: Routledge.

1. A user's guide to contrasting theories of HIV-related risk behaviour

Michael Bloor

Introduction

It is probably the case that most sociological interest in the field of risk has recently attached to the analysis of public discourses of risk; this is readily seen in the enthusiastic reception for Ulrich Beck's work (Beck 1992). In respect of discourses on HIV risk, there has been a great number of publications which have sought to analyse these discourses and to link them to power relations (for example, Patton 1985, Treichler 1992, Watney 1987). The sociological theorising of HIV-related risk perception and management has received less attention: the most influential work has been conducted by social psychologists; even the work of the social anthropologist, Mary Douglas (for example, Douglas 1985), seen by many as pre-eminent in the conceptualisation of risk behaviour as a cultural product, has been quite without practical influence on the design of HIV/AIDS prevention programmes.

This chapter provides a short critical overview of the main theoretical approaches to understanding risk perception and risk management. The approaches addressed are: firstly, the Health Beliefs Model (HBM), the most widely used of the psycho-social models; secondly, what I have chosen to call 'The Situated Rationality' Approach; and thirdly, Douglas's 'Culture of Risk' Approach. Finally, a phenomenological alternative is conceptualised which, although heuristic rather than predictive, overcomes some of the difficulties apparent in the preceeding models.

The chapter is entitled 'A User's Guide . . .' because it is written from the perspective of an empirical researcher attempting to use theories of risk perception and risk management to deepen and elaborate his understanding of research findings. The research in question was a study of HIV-related risk behaviour by Glaswegian male prostitutes. The methods of the research have been described in detail elsewhere (Bloor *et al.* 1992, Bloor *et al.* 1993); only a summary account of the methods need be supplied here. The project was an ethnographic study and fieldwork was planned so as to ensure that a range of prostitution practice was included: the eventual sample of 32 respondents included both street and off-street prostitutes, novices and experienced prostitutes, drug injectors and non-injectors, gay-identified prostitutes and those who did not identify as gay. All contacts were offered free condoms suitable for anal and oral sex and a leaflet with advice and contact numbers. The data related to 240 hours of fieldwork spread over 16 months.

The health beliefs model

The HBM is only one of several psychological models of risk behaviour (others include the Theory of Reasoned Action, Social Learning Theory and the 'Precaution Adoption Process'). All these models are essentially similar in that they seek to explain variations in risk behaviour by references to variations in individuals' *perceptions* of risk. For simplicity of exposition, I have chosen here to concentrate on the HBM, the model most widely used to explain HIV-related risk behaviour; accounts of the other psychological models can be found in reviews by Kronenfeld and Glik (1991) and by a Royal Society working group (Royal Society 1992).

With intellectual antecedents in the work of Kurt Lewin, the HBM views health behaviour, including the practising of safer sex, as arising out of a number of interlinked perceptions. Firstly, the individual must perceive him/herself as vulnerable or susceptible to a health threat, such as HIV infection. Secondly, that health threat has to be perceived as having serious consequences. Thirdly, the protective action that is potentially available to avoid that health threat has to be perceived as an effective safeguard. And fourthly, taking the protective action has to be perceived to have benefits which outweigh the perceived costs. Early applications of the model were designed to address topics such as the under-use of preventive dentistry and variations in the uptake of child immunisation programmes (for example, Kegeles 1963). The best known application in the field of HIV-related risk behaviour is found in the study of associations between perceptions of risk and safer sexual practices among a large sample of Chicago gay men: only a modest association was found (Joseph *et al.* 1987).

The main difficulty with this kind of approach can be succinctly stated: theories of risk behaviour which conceptualise risk behaviour as a volitional and individual act are inappropriate where risk behaviour involves two parties, not a lone individual, and where practice may be characterised by constraint, rather than by free choice. Sexual relationships self-evidently involve (at least) two parties and sexual risk behaviour is a social rather than an individual activity.

The limitations of a conceptual focus on the individual are seen clearly in the male prostitution data. Here a third of the respondents were currently engaging in unsafe commercial sex with at least some of their clients ('unsafe sex' is defined here, following the Terrence Higgins Trust and other authorities, as protected or unprotected anal sex, reflecting the greater propensity for condom failure in anal sex). With one exception, all those engaging in commercial anal sex did so because they were constrained to do so by clients. Unsafe sex was reported to be a matter of client volition, not prostitute volition, as the following fieldnote illustrates:

'Simon' would do anal sex but *asked* the punter to wear a condom. He also said, at a different point, that the punter was in control – things like type of sex and location were matters for the punter's discretion.

Indeed, some of the client-prostitute relations reported were highly exploitative:

He said his sixteen year-old nephew had been coming down here [to the public lavatories] and getting four pounds for 'doing everything'. Punters were ripping him off: taking him away in cars and dumping him in places like Cumbernauld [ten miles away] without any money.

This is not a situation peculiar to male prostitution. Studies of private heterosexual encounters have also reported that unsafe sex arises out of the strategic power relationship between male and female partners (Holland *et al.* 1992).

It is possible, in principle, to amend and elaborate the HBM to take account of social constraints. The perceptions of the sexual partner of the respondent could be incorporated into the model as facilitating or inhibiting safer sexual practices. But there seems little virtue in grafting social factors onto a health behaviour model based on individualistic decision-making. The argument here about models of health behaviour is analogous to that advanced some years ago in relation to models of illness behaviour: attempts to explain variations in the use of medical services by reference to variations in patients' perceptions were superceded by models which emphasised the importance of social structural and cultural factors in producing differential consultation rates (for example, Suchman 1965, Strauss 1969). Collectivity-orientated models of risk behaviour may be more appropriate models than individualistic models to understand group and dyadic behaviours.

The situated rationality approach

Quite separate from the psycho-social studies have been a number of important empirical studies which have had the laudable aim of throwing light on risk behaviour by the analysis of risk-takers' accounts. This is an approach which is heir to a long tradition in sociology and which traces its beginnings back to the old dictum: 'If men define situations as real, then they are real in their consequences'. Previously, in the field of risk behaviour, the approach has been particularly influential in studies of reproductive risk behaviour – for example, Luker's (1975) study of women's accounts of their 'failure' to use contraception, and Parsons's analysis of variations in the reproductive decision-making of women at risk of bearing a child with muscular dystrophy (Parsons 1990, Parsons and Atkinson 1992).

Such studies have been an invaluable counterweight to the pathological view of risk-taking which sees risk behaviour as merely irrational. Instead, researchers have stressed the situated rationality of their subjects' decision-making in terms of the subjects' own definitions of the situation – for example, the willingness of women to bear a male foetus with a high mathematical risk of a future genetic disorder may be understandable by reference to the high value they place on family formation, or to their positive memories of a sibling who developed the disorder.

Studies of HIV-related risk behaviour which have followed this situated rationality approach include, for example, those studies of men who have sex with men which have stressed the important distinction in sexual behaviour between different types of relationship, with many men practising safer sex with casual partners and unprotected anal intercourse with their regular partner (see, for example, Hickson *et al.* 1992). For these men, the risk of HIV infection may be viewed as non-existent where they and their regular partner are HIV-negative. Or alternatively, willingness to engage in anal intercourse with one's regular partner may be viewed as emblematic of mutual intimacy and trust. In this view it is one's relationships and the meaning of sexual acts within one's relationships which pattern one's 'sexual risk behaviour'. The same point applies to much heterosexual risk behaviour and to syringe-sharing: syringe-sharing is no random activity, but is socially patterned, with one of the commonest patterns of syringe-sharing occurring between drug injectors who are also regular sexual partners (see, for example, Kane 1991).

Empirical studies which have stressed the situated rationality of risk behaviour have, of course, been concerned to explain their own data rather than to elaborate a broadly applicable theory of risk behaviour. It is therefore no surprise that there are limits on the applicability of a situated rationality approach. It might be argued that the very strength of these studies, their stress on the immediate benefits of risk behaviour – the calculative rationality of risk-taking – is also a brake on wider applicability. In this respect the situated rationality approach resembles some of the psycho-social models listed earlier, indeed Social Learning Theory has focussed on how the immediate incentives of risk-taking (the immediate gratification of a cigarette) may outweigh the more distant gratifications of risk avoidance (such as longevity). It will already be apparent to readers that an approach which focusses on the situated rationality of unprotected anal intercourse with a regular partner, where risk-taking is *chosen* as a signifier of intimacy, has little explanatory value for the contrasting case of male prostitution, where prostitute risk behaviour is an involuntary act reflecting client domination of the commercial sexual encounter.

Every sexual relationship (and every syringe-sharing relationship) may be conceived of as a 'strategic' relationship in the Foucauldian sense of the term. Foucault, in contrast to Marx and Weber, viewed power as consisting solely in its exercise, as being located in relationships rather than being a commodity possessed by an individual or group (Cousins and Hussain 1984). Power cannot be wished or legislated away; it is inherent in all relationships (Foucault 1980).

It might be responded that commercial sexual encounters (like private sexual encounters) are also patterned by type of relationship: a study of male prostitution in South Wales shows that reports of anal intercourse are more common with regular clients than with casual clients (Davies and Feldman 1991). However, anal intercourse was by no means confined to regular clients: 77 male prostitute respondents reported 41 sessions of anal intercourse with casual clients in the previous month (ibid: 11). It may be that the apparent patterning of risk behaviour by type of relationship is an artefact of the greater likelihood of encounters with regular clients taking place in comparative privacy such as the client's home. Commercial sex between prostitutes and casual clients is much more likely to occur at venues such as parks and public lavatories, where limited privacy makes anal intercourse a less popular option. Project Sigma's study of a large sample of gay men similarly shows that a very low proportion of sexual encounters with those partners met at gay cruising grounds or 'cottages' (public lavatories) involved penetration: sexual encounters involving those partners met in gay pubs and clubs were relatively more likely to involve penetration because the participants must retire from the pub/club to the privacy of a partner's home (Davies *et al.* 1993: 154–7). The possible impact of situational constraints on risk behaviour is one to which I shall return.

One further difficulty with the Situated Rationality approach should be stated. The implication of a calculative orientation to risk behaviour, like all approaches with their antecedents in models of economic rationality, understate the unconsidered and frequently habitual character of much behaviour. Some Glaswegian male prostitute respondents were averaging six clients a day and working six days a week. Under these circumstances, the deliberation of the costs and benefits of different courses of action may be less likely to occur as a degree of routinisation of behaviour develops. In a similar fashion, syringe-sharing is unlikely to be deliberated when it occurs, say, between long-standing sexual partners who, in order to maintain their habits, must inject opiates several times a day: risk behaviour, through repetition of circumstances, can become an habitual and taken-for-granted aspect of daily lives. A rounded explanation of risk behaviour would need to embrace both routinised and calculative risk behaviour.

Cultures of risk

In a series of publications (Douglas and Wildavsky 1982, Douglas 1985 op. cit., Douglas 1992) the anthropologist Mary Douglas has developed a view of risk behaviour as a culturally variable product. In an article in 1990 she explicitly applied this approach to HIV-related risk behaviour (Douglas and Chavez 1990). It is argued that variations in risk recognition, risk assessment and response are the product of differential socialisation in various sub-cultures and complex social institutions. Douglas's approach is sometimes called the grid/group approach because this differential socialisation in risk perception and risk management is shaped, both by the variable groups to which the individual belongs and by the variable pattern of constraint ('grid') by which groups require uniformity of conduct among group members. Variations in risk behaviour can be represented schematically in a four-box table where the two axes represent, firstly, the variable degree to which the individual is integrated in bounded groups (the 'group' axis), and secondly, the variable degree to which those groups require adherence to particular rules of conduct (the 'grid' axis). Each box at the intersection of these axes is characterised by a particular 'cosmology', or world-view, in respect of risk – the individualist approach, the fatalist approach, and so forth. Douglas's scheme has been followed by several empirical investigators, notably Rayner's (1986) study of how responses to occupational radiation hazards varied systematically between different occupational groups (radiologists, nurses, technicians, and maintenance workers) in an American hospital.

The Royal Society review (op. cit.) recapitulates a number of difficulties that have been raised with the grid/group classification, but these difficulties do not seem particularly serious: if the two axes of 'grid' and 'group' are seen as continua and the four cosmologies are no longer viewed as discrete, then most of the classificatory problems recede. More important problems have been raised by Bellaby (1990), who argued that a more dynamic and situated model is required. Certainly, it is difficult to conceive how behaviour change occurs in Douglas's model; it is perhaps no accident that the successful 'gay hero' peer-influence interventions developed by Kelly and his associates (Kelly *et al.* 1992, Kelly *et al.* 1993) owe nothing to Douglas's work, having their antecedents in earlier work on the cultural diffusion of innovations (Rogers 1962).

It may also be the case that the normative expectations and cosmologies that people bring to the situation of risk may be a less important determinant of risk behaviour than aspects of the situation itself. Risk-taking may follow less from learned orientations than from strategic relationships in the immediate risk situation. In respect of male prostitution, it may be a mistake to characterise the failure to contest client domination of the commercial sexual encounter as passivity arising out of a fatalistic cosmology. Among Glaswegian male prostitutes, safer commercial sex was practised by those prostitutes who used specific techniques of power to resist client domination:

> His procedure was to stand at the urinal. The client would come and stand beside him. When the coast was clear the client would put out a hand and he would immediately say, 'I'm sorry but I charge'. Some would leave at that point. With the remainder he'd negotiate a rate. He would accept £10 but sometimes got £20. . . . He always did hand jobs or oral sex. . . . If clients asked him for anal sex he told them to eff off.

Among Glaswegian female prostitutes, who overwhelmingly practise safer commercial sex, it is the universal practice to demand prior payment for sexual services (McKeganey *et al.* 1990); likewise, none of those Glasgow male prostitutes (a minority) who also sought their money up front were currently engaging in receptive anal intercourse with clients:

> I asked him if he took the money up front. He said he did and explained that it had happened this way. The first time he got a customer he wasn't too sure how to proceed: the customer asked him how much he charged and he answered, 'how much will you pay?' Eventually they fixed a price. When they got to the venue, he asked the customer for the money. The customer refused. So he said: 'No money, no deal'. And he got the money. He guessed from the customer's surprised reaction that it was more usual to ask for the money afterward. But since he'd been successful, he'd continued to work on this principle.

Unsafe commercial sex among male prostitutes is associated with the absence of countervailing techniques of power which wrest the interactional initiative from the client. Safer commercial sex is associated, not with learned orientations, but with local strategic relationships. While these countervailing techniques can be learned by participants in particular sub-cultures, rather than be simply stumbled upon (as in the case of the 'No money, no deal' respondent), they are situated and specific rather than components of a generalised world-view.

A phenomenological alternative

The argument so far can be summarised as requiring from any successful theoretical scheme that it embrace at least two sets of oppositions: an approach is needed which embraces habituation as well as calculation and constraint as well as volition. It is the phenomenological approach, rather than any other, which focuses on unconsidered action and taken-for-granted understandings, that is, habituation. The 'phenomenological attitude' involves the suspension of taken-for-granted understandings and a focus on the previously implicit as an explicit analytical topic.

The social world of unconsidered certitudes and implicit understandings has been conceptualised most systematically by Alfred Schutz, an author perhaps now more quoted than read. Central to Schutz's work is a conceptual distinction between two modes of social action, derived from two modes of cognition: on the one hand the 'world of routine activities' (Schutz 1970), on the other hand a world of considered alternatives and calculative action. The distinction, derived originally from Husserl's monothetic/polythetic division, is not an absolute distinction, rather it represents a range along a continuum. Schutz's scheme of 'systems of relevances' (ibid) is a heuristic device which orders into one conceptual framework both this routinised/calculated distinction and the temporal development or unfolding of cognitive acts.

It might be objected that while the systems of relevances are clearly designed to embrace the habituation/calculation distinction, their utility for addressing the volition/constraint distinction is less evident. However, Schutz is clear that all the different systems of relevances are divisible into 'intrinsic' and 'imposed' relevances. Indeed, it is partly this recognition by Schutz of how relevances may be socially constrained that gives his approach to cognition a distinctively social character. Constraint may be absolute or only partially restrictive. In instances of the latter, for example, the person may need to focus on which of those potential actions are actually allowable in the situation of action and, of these allowable actions, which is the most preferable.

Previously, both Robert Dingwall and I (Bloor 1970, Dingwall 1976, Bloor 1983) have suggested that Schutz's systems of relevance could be used to conceptualise variations in 'illness behaviour'. The suggestion here is that the same scheme might be used also to understand variations in 'health behaviour', including risk behaviour and risk reduction.

The sequence of cognition can be represented as follows:

TOPICAL RELEVANCES
|
INTERPRETATIVE RELEVANCES
|
MOTIVATIONAL RELEVANCES
|
INTERPRETATION OF THE SITUATION
|

RECIPE FOR ACTION
|
RISK MANAGEMENT

Topical relevances determine whether or not a situation becomes problematic for an individual. Interpretative relevances are the limited range of elements in the individual's stock of knowledge to which the individual's current situation can be compared. Motivational relevances determine how far the search for an interpretation is pursued – the degree of certitude that is required. Having arrived at an interpretation, there may be a number of different recipes for action attached to a given interpretation. In the world of routine activities this step-wise cognitive sequence is collapsed as cognition occurs monothetically, in a single flash.

At each stage in the above cognitive sequence volition and constraint are conceptually differentiated. Thus, topical relevances are divided into 'intrinsic topical relevances', where topics are constituted as problematic by self-selection, and 'imposed topical relevances', where topics are constituted as problematic by the actions and utterances of the individual's significant others. Again, the selection of a suitable recipe for action may turn on which of those recipes associated with a given interpretation of the situation are in fact 'performable' in that situation: choice of recipes may be restricted or eliminated.

Returning to HIV-related risk behaviour among male prostitutes, the schema embraces a range of activities previously reported – the routinisation of risk behaviour through daily repetition where safer commercial sex is no longer a topically relevant pursuit, the imposed adoption of risk behaviour, motivational relevances which give greater or lesser urgency to the topic of safer commercial sex, and the strategic choice of performable recipes for action which countervail clients' preferences for unsafe sex.

Conclusion

Many of the studies overviewed here have yielded important empirical findings and Douglas's work on cultures of risk has been rightly described by the Royal Society working party (op. cit.) as 'revolutionary'. Nevertheless, considered as models of HIV-related risk behaviour, the earlier studies have multiple deficiencies, some of them highlighted by their lack of congruence with qualitative data on risk behaviour among male prostitutes. In view of these several deficiencies it may be premature to seek to elaborate a predictive model of risk behaviour. A more readily achievable goal might be the specification of a conceptual scheme which provides a heuristic framework for the description of various diversities of risk practices and risk reduction.

Schutz's 'system of relevances' seems a suitable candidate for the basis of such a heuristic framework. The conceptual focus is on the immediate situation of action – local strategic relationships as well as orientations brought to the situation. Further, the framework incorporates both automatic activity and the rational weighing of costs and benefits. And finally, the same framework incorporates both volitional actions and constrained responses.

Discussions of phenomenology may seem some distance from the daily toll of infection and death that is the reality of the HIV/AIDS epidemic. But, in fact, all health education and health promotion activities operate with implicit theories of risk behaviour. Campaigns which seek to alter perceptions of risk, for example, are in fact operating with a psycho-social model of risk behaviour, such as the Health Beliefs Model. A different kind of theory might suggest different kinds of interventions: the earlier discussion implies that successful HIV intervention campaigns would need to address the situations in which risk behaviour occurs and, not least, the power relations which limit or eliminate health choices. There is nothing so practical as a good theory.

Acknowledgements

I wish to thank Marina Barnard, Andrew Finlay and Neil McKeganey for their assistance with the fieldwork on the prostitution study, which was supported by the Medical Research Council. Greater Glasgow Health Board supplied the free condoms distributed to respondents. An earlier and briefer version of this chapter was presented at the 1994 British Sociological Association Annual Conference at Preston. A more extensive discussion of the topic is to be found in M. Bloor (1995) *The Sociology of HIV Transmission*. London: Sage.

References

Beck, U. (1992) *Risk Society: Towards a New Modernity*. London: Sage.
Bellaby, P. (1990) To risk or not to risk? uses and limitations of Mary Douglas on risk acceptability for understanding health and safety at work and road accidents, *Sociological Review*, 38, 465–83.
Bloor, M. (1970) Current explanatory models of pre-patient behaviour: a critique with some suggestions on further model development. M.Litt. dissertation, University of Aberdeen.
Bloor, M. (1985) Observations of abortive illness behaviour, *Urban Life*, 14, 300–16.
Bloor, M., McKeganey, N., Finlay, A. and Barnard, M. (1992) The inappropriateness of psycho-social models of risk behaviour for understanding HIV-related risk practices among Glasgow male prostitutes, *AIDS Care*, 4, 131–7.

Bloor, M., Barnard, M., Finlay, A. and McKeganey, N. (1993) HIV-related risk practices among Glasgow male prostitutes: reframing concepts of risk behaviour, *Medical Anthropology Quarterly*, 7, 1–19.

Cousins, M. and Hussain, A. (1984) *Michel Foucault*. London: Macmillan.

Davies, P. and Feldman, R. (1991) *Male Sex Workers in South Wales*. Project Sigma Working Paper No. 35. London: Project Sigma.

Davies, P., Hickson, F., Weatherburn, P. and Hunt, A. (1993) *Sex, Gay Men and AIDS*. Brighton: Falmer.

Dingwall, R. (1976) *Aspects of Illness*. London: Martin Robertson.

Douglas, M. (1985) *Risk Acceptability According to the Social Sciences*. New York: Russell Sage Foundation.

Douglas, M. (1992) *Risk and Blame*. London: Routledge.

Douglas, M. and Calvez, M. (1990) The self as risk taker: a cultural theory of contagion in relation to AIDS, *Sociological Review*, 38, 445–64.

Douglas, M. and Wildavsky, A. (1982) *Risk and Culture: An Essay on the Selection of Technical and Environmental Dangers*. Berkeley: University of California Press.

Foucault (1980) The eye of power. In C. Gordon (ed) *Michel Foucault: Power/Knowledge*. Brighton: Harvester.

Hickson, F., Davies, P., Hunt, A., Weatherburn, P., McManus, T. and Coxon, A. (1992) Maintenance of open gay relationships: some strategies for protection against HIV, *AIDS Care*, 4, 409–19.

Holland, J., Ramazonoglu, C., Sharpe, S. and Thompson, R. (1992) Pressured pleasure: young women and the negotiation of sexual boundaries, *Sociological Review*, 40, 645–74.

Joseph, J., Montgomery, S., Emmons, C., Kirscht, J., Kessler, R., Ostrow, D., Wortman, C., O'Brien, K., Eller, M. and Eshleman, S. (1987) Perceived risk of AIDS: assessing the behavioural and psychosocial consequences in a cohort of gay men, *Journal of Applied Social Psychology*, 17, 231–50.

Kane, S. (1991) HIV, heroin and heterosexual relations, *Social Science and Medicine*, 32, 1037–50.

Kegeles, S. 91963) Why people seek dental care: a test of a conceptual formulation, *Journal of Health and Social Behaviour*, 4, 166–73.

Kelly, J., Sikkema, K., Winett, R., Solomon, L., Roffman, R., Kalichman, S., Stevenson, Y., et al. (1992) Outcomes of a 16-city randomised field trial of a community-level HIV risk reduction intervention. Paper presented at VIII International Conference on AIDS, Amsterdam [abstract TuD 0543].

Kelly, J., Winett, R., Roffman, R., Solomon, L., Kalichman, S., Stevenson, Y., et al. (1993) Social diffusion models can produce population-level HIV risk behaviour reduction: field trial results and mechanisms underlying change. Paper presented at IX International Conference on AIDS, Berlin [abstract Po-C23-3167].

Kronenfeld, J. and Glik, S. (1991) Models of preventive health behaviour, health behaviour change and roles for sociologists, *Research in the Sociology of Health Care*, 7, 303–28.

Luker, K. (1975) *Taking Chances, Abortion and the Decision not to Contracept*. Berkeley: University of California Press.

McKeganey, N., Barnard, M. and Bloor, M. (1990) A comparison of HIV-related risk behaviour and risk reduction between female street-working prostitutes and male rent boys in Glasgow, *Sociology of Health and Illness*, 12, 274–92.

Parsons, E. (1990) Living with Duchenne Muscular Dystrophy: women's understandings of disability and risk. PhD thesis, University of Wales, Cardiff.

Parsons, E. and Atkinson, P. (1992) Lay constructions of genetic risk, *Sociology of Health and Illness*, 14, 437–55.

Patton, C. (1985) *Sex and Germs: the Politics of AIDS*. Boston: Southend Press.

Rayner, G. (1986) Management of radiation hazards in hospitals: plural rationalities in a single institution, *Social Studies of Science*, 16, 573–91.

Rogers, E. (1962) *Diffusion of Innovations*. New York: Free Press.

Royal Society (1992) *Risk Analysis, Perception and Management: Report of a Royal Society Study Group*. London: Royal Society.

Schutz, A. (1970) *Reflections on the Problem of Relevance*, (ed) R. Zaner. New Haven: Yale University Press.

Suchman (1965) Socio-medical variations among ethnic groups, *American Journal of Sociology*, 70, 319–31.

Strauss, A. (1969) Medical organisation, medical care, and lower income groups, *Social Science and Medicine*, 3, 143–77.

2. Risk, the real world and naive sociology: Perceptions of risk from occupational injury in the health service

Anne Grinyer

Introduction

Of the various sociological approaches to the understanding of risk and its management, this chapter takes as its starting point the theories of risk and the public understanding of science as developed by Wynne (1989, 1991, 1992). Wynne argues that central to the compilation of official information on risk, appears to be a deeply embedded assumption that it is only scientific knowledge which merits the status of 'expertise'. However, it must be recognised that in the context in which information based on technical expertise is to be implemented, it is frequently the public who are the experts. This lay expertise, founded on experience in a particular social world, does not of necessity invalidate technical expertise, rather it brings an added dimension of understanding to the complexity of social life, essential if official information on the avoidance of risk is to be followed successfully. However, this dimension seems to be a factor which remains largely disregarded or unrecognised when risk information on scientific or technical matters is delivered to the public. Risk, it could be argued, is seen by the policy makers in a one-dimensional context, rather than being part of a multi-dimensional, complex and socially embedded process.

The term 'expert' is in itself problematic and, where it is used, needs to be qualified to distinguish technical expertise from lay expertise. Managers and policy makers, it could be argued, are themselves experts in neither the technical sphere nor the social or working environments which are the settings of application. They are, however, frequently the purchasers of the technical expertise which forms the basis of policies on risk and safety, although it is usually the workers who face the risk. Whether the technical expert knowledge would be different if commissioned by the workers rather than the managers is not the focus of this study, but given the socially negotiated nature of scientific knowledge, and the role of vested interests (Bloor 1978, Pinch 1981, Latour 1987, Latour and Woolgar 1986), it is an important issue which underlies the following discussion.

Wynne (1989) argues that both technical expert and lay risk

perceptions are based upon social models and assumptions which are much deeper than is generally recognised, and claims the following:

> Expert assumptions about the social world of risk practices are necessary in order even to frame a technical risk analysis. Yet their assumptions and commitment in this domain may be no better than those of the lay public's – indeed they may be worse (1989: 33–4).

According to Wynne, there is an assumption on the part of technical experts that it is the public's scientific illiteracy which is responsible for anxiety and concern over issues such as bio-technology and nuclear power. As polarisation between public and experts becomes more extreme, so experts engage in ever more elaborate programmes of information on the basis that more information will convince the public to take certain actions, or that risks are insignificant. Thus information programmes are likely to be intensified before the assumptions upon which they are based are questioned. It may be that policy makers have greater anxiety over causing alarm than over the risks involved in any particular course of action. This policy stance seems to be based on the conviction, which may be institutionally necessary, that it is only technical experts who understand the 'real' risks, while the public have merely a perception of them. Such expert assumptions may also serve to shape the public perception of an issue.

Wynne offers a different interpretation of public risk perceptions that 'grounds their rationality in social experiences and processes' (1989: 35). He argues that the dominant perception of the problem – how to defend scientific rationality against uninformed and disorderly subjectivism – is fundamentally flawed. What is taken by technical experts and policy makers to be an irrational rejection of scientific information, may instead be a rejection of naive assumptions about an ideal world, both social and material, which is embedded in the 'expert' model of risk taking. Wynne calls this a 'naive sociology' on the part of expert bodies who construct a model of an idealised social world which is embedded in their technical analysis of risk management. There is of course a danger of idealising lay expertise and it is necessary to acknowledge that lay experiences may be subject to the same process of construction as the experts' knowledge. This does not, however, invalidate the central thesis.

This naivety on the part of experts is made manifest through a review of the literature on education and information programmes on a variety of risk situations by Sims and Baumann (1983) who conclude that there is a history of consistently failed connections between education and awareness and between awareness and behaviour. As a result of the need to manage a number of possibly competing and cross cutting agendas, the breakdown in the causal chain of 'education causes awareness causes behaviour' becomes apparent. It is both the logical flaw and empirical failure of such a simplistic model which needs to be demonstrated if risk information usable to a public audience is to be constructed.

The construction of such policies on risk could be seen to reflect the way the structuration of an organisation informs the way in which a text is interpreted, and feeds back into the organisation to reproduce the organisation in a circular process. Thus particular discourses lie at the heart of what constitutes an organisation, and what acts to sustain its continuation. The process of structuration, as defined by Giddens, is the 'structuring of social relations across time and space, in virtue of the duality of structure' (1984: 376). His main proposition is that the rules and resources drawn upon in both the production and reproduction of social action, also act to reproduce the system. Thus in reproducing structural properties, the conditions that make such action possible are also reproduced. He suggests that the flow of action continually produces consequences which are unintended, and these may in turn form unacknowledged conditions of action and response in feedback form.

Using a similar analytical approach Manning (1986) argues that organisations are formally constituted systems which process information, utilise technology and structure roles and practices. It is these processes which, he claims, convert equivocal and uncertain messages into organisationally workable procedures. Thus it is the context in which this process occurs which governs the way in which the information will be interpreted.

The texts used by Manning are calls from the public to the police. Having addressed the nature of the constraints on communication which are affected by the organisational context in which the messages occur, he concludes,

The text can be viewed . . . as representing both organisation, or the internal perspective, and the environment or the external perspective. A text of a citizen's call contains a double referent in that it refers to itself whilst moving through the police communicational system and to the environment of citizens' calls from whence it came (1986: 299).

Based largely upon empirical data, the focus of the investigation in this chapter lies in an exploration of the different perceptions of risk between expert and lay frames of reference, the rationalisation of anomalous information and the interpretation of scientific and medical opinion, particularly in relation to the risk from HIV infection amongst occupational groups in a hospital setting. Extensive fieldwork amongst both policy makers and the workforce in two health authorities provides the source of much of the material, and it is the different perceptions of risk from occupational injury as it is constructed by management, and as it is perceived and experienced by the workforce, which is the subject of analysis. Before turning to this fieldwork, however, it is necessary to clarify my use of the terms 'expert' and 'lay' in relation to management and workers in the two health authorities.

'Expert' knowledge and 'lay' knowledge in a working environment

The distinction between, and definition of 'expert' and 'lay' in an institutional setting where the 'lay' group are members of a workforce is complex, and the categories may on occasions overlap. However, for the purposes of analysis, I define 'expert' as those responsible for compiling official information and safety regulations for use in the hospital. They are the managers and policy makers who may or may not have scientific and medical training, but whose job it is to construct information and safety programmes for use in a working environment – thus setting themselves up as 'experts' on risk and safety. It is the recipients of this advice whom I define as 'lay', although in some cases they may be members of a professional medical group within the health service.

This situation clearly differs considerably from the more general provision of risk information in which technical experts devise information for use by lay audiences in their private or social lives. However, the principle remains the same, as evidenced by the examples chosen by Wynne (1989) who demonstrates the misunderstanding of the social world shown by the Pesticides Advisory Committee in drawing up safety regulations for the use of 2,4,5-T on farms, and the European Commission's Expert Advisory Committee who drew up guidelines for the use of animal growth hormones. In both these instances the 'expert' committees had failed to take into account the reality of the working environment and the consequent impossibility of their regulations being implemented effectively. As a result safety policies, devised for use under ideal conditions, were found to be unworkable in practice under conditions which prevail in the working environment of which the expert committees had no understanding. As one worker is reported as saying, it was like asking someone to work in the laundry but to keep out of the steam.

Similar findings are documented by Nelkin and Brown (1984) whose interviews with a range of workers including a laboratory technician, deckhand, sculptor, gardener, hair stylist, dry cleaner, chemical pipe fitter, industrial painter and computer assembler, demonstrate the considerable constraints imposed by both social and practical problems. For example, the hair stylist whose lungs had been damaged by the chemicals of her trade but whose customers were 'turned off' if she wore a mask. Neither was she able to wear rubber gloves as they made it impossible to feel how the chemicals were reacting with the hair.

Nelkin and Brown also demonstrate the suspicion which workers feel towards management's control of information, and the effect this has on the credibility of safety policy. The evidence of the computer assembler whose management tested for dust levels, but refused to disclose the results, apart from telling the workers that the levels were within 'company and OHSA specs' (1984: 158), shows that such assurances do no more than make the workers believe that if they fought for more information they would be stone-walled and labelled trouble makers.

It is these issues of trust and credibility, practical and social constraints, and 'lay' and 'expert' knowledge which are examined in a health care setting in this chapter.

Methodology

Interviews were carried out amongst health care workers (HCWs) in two health authorities (HA 1 and HA 2). The major difference between HA 1 and HA 2 was that HA 1 already had an AIDS education programme running, while HA 2 had put out only limited information on the avoidance of AIDS and was planning a more structured programme of information. Where this difference is relevant to the findings it will be discussed.

Interviewees included the same categories of worker in both HA 1 and HA 2, and covered a range of occupations from kitchen assistants to junior doctors selected at random. The interviews focused on the workers' perceptions of the risk associated with their employment, and their ability to implement risk information as provided for them by their health authority. Extracts from the fieldwork used in this chapter are representative of many other responses reflecting similar views and experiences. Considering the disparity between the education programmes in HA 1 and HA 2, responses were surprisingly consistent across both health authorities. No significant difference in either knowledge or risk perception was found between HA 1 and HA 2 when comparing the same occupational categories. Distinction will be made between the health authorities only where it is relevant to the analysis of the findings.

Data in both HA 1 and HA 2 were collected through the use of informal, focused, qualitative interviews lasting an average of one hour each, and anonymity was guaranteed. This method overcame the inflexibility of a more formal method, such as a postal survey, while retaining some consistency of format between respondents, thus assuring that relevant topics were covered. According to May, while the use of a structured questionnaire is likely to result in the nature of the answer being guided by the interview schedule, the focused interview instead,

> . . . rests its strength upon eliciting answers which are, as far as possible, in the person's own words and frame of reference (1993: 97).

On the practice of focused interviews, Spradley (1979) suggests that a process of building up trust and cooperation should enable the interviewer to explore in depth the respondents' experiences, and can be used both to validate and disconfirm the researcher's existing ideas. This is clearly a time consuming process, and while numbers using this method of necessity remain relatively small – in my study, 75 from a combined workforce of approximately 10,000 – it could be argued that the quality of the data outweighs the limitations of a quantitative method. The relative merits of qualitative versus quantitative methods are summed up by Hughes and Ackroyd as follows:

> This contrast is sometimes expressed by saying that there is a fundamental methodological dilemma: either you are sure that your data are true, but you are not sure how general they are (observation); or you are sure that your data are general, but you are not sure how true they are (surveys) (1992: 170).

However, the consistency of findings across both health authorities when comparing occupational categories suggests a commonality of experience which could reasonably be assumed to represent a wider section of the workforce.

The fieldwork was not, however, limited to those selected for interview; it also included those who had commissioned the research. Being locally powerful this group could be described as the 'controllers' (Bell and Encell 1978). The usual problems described in studying such a group were to some extent circumvented by the fact that they had engaged me as a researcher to study those they controlled. They were in effect the 'gate-keepers' (Barnes 1979) without whom I would not have had access to the workforce. There were of course ethical problems associated with the fact that they too, particularly in HA 1, became the subjects of my research. So while my research amongst the workforce was overt, my research of its commissioners was, to some extent, covert. Although my identity was not concealed, to some degree my purpose was (Dunsmuir and Williams 1991). It was however, only as my research amongst the workers progressed that the discrepancies between management assumptions and the experiences of the workers began to emerge. Thus, during much of my initial attendance at management meetings in HA 1, I was genuinely unaware of the use to which the information to which I was privy, would be put.

An additional ethical problem was posed by the fact that I had been commissioned to interview members of the workforce by their employers. This inevitably raised the question 'whose side am I on?' While I had initially, and somewhat naively, supposed that I would simply be collecting information, the interviews exposed many pre-existing resentments and fears amongst the workers. On a number of occasions in HA 1 I was asked by respondents if I could obtain supplies of safety equipment, or information on risks from management. While being aware of the importance of remaining as objective as possible, it was difficult to refuse such requests. I did however, try to avoid becoming identified as a 'champion of the workers', and passed on complaints and requests in the context of my research. However, when my research findings ran counter to the expectations of management, I had to make clear the fact that their commissioning of the research could in no way influence the outcome, thus maintaining my professional commitment to represent my respondents without bias.

At the beginning of each interview I made it clear to the respondent that it was the health authority which had commissioned the research, but that I was based in a university department, and was not an employee of the health authority. Coupled with the fact that I assured anonymity to my respondents, this appeared to free them from the fear of repercussions if they criticised or complained about their employers or their working conditions. In fact the research was regarded by a number of respondents as a way of articulating their needs in a way which protected them.

Such research can of course be subject to interviewer influence and bias. As Bell and Newby (1977) argue, all social research takes place within a political context which virtually determines the design, implementation and outcome of the investigation. In attempting to ascertain risk perceptions amongst the workforce it is possible to 'plant' the notion of risk in the respondents' minds, thus eliciting responses unrepresentative of their everyday concerns, and creating an additional layer of ethical problems. However, through the use of interviews which, while unstructured, were based on a checklist of topics I hoped to address, the information I received appeared to be spontaneous and representative of the respondents' concerns about the risk encountered on a daily basis in their working practice. Indeed, I was given information of a kind that I had not been expecting, and could not have elicited simply through the use of biased questioning.

The data from the policy makers are based not only upon attendance at policy making meetings and the content of safety information issued to the workforce, but also upon the policy makers' resistance to my research findings which challenged their construction of the working environment and its attendant risks. This resistance, particularly notable in HA 1, should perhaps have been expected, for as Becker points out, as sociologists, we provoke the charge of bias by refusing to the established status order. After all, as he states ironically, 'everyone knows' that it is the responsible professionals who know more about things than laypeople (1967: 128). Thus research findings which indicated that the recipients of safety advice found it impractical or irrelevant, were likely to be rejected.

Risk as defined by health authority policy makers and as experienced by the workforce

The lack of applicable advice on risk, particularly notable in HA 1, does not, of necessity, denote a lack of concern about the safety of the recipients. There appeared to be genuine concern for the welfare of the workforce amongst those responsible for drawing up safety procedures and policies to protect staff from accidental infection with HIV and other infective organisms. However, risks, as they were assessed in the committee room by management in both HA 1 and HA 2, frequently bore little relation to risks as they were experienced in the working environment, thus bearing out much of the evidence from Wynne (1989) and Nelkin and Brown (1984). An ideal model of working practice appeared to be the basis for advice and for policies which consequently failed to address the needs of their recipients. The complexity of risks involved was rarely recognised and the messages designed to protect staff were kept simple because, in the words of a Health Promotion Officer in HA 1, 'A simple message is all people can deal with'. This approach had resulted in the compilation of a safety leaflet in HA 1, designed to provide staff at all levels with the basic information needed to avoid infection. Advice included the following:

'Prevent puncture wounds, cuts and abrasions in the presence of blood.'

'Take simple protective measures to avoid contamination of person and clothing.'

'Protect mucous membrane of eyes, mouth and nose from blood splashes.'

Here we are reminded of the impossibility of working in the laundry whilst being required to keep out of the steam. Clearly all the above advice is sound, but how practicable is its implementation in a busy Accident and Emergency department, or in the even less controlled conditions at the scene of an accident? To the ambulance crew member from HA 1, accidentally stabbed in the cheek with a hypodermic syringe by a doctor who had just used it on an injured man trapped under a lorry, advice such as this would appear entirely to misunderstand the nature of the risks attendant in the job. As another ambulance crew member said:

> Yes, we are at risk . . . The health authority 'cover the back door' by issuing gloves and masks, but it's not always practical to use them . . . it's a profit making organisation now, so if it'll cost money it doesn't matter about the staff or the patients, we're just a number.

Such a response demonstrates not only the manner in which the existing relationship between management and workers shapes the reaction to safety advice (Nelkin and Brown 1984), but also the mismatches between risks as constructed by management, and risks as experienced by the workforce (Wynne 1989). These mismatches were many and varied. To the staff in the X-Ray department in HA 1 who were required to mop up significant amounts of blood, the lack of granules designed to make the job safer was interpreted as management failing to understand the nature of their working practice. To the van drivers in HA 1 who had repeatedly requested strong rubber gloves and other protective clothing, to no avail, the assumption was that management had no understanding of their working conditions, or were unconcerned that they were at daily risk of injury and infection. The following quote from a van driver in HA 1 typifies the general feeling:

> We had to go on bended knee to be allowed hepatitis B vaccinations, they just don't realise the nature of our work.

In a potentially serious incident, again in HA 1, a van driver had been stabbed in the leg by five used hypodermic syringes while on the clinical waste run. Safety measures under ideal circumstances should have prevented an accident such as this from occurring, however working conditions are frequently far from ideal. In this instance a sharps box had been emptied into a waste bag by a cleaner who was unaware of the need to keep used sharps in a strong rigid container.

In similar incidents porters in HA 1, another occupational group not immediately associated with the risk of HIV infection, had been required to carry laboratory and mortuary specimens which had been badly sealed by medical staff, and which had subsequently leaked body fluids onto their skin and clothing. Kitchen staff too might be assumed to be at little risk from such contamination, yet the accidental presence of bloodied swabs and used bandages on trays returned to the kitchen, was reported by several of my respondents.

Cleaners, technically not supposed to come into contact with blood, asked me during my research whether they were at risk when clearing up 'large quantities' of blood. They were also concerned that chapped hands might constitute a breach in the skin which could put them at risk of infection. As one cleaner in HA 1 said:

> It's all very well being told not to allow blood to come into contact with cuts and abrasions, but sometimes you can't tell until its too late, like when you put your hands in lemon juice.

It is not, however, simply the reporting of such accidents and incidents and the reality of the risks they represent which is of interest. It is also the response from management and policy makers to my research report detailing the risks encountered by the workforce. In HA 1, where all these incidents took place, rather than welcoming the information that they were unaware of when compiling their initial safety information on the risk of HIV infection, they instead questioned the validity of research results which challenged their assumptions.

When informed of the need various working groups expressed for protective equipment, the response in HA 1 was dismissive, as demonstrated by the Infection Control Nurse's comment:

> That's ridiculous, they've only got to ask and we'd give them what they want.

It was, however, unclear what the process of 'simply asking' for them would have been, given that clearly expressed needs had already met with failure. When the management committee was faced with the incident of the van driver stabbed by the used hypodermics, they could not deny the veracity of the incident as it had been officially reported. However, as it could be explained – the cleaner had not been properly trained in the use of sharps boxes – it could be dismissed as an anomalous occurrence, therefore not of relevance to general safety policy, as the comment of the Infection Control Nurse demonstrates:

> Oh yes, we know about that, but we know why it happened. It's not the disposal system that's at fault, and it won't happen again.

As far as the risk to cleaners was concerned, the response was that 'cleaners were specifically told not to clean up blood spillages'. The cleaners, however, appeared to be unaware of this regulation. In response to other examples of risk situations, the Senior Microbiologist from HA 1 said in a written reply that he was reasonably certain that a number of the incidents I reported had not occurred locally, thus implying that they were fabricated either by the respondents or based upon biased research.

While the commissioning of research such as mine might be expected to shape what comes to be defined as 'expert' knowledge, clearly in HA 1 my research report or 'text' could not be used to reinforce the existing culture, but was instead seen as a threat to it. Therefore, rather than becoming part of the 'structuration' of the institution, it had to be rejected. The response in HA 2 to very similar incidents was less hostile. While there was still evidence that management in HA 2 had had little awareness of the practical problems and risks faced by the workforce, their greater willingness to accept my findings could be attributed to their need to support a bid for funding to implement an AIDS education programme. Thus, while criticisms in HA 1 had run counter to the prevailing culture, similar criticisms in HA 2 were used to support a culture managing a different agenda.

The source of risk information

In the absence of any appropriate or accessible information in either HA 1 or HA 2, risk assessments, founded on experience and a knowledge of working practice, were made on a daily basis by members of the workforce. This suggested an ability to manage complex risk situations in a sophisticated manner, thus throwing the experts' assumption of a requirement for 'simple messages' into doubt.

While the majority of respondents would have welcomed further information on the avoidance of risk from their health authority, they recognised that this could only be of value if delivered in a personal or interactive format. There was an awareness amongst the workforce that many of the risks encountered through their work remained hidden from management. As a result there was no belief that the usual methods of the dissemination of information, such as leaflets or posters, could be of significant use. Indeed, the lack of difference in levels of knowledge between workers in both health authorities suggests that HA 1's programme of education had had little, if any, effect. Responses similar to the following were common in both HA 1 and HA 2:

Not a leaflet. Someone coming round to give a talk like the fire brigade do. Then we could ask questions (Medical Laboratory Scientific Officer HA 2).

However, it seems that even if the information included in the 7,000 leaflets distributed by HA 1 to all members of staff in their wage packets had been appropriate, it would have been of little use. Enclosures in wage packets, which advertise services and goods ranging from insurance to double glazing, are resented and routinely thrown away unread by their recipients. Again responses from HA 1 and HA 2 were remarkably similar:

People are only interested in how much they've been paid, so this wouldn't be an effective way of communicating information (Clerk HA 1).

Another leaflet in a wages packet – forget it, it'll just get thrown away (Ambulance crew member HA 2).

The problem was further compounded by the belief that any attempt to provide effective protection from risk either through the provision of information or equipment, was unlikely to be forthcoming as it would cost money which would be begrudged (as shown by the quote from the ambulance crew member cited on p. 38). This raises an additional factor when untangling risk perceptions and the response to risk information. Clearly the source of information needs to be one which can be both trusted and respected. If information designed to reassure is received from a source which has already had its credibility damaged, or which the recipients of the information believe has a vested interest in cutting costs, any further attempt to inform, however accurate and well-intentioned, may be mistrusted and therefore rejected.

A prime example of this is provided by the experience of ambulance crews in HA 2 at a routine training lecture. When expressing concern about the possibility of their blood soaked clothing presenting a risk to them and their families, the lecturer's response was to take off his jumper, throw it from the first floor window, and claim that by the time it had reached the ground below, any HIV contamination on it would have died. Paradoxically, far from reassuring the ambulance crews that they were at minimal risk, they interpreted this gesture as an attempt to fob them off with platitudes. Consequently, all further information on risk supplied by the health authority was dismissed. Indeed, bulletins were routinely disregarded as being 'useless'. Having themselves experienced a lack of adequate protective clothing from the health authority, they assumed, rightly or wrongly, that any information emanating from them would be of little relevance.

The social risk

To assume that risk to health could be separated from social risks would be to minimise the complexity of the response to risk information. On occasions the social risks entailed in following safety advice outweigh the possible benefits, and the health risk is deemed the lesser of two evils. Clearly, with advice on the avoidance of HIV infection, the risks are multi-dimensional from both sexual and occupational infection.

It was apparent from the interview data that while the risk of HIV infection from unprotected sexual encounters was well understood by the majority of respondents, the risk of damaging a relationship was deemed even greater. Thus, while Family Planning Clinic (FPC) staff in HA 1 and HA 2 routinely advised those clients who were either married or in long term, supposedly faithful relationships, to practise safer sex with their partners, the staff themselves were unable to implement such strategies. When presented with this inconsistency they admitted the discrepancy, but believed the risk of damaging their relationships was greater than the risk of being infected by an unfaithful partner.

Here a direct comparison can be drawn between the safety guidelines on the avoidance of risk as devised by the health authority for use by the workforce, and the safety advice on the avoidance of risk as devised by the FPC staff and delivered to the client group. In both instances an ideal model of the recipient group had been constructed, and while it was possible for the FPC staff to see the flaws in the advice *given* to them, it did not lead to their ability to identify the flaws in the advice they *gave*.

The social risk also extended to the means which the health authority had provided for HIV testing. While respondents in both HA 1 and HA 2 expressed a wish for routinised and therefore unstigmatised testing[1], the provision made by the Genito Urinary Medicine (GUM) Clinic was perceived as adequate by management in both health authorities. However, despite the change in nomenclature from 'VD' Clinic, to 'Special Clinic' to 'GUM Clinic', the stigma remains. The attitude of staff who feared they had been put at risk from accidental occupational exposure to HIV can be summed up by the following quote from a van driver in HA 2:

> Everyone knows why people sit along that corridor at a certain time. You walk past and think 'oh dear they're busy today', there's no way you'd catch me sitting there.

The importance of stigma was also recognised by staff in the GUM Clinic in HA 1, if not by management, as evidenced by the following quote from a member of the GUM Clinic's nursing staff:

> When I used to work in Accident and Emergency, people I had treated would come up to me in the street and speak to me. Now I work here no one who has been to the clinic would risk saying 'hello' in case people knew where they had been. It's the same with staff in other departments, they don't want to have anything to do with us. They don't even walk by if they can help it in case anyone thinks they're coming here.

The result of the perceived social risk of attendance at the GUM Clinic led, in some instances, to a number of staff in both health authorities electing to donate blood in order to be tested for HIV without any attendant stigma. This action, while minimising the social risk for the individual, and possibly providing an effective solution at the micro level, has the potential for increasing risk at the macro level. For while any HIV positive blood would of course be rejected by the Blood Transfusion Service, and the donor informed of their serostatus, not all potential donors were aware of the time-lag between infection and the ability to detect HIV antibodies, thus posing a small, but significant risk of donating infected blood which remained undetected.

However, once again, in spite of being informed of both the social risk as experienced by the staff, and the possibly risky solution to the problem, the response from a member of the policy making body in HA 1 was:

> Well, I went to the GUM Clinic for a colposcopy and I didn't mind going there. They do all sorts of things now as well as treating sexually

transmitted diseases. People may say they want freer access to testing, but people want all sorts of things that aren't good for them, like unsafe sex. We can't just let them have what they want. Anyway if lots of people had tests, we wouldn't be able to cope with the hysteria from the number who'd be positive, and if they were negative they'd just go and behave in the same way again because they'd think they were safe. I don't see anything wrong with the present system (Health Promotion Officer).

This comment would appear to demonstrate an institutional response which denies the very particular social complexities associated with AIDS. Even when presented with evidence which challenged the risk as constructed by the policy making body of the health authority, the deeply embedded assumption appeared to be that by virtue of being 'experts' they had a better understanding of the risk, and that any departure on the part of the workforce in conforming to this model denoted fault or inadequacy.

However, the social risk is not confined to that posed by stigma. Rather it extends to the relationship with the patient or client group, and affects calculations about the probability of health risks in relation to other social and professional considerations. Thus, a calculated decision to risk a small chance of infection might be taken in preference to following safety procedures. This is evidenced by the actions of midwives in both HA 1 and HA 2, advised to wear goggles during deliveries to avoid the possibility of HIV infection through eyesplash:

We know that the fact that our patients are on the maternity ward means that they are sexually active, and we know that some of them might be HIV positive, but we'd rather put the patient before the risk. So we don't want to wear goggles and masks while attending women in labour (Midwives HA 1).

Whether or not the midwives' relationship with patients would actually have been damaged by taking this safety precaution is arguable, but the fact remains that safety advice was deemed inappropriate and unworkable.

Similar judgements, although not based on prior calculation, were made by staff in Accident and Emergency in both health authorities, who might be faced with the choice of giving immediate life-saving treatment to a seriously injured patient, or to stop and put on protective gloves before attempting to stop a haemorrhage. It seems that under such circumstances the majority of staff would act instinctively to save life, and worry about the risk of infection later, thus demonstrating that the risk of a patient dying is likely to override any calculation about the risk of infection by HIV, hepatitis B or any other infective organism[2].

It is daily judgements such as these which are not, and indeed possibly cannot be, addressed in policy documents, safety manuals and leaflets. But they are the stuff of which hospital life is frequently made.

A risky solution

Despite the tendency on the part of policy makers to address risk through means likely to be less than satisfactory and to minimise the complexity of adhering to safety advice, there was a recognition that accidents did indeed occur from time to time, and that staff were on occasions put at risk from infection by HIV through accidental injury.

In an attempt to minimise the risk of seroconversion from an infective needle stick or sharps injury, an immediate course of AZT was offered in HA 1. Indeed the possibility of offering prophylactic treatment was referred to in the 7,000 leaflets advising on safety. The unsatisfactory nature of AZT's use as a prophylactic treatment, the risk of long-term and toxic side effects, the problematic nature of the scientific evidence upon which such a policy was based, and the fact that HA 2 considered such treatment to be too risky to employ, are the subject of another study (Grinyer 1994). Suffice it to say at this point that the risk assessment exercise entered into after such an accident posed enormous problems.

The rationalisation of anomalous scientific information and the representation of a drug as minimally toxic may not be unusual in health policy and is well documented by Abraham's (1994) study of the use of *Opren* amongst elderly arthritis sufferers. Paradoxically, in this instance the policy of offering treatment with AZT had been implemented in order to demonstrate that the health authority was doing something rather than nothing for an injured health care worker. However, the risks associated with this treatment seem likely to outweigh either the unproven benefits or the small chance of infection.

Cultural attributes of blame and responsibility could be seen to be in operation here. Attitudes towards those infected with HIV have been commonly characterised by the means of infection. As Lupton (1993) argues, health risk can focus upon risk as a consequence of 'lifestyle' choices, and as such may be constructed as the self-imposed result of a lack of will power, moral weakness, venality or laziness on the part of the individual. In addition, with particular reference to AIDS, Douglas and Calvez say:

> If it is cancer or heart disease, enormous sums will be forthcoming. If the disease is categorised as something outsiders are prone to, along with their outsidership and reprehensible behaviour, the same outlay

will be sanctioned less readily. So the fears of those working with
AIDS victims that they will be segregated, marginalised, and discriminated against, are not unreasonable (1990: 463).

As Fumento (1990) argues, it is only the non-drug abusing, non-homo-
sexual sufferers who are regarded as innocent victims. Thus those whose
infection stems from sexual contact, particularly homosexuals, are
labelled 'guilty', whereas those infected through blood transfusions or
other medical procedures are deemed to be 'innocent' victims. This cate-
gorisation of 'guilt' and 'innocence' may unwittingly inform attitudes to
injured HCWs, and thus provoke a need to be active in the attempt to
minimise seroconversion.

If an injured HCW is constructed as an 'innocent' victim, as a result he
or she is therefore entitled to expensive treatment. This, however, can be
contrasted not only with the lack of routine (and much less costly) protective equipment provided to my respondents; it can also be contrasted
with the likely treatment of a 'guilty' victim. Thus a gay man arriving at
the hospital after an unsafe sexual encounter and asking for prophylactic
treatment would be unlikely to be offered a course of AZT. In an ironic
twist, although the gay man might be denied treatment with AZT, and
the HCW given it, more harm than good might be done by such an intervention at an early stage when seroconversion has not even been established (Grinyer 1994).

It seems that the construction of risk after an unsafe incident is
extremely complex. The health authority is having to manage a number
of agendas. Evidence from a separate survey of 35 health authorities
across the country (Grinyer 1994), suggests that even those health authorities who fear that the risks from a course of AZT outweigh any possible
benefits, are concerned about legal action. As a result, many feel obliged
to offer treatment in order to prevent the possibility of litigation at a
later date. That the majority of injured HCWs offered such treatment
appear to decline AZT, instead taking the probably smaller risk that they
will not seroconvert, is probably due to the manner in which the risks are
presented when the HCW is counselled. Existing relationships between
staff and management may also colour the manner in which such advice
is interpreted and acted upon.

The problem of institutional bias and a need for certainty

As demonstrated through the evidence already presented, naive expert
assumptions which lack recognition of the complex nature of social and
working practice may fail to address crucial issues governing the ability
to utilise official information. In the case of both health authorities, not

only had the social risk entailed by following official advice been neglected by policy makers, a similarly idealised model had been constructed which failed to address the physical risks as perceived and experienced by the workforce. As Wynne (1989, 1992) shows us, bland assurances that no danger exists are likely to be both unconvincing, and in some cases even dangerous. They may also lead to a mistrust of the institution which becomes impossible to repair. However, from the institutional responses to my research findings, it is clear that an assumption that the workforce demand 'no risk' assurances underpinned many policy decisions.

The prevalence of minimal effort at prevention, being combined with an expensive, unproven and potentially toxic remedy, is recognised in the following comment from a somewhat disillusioned Health Promotion Officer from HA 1:

> You could say that health promotion was like having a doctor just past the bend of a river pulling out half-drowned people and reviving them. If only he'd walked upstream a bit he could have stopped the person who was pushing them in.

It could be argued that the prevalence of this failure to recognise areas in which, with far less resources, greater impact could be made, represents a systematic bias in the construction of victims, and that this bias might account for the naivety of naive sociology.

It seems unlikely that this resistance to addressing the risks as they were experienced and perceived by the workforce was based on any unwillingness to provide adequate information or protection. Indeed, the attempt to provide prophylactic treatment in the form of AZT in HA 1, however unsatisfactory its effect, demonstrates not only a need to be seen to be acting in the interests of injured HCWs, but also a concern for the staff in question. The resistance, I would argue, was instead based upon an institutional inability to acknowledge the complexity of the working environment, the concomitant complexity inherent in the production of effective information programmes, and the multi-dimensional nature of the risks encountered. This might of course be exacerbated by the policy makers' wish to monopolise the accredited account of risk, thereby reinforcing institutionalised bias.

It could be argued that the political need for closure, both in terms of the science upon which the AZT policy was based, and around which social assumptions were made, led to a rationalisation of seemingly apparent anomalies. This could be interpreted as symptomatic of the way in which the structure of an organisation both informs the way in which a text is interpreted and feeds back into itself to reproduce the organisation in a circular process (Giddens 1984, Manning 1986). Thus, particular discourses lie at the heart of what constitutes an organisation, and what acts to sustain its continuation. In addition, the governance of expertise is a way in which organisations reproduce their power structures. In this instance it has resulted in the offering of an extremely expensive treatment of dubious efficacy which reflects the way in which managers' beliefs structure workers' experiences.

The texts used by Manning (1986) to demonstrate this point are the public's calls to the police. However, in relation to this study, it could be argued that the texts are the information on the use of AZT as a prophylactic treatment, and my research report on the risks as perceived and experienced by HCWs. These texts, it seems, were interpreted differently in HA 1 and in HA 2, but in such a way as to reinforce existing culture, thus turning anomalous material into organisationally actionable working practice which, in a process of circularity, not only reflected or echoed the existing organisational culture, but also served to reproduce it.

It is unclear precisely what mechanism would result in policy change, but, from extensive interviews among 35 other health authorities (Grinyer 1994), it appears that there is a strong desire for consensus and conformity. Many respondents asked me what policy other health authorities were employing, and insecurity at being different was evident. Thus, pressure to implement a coherent national policy might serve to undermine existing practices, and by extension, organisational culture.

To account for the management's construction of working practice only through the structuration of the organisation may, however, in this instance be to miss the point. An alternative analysis might be provided through the reflexive questioning of the implicit assumptions of my analysis regarding the manner in which policy making *should* be carried out. Such an analysis might expose a parallel process of ideal construction in operation. Much of this chapter has focused on the ways in which policy makers have constructed an ideal model of both working practice and response to safety information. It has been demonstrated through empirical evidence that this construction frequently bears little relation to the experience of the workforce. It would be easy to fall into the trap of fabricating a similarly constructed ideal model of how the policy makers in the health authority *ought* to function. While it is not the main focus of this study, it still needs to be recognised that the constraints within which the policy makers and experts operate, and the complexities with which they have to deal, affect their working practice in a manner which can be paralleled with that of their workforce. These complexities also include cultural factors beyond the confines of the institution such as professional training and science orientation.

Conclusion

This chapter has considered the perception of risk from a number of different perspectives. The risk as constructed by health authority policy makers has been compared with that experienced by the workforce, and a considerable gap has been identified between the two. Despite the fact that policy makers have little notion of the conditions in which the workforce themselves are 'expert', when faced with failures of safety procedure, it is the workforce who are criticised rather than the procedures. Though the extent to which this applies varies between HA 1 and HA 2, both health authorities shared this attitude to some degree.

The multi-dimensional nature of risk has also been demonstrated. Risk it seems is not confined to the physical, but extends to the social involving both professional and social relationships in a manner which appears to be overlooked by the 'experts'. Not only are risk perceptions multi-dimensional, but, at any given time, people are managing a number of different agendas which may conflict with the official ones and can be contradictory. Official information is only one of a number of different routes through which a hazard is understood. Powerful social forces shape the way in which information is perceived and acted upon in a way which may be underestimated by those responsible for risk assessment and the compilation of official information. Connections may be made by the recipients in unexpected ways, and the resulting interpretation of official data may be substantially different from official predictions.

The interpretation of risk information may also, it seems, be affected by previous experience of the institution responsible for disseminating the information. Thus, as we have seen, when trust and respect are damaged, any further attempt on the part of the institution to provide advice may be dismissed. This is an issue which clearly has profound implications for the receipt of risk and safety information.

The adoption of a particular theoretical and political approach to this study might warrant an accusation of bias which idealises the public's ability to manage risk. Clearly, amongst the lay public there is a wide differential in the ability both within and between individuals, under a variety of conditions, to manage information and risk situations. While acknowledging this, it would still seem to be justifiable to argue that whatever their social position, lay people can possess an understanding or knowledge of social complexities and practical constraints which could be described as 'expertise'. Thus they hold an expertise different from, but additional to, that of the technical experts.

Many of the findings of the fieldwork discussed in this chapter endorse other work in the field (Wynne 1989, 1991, 1993, Nelkin and Brown 1984). There would, therefore, appear to be a need for technical experts to recognise and integrate the two spheres of expertise before information on risk and safety measures could practicably be implemented by lay groups. This, however, raises the problem of how to integrate this additional knowledge when it does not simply supplement, but challenges or contradicts technical expertise. In such circumstances the existing relationship between the technical experts and the lay group may determine whether or not the lay expertise can be accommodated. In the case of the health authorities, particularly HA 1, it seems that deeply embedded social relationships served to mutually reinforce both the policy makers' construction of the workforce and vice versa.

Acknowledgement

I would like to thank Mike Michael for his helpful comments on an earlier draft of this chapter.

Notes

1 I do not wish to suggest that routine testing would be unproblematic. Clearly the ethical implications and the potential threat to employment if an HCW is found to be HIV positive through such testing pose problems. However, the point here is that the existing testing facilities were perceived as being unacceptable, and that rather than addressing the expressed needs exposed through my research, the experience of the HCWs was interpreted by policy makers as denoting ignorance.
2 The risks addressed in this chapter have been largely confined to those posed by HIV infection. However, many respondents had an underlying knowledge that by virtue of working in a hospital setting they were at constant low-grade risk. This was not frequently or consciously addressed, and although feared more than other hazards, the chance of encountering AIDS/HIV was considered to be fairly low down the list of potential hazards. Risk hierarchies were informally constructed by different occupational groups and varied from a general fear of 'germs' to more specific concerns over infection from TB, and hepatitis B. Nursing staff also feared back injury, and radiography staff were constantly aware of the risk from radiation. Risk management strategies, unobserved by management, were frequently employed. These provide evidence of expert knowledge of the working environment used as a basis for a sometimes sophisticated and complex approach to the avoidance of risk.

References

Abraham, J. (1994) Bias in science and medical knowledge: the Opren controversy, *Sociology*, 8, 717–36.

Barnes, J. (1979) *Who Should Know What?* Harmonsworth: Penguin.

Becker, H. (1967) Whose side are we on? *Social Problems*, 4, 239–47.

Bell, C. and Encell, S. (eds) (1978) *Inside the Whale*. Oxford: Pergamon. Press.

Bell, C. and Newby, H. (1977) *Doing Sociological Research*. London: Allen and Unwin.

Bloor, D. (1978) Polyhedra and the abomination of Leviticus, *The British Journal for the History of Science*, 11, 245–72.

Douglas, M. and Calvez, M. (1990) The self as risk taker: a cultural theory of contagion in relation to AIDS, *Sociological Review*, 38, 445–64.

Dunsmuir, A. and Williams, L. (1991) *How To Do Social Research*. London: Collins Educational.

Fumento, M. (1990) *The Myth of Heterosxual AIDS*. New York: Basic Books.

Giddens, A. (1984) *The Constitution of Society*. Cambridge: Polity Press.

Grinyer, A. (1994) AZT kill or cure? The social essences of scientific authority, *Sociological Review*, 42, 686–702.

Hughes, J. and Ackroyd, S. (1992) *Data Collection in Context*. Harlow: Longman.

Latour, B. (1987) *Science in Action*. Milton Keynes: Open University Press.

Latour, B. and Woolgar, S. (1986) *Laboratory Life*. New Jersey: Princetown University Press.

Lupton, D. (1993) Risk as moral danger: the social and political functions of risk discourse in public health, *International Journal of Health Services*, 23, 425–35.

May, T. (1993) *Social Research: Issues Methods and Process*. Milton Keynes: Open University Press.

Manning, P. (1986) Texts as organizational echoes, *Human Studies*, 9, 287–302.

Nelkin, D. and Brown, M.S. (1984) *Workers at Risk*. London: University of Chicago Press.

Pinch, T. (1981) The Sun-set: the presentation of certainty in scientific life, *Social Studies of Science*, 11, 131–58.

Spradley, J. (1979) *The Ethnographic Interview*. New York: Holt, Rinehart and Winston.

Sims, J.H. and Bauman, D.D. (1983) Educational programmes and human response to natural hazards, *Environment and Behaviour*, 15, 165–89.

Wynne, B. (1989) Frameworks of rationality in risk management: towards the testing of naive sociology. In Brown, J. (ed), *Environmental Threats*. London: Belhaven Press.

Wynne, B. (1991) Knowledges in context, *Science, Technology and Human Values*, 16, 111–21.

Wynne, B. (1992) Misunderstood misunderstanding: social identities and the public uptake of science, *Public Understanding of Science*, 1, 281–304.

3. The medical model of the body as a site of risk: a case study of childbirth

Karen Lane

Introduction

[Looking back on the experience] I think they're really trying hard to make it a different sort of experience than what had happened there before . . . I can't really complain. I'm a little bit worried – and I guess this goes for any hospital situation – I'm a little bit concerned about the technology and what it actually does to babies, to a natural event – or it should be natural – and the intervention. I asked for too much and I think perhaps maybe this wouldn't have happened if I'd just gone into labour naturally and had less intervention. But I'm not ever to know that . . .

I'd planned on sort of being mobile and that was a disappointment as well. Yes, I guess consenting to things that were really against my better judgement – well, things that I hadn't wanted to happen and then being forced on me, well, in a manner of speaking – was really what disappointed me the most. I guess I wasn't being very assertive, but I suppose in that sort of situation one wouldn't really be expected to . . .[1]

These statements came from women who gave birth in Australian hospitals where the medical model was the dominant principle. The women expressed retrospective uneasiness and disappointment because they had wanted a 'natural' birth (that is, one free from intervention) and they had wanted to maintain control over events and procedures. Whilst the women had attempted to exercise agency during their labour and delivery, a medicalised approach to childbirth under the hospital regime had virtually squashed their ambitions. Although they remained unsure whether the interventions had really been necessary, what is ultimately interesting about their testimonies for the purposes of this chapter is an element of reflexive criticism towards medical authority.

The above comments may be located in the now voluble level of reaction against the cult of the expert in diverse professional spheres. In this sense, Beck (1992) has been correct to argue at a macrotheoretical level that the private sphere has become politicised. Business, industry and science were areas previously accorded to the bourgeois private sphere and therefore free from political intervention. However, the expansion of the welfare state and the possibility of future hazards of large-scale technological innovation have encouraged a mass critique of state and corporate legitimation. The novel contribution by Beck in the debate about risk is that reflexive modernity and risk society are analogous. Classical industrial society, or simple modernity, was characterised by the dominance of the logic of wealth production over risk production because it was driven by an ideology of scarcity. By contrast, in this new phase of modernity, 'progress' is increasingly overshadowed by the production of risks. The risks are beheld as irrevocable threats to all forms of life. Unlike the personal and visible risks facing earlier societies, the risks of high modernity are the risks of self-destruction. They are no longer limited to specific localities or groups, but are globalised, hidden to the senses, non class-specific and supra-national. Whilst they remain imperceptible to the senses, their universality is evident in localised side-effects – the toxins present in foodstuffs, pollutants, radio-activity or the nuclear threat. Thus, the realisation that the threats are universal breeds a novel type of social and political dynamism. Such 'methodical skepticism' within reflexive modernity attacks the very foundations of modern science to the point where science is both 'generalised' and 'demystified' (Beck 1992: 14). The socialisation of risk produces social risk positions, or a differentiation in the degree of risk experienced. Some nations, notably those in the Third World, are more at risk than advanced nations. Also some are more knowledgeable about risks than others. Ultimately, the knowledge about risk-inducing production decisions of big business flows through to the public sphere so that citizens and governments have a mandate to intervene in the industrialisation process itself. However, Beck has inserted a sub-thesis which argues that mass politicisation cannot be applied to medical science.

Beck designates medicine as an extreme case of sub-politics because in the medical field there is no equivalent institutional separation of powers which may foster the emergence of critical social movements. This is because successful professionalisation since the turn of the century has prevented the delegitimation of medicine, both externally and internally. Professionalisation has successfully protected its research institutionally; it has been able to determine its own standards and training procedures for future generations of medical students; and it has been able to control the practical application of the knowledge within its own institutions. Hospitals represent 'the organizational roof under which research, training and practice are interconnected' (Beck 1992: 209–10). Consequently, he argues, the medical profession has been able to convince the public that it is conceptually 'uninformed', and that it lags hopelessly behind medical innovation and medical knowledge. In effect, the assertion of mastery over nature has accomplished the most thorough-going mastery over the subject. As Foucault (1973) argued, medicine is a parable about social control.

Beck can be criticised for the failure to distinguish between hazard and risk. He wants to use 'risk' to describe social relationships, but most of his examples refer to environmental hazard (Turner 1994). While it is recognised in this chapter that birth involves hazard, the main focus is on the risk of birth which is produced by precipitous medical intervention, by the bureaucratisation of birth which ignores the importance of the social relations surrounding birth, and by social and historical factors, such as poor diet, poor health, poor income and housing (Oakley 1986). Thus, Beck's thesis provides a useful paradigm for research in medical sociology. There are, of course, difficulties with Beck's historical argument regarding palpable risk, but these issues are beyond the scope of this chapter.

Medical science and childbirth

It is argued here that Beck's thesis must be treated with caution in relation to childbirth. It is the case that under the medical model of childbirth, risk has been assigned to individuals rather than structural and social conditions. The individualisation of risk has, therefore, legitimated the routine use of interventions such as amniotomy (artificial breaking of fetal membranes); pharmacological induction of labour; adoption of the lithotomy position in delivery or labour (still practised in Eastern Europe but losing favour in Western Europe, the United States and Australia); drugs for pain relief and epidural; routine intrapartum electronic fetal monitoring; and episiotomy (Marsden 1994). Consumer dissatisfaction with antenatal care has always existed. However, organised protest by women's lobby groups, by concerned doctors and academics, and other consumer groups generally, of medical practice relating to women's health began mainly in the UK and the USA in the 1960s and 1970s. Medical and state responses to the 'vocal minority', as they were labelled, have included co-option of dissent, a more rationalised approach to antenatal care, an acceleration towards more technical controls of the kind mentioned above and even greater specialisation within obstetrics (Oakley 1986). These responses at the same time both increased state and medical surveillance over women and individualised the blame for adverse outcomes. Beck's argument is that it is only in recent years that medical practices and interventions have received systematic scrutiny by state agencies. Previously, as Oakley (1986) has shown, the state and medical science formed an unholy alliance. The state exercised indirect control over medicine through the construction of social and economic policy, but left the profession to control technological development and assessment. Beck has been correct to argue, in one sense, that medical science has proceeded largely undeterred by widespread democratic evaluation.

   Critics of the medical model have not denied the utility of risk assessment. That is, an alternative, social model of childbirth, would not dispense with risk criteria in evaluating level of risk, although the kinds of criteria and measuring devices may well be challenged. For example, the value of electronic fetal monitoring and ultrasound scanning as early screening devices have come under attack for their unreliable predictive properties and possible harmful effects (Marsden 1994). Extra-medical criteria such as emotional equilibrium may also be used to supplement obstetric factors in the designation of risk status. However, the assessment of risk will continue to organise the delivery of maternity services. Beck would appear to be correct, therefore, at least at the more general level of his framework about late modernity.

   However, Beck's thesis regarding the impenetrable nature of medical science cannot be confirmed. Internal and external critiques of medicine have led to two policy documents in Britain – the Winterton Committee report (Health Committee 1992), and a new government paper entitled *Changing Childbirth* (Department of Health 1994). In Australia, also, the National Health and Medical Research Council (NH&MRC 1994) has challenged medical dominance in childbirth. These reports have recommended a greater role for midwives, an expanded set of options for women and a plurality of models of care for low-risk women. Significantly, the documents have been very critical of routine obstetric interventions. Such interventions have been employed, according to the NH&MRC document, more on the basis of 'myth and fashion' rather than rigorous scientific assessment (1994: 16). The World Health Organisation meeting in Brazil in 1994 endorsed that view (Marsden 1994).

   The argument in this chapter both refutes and supports Beck's thesis. Medical science has not remained immune from internal and external critique. However, Beck has identified a characteristic feature of late modernity – the prominent nature of debates about risk. It is the case that debates about childbirth will most likely continue to pivot around the notion of risk despite the low rates of mortality and morbidity relative to pre-war figures in advanced Western economies. What is at issue in childbirth, therefore, is not the question of risk or no risk, but i) the iatrogenic risk of medical interventions ii) the realisation of social control over women by the use of a risk vocabulary to describe maternity iii) what additional criteria should be used to assess risk, (such as women's perception of their physical and social environment) and iv) whether risk has monopolised the debates about childbirth to the exclusion of other factors such as emotional satisfaction and control over the events and procedures surrounding birth. This chapter will consider these issues.

Bodies at risk

Interventions

I am not concerned here with the intention of doctors, but with the central assumptions of the medical model. The medical model assumes that the body is always ready to fail, even in ostensibly low-risk cases. As Douglas (1990) has argued, risk is not a neutral term. Doctors do not talk about a 'good' risk. The term is used negatively – and with negative consequences for women. For example, the following table (Table 1) is indicative of the higher rates of intervention experienced by women in Victorian hospitals compared with women who delivered in a midwifery-run birth centre (Health Department Victoria 1990, Monash Medical Centre 1993).

Findings of major studies cited below also support the view that midwifery care within the home or birth-centre (where a social model, or woman-centred model is adopted) demonstrate lower mortality rates, better Apgar scores (these scores include heart rate, respiratory effort, muscle tone, reflex irritability and colour of skin) and lower intervention rates, including forceps and ventouse delivery, augmentation, caesarean, episiotomy and pain relief (Elliott 1992, Duran 1992, Declercq 1984, Hemminiki *et al* 1992, Campbell *et al* 1984, Cavero *et al* 1991, Haire and Elsberry 1991, Tew 1990, Tew and Damstra-Wijmenga 1991).

Table 1. *Comparative rates of interventions – hospital and birth centre*

	Rep. study of 100 women in Vic hospitals[1] %	Birth Centre (Moorabin)[2] %
Spon. labour	62.0	89.0
Induction	27.0	4.7
Augmentation	11.0	5.4
Forceps	6.0	4.7
Caesarean	14.0	5.1
Episiotomy	14.0	0
Tears, stitches	16.0	33.0 (11.5% 1st degree)
No intervention	11.0	44.7

1. Health Dept. Victoria 1990
2. Monash Med. Centre 1993

Mortality: home versus hospital

The most persuasive and most recent arguments for lower mortality rates associated with midwifery care (and GP care) can be found in: Tew (1990), Tew and Damstra-Wijmenga (1991), Campbell *et al* (1984),

Campbell and Macfarlane (1987), Duran (1992), Albers and Katz (1991), Morris *et al* (1986), Biro and Lumley (1991), Street *et al* (1991), Cavero *et al* (1991), Elliott (1992), Ford *et al* (1991), and Tyson (1991). All of the above are large studies and all conclude that midwifery care (sometimes in collaboration with a GP) achieves comparable or better perinatal mortality rates (PNMR's) than obstetric care.

Bundy (1993), in arguing the case for obstetrics and hospital birth, has responded to this kind of statistical evidence by saying that the homebirth rate is, in fact, not favourable because homebirths exclude high-risk women and babies. Hospitals are obliged to accept all categories, he argues, including high-risk categories for both infant and mother, including pre-term, low-birthweight infants (the highest cause of perinatal death). Hence, the homebirth rate should be much lower. Several rejoinders need to be made. The authors of the studies above dispute the claim that hospital is safer when calculated on crude PNMR's. However, it is correct to argue that proper comparisons of childbirth by location can only be accurately assessed when standardised studies are undertaken. Tew (1990) is one of the few researchers to have carried out this test.

Tew (1990) found that it was safer to give birth in Britain at home with a midwife than in an obstetric unit in a hospital. She also found that it was eleven times safer to give birth in The Netherlands at home attended by a midwife than by an obstetrician in hospital (Tew and Damstra-Wijmenga 1991). Tew's extensive studies of comparative national perinatal rates took into account the high maternal risk due to age and parity associated with hospital births. She found that hardly any of the hospitals' excess mortality was due to their excess of births at high risk on account of maternal age and parity. She also found that the greater safety of homebirth pertained at all levels of risk status of the mother (low, medium or high) on a number of obstetrical and sociological indicators – parity, social class, toxaemia and fetal gestation (Tew 1990). Campbell and MacFarlane (1987) also examined standardised rates in Britain and agreed with Tew that the greater safety of hospital birth could not be supported by statistical analysis. However, they disputed the degree of safety claimed by Tew, because Tew attributed mortalities arising from transferred cases to the hospital.

It is unlikely that the debate about safety relative to setting and location will be resolved satisfactorily because the definition of risk, or what criteria should be employed to determine level of risk, is a contested terrain. There are different discourses of risk around differing views of the body, women and the nature of childbirth. Some obstetricians (for example, Permezel *et al* (1987) reported below) extrapolate levels of interventions received by women who deliver in hospital, or rates of transfer from birth centre to labour ward, as an adequate rationale that all women are at risk and that the site of the risk cannot be fully anticipated prior to birth. Therefore, they conclude, all women should give birth in hospital in close proximity to life-saving, high-technological aids. Others argue that it is impossible to carry out rigorous assessment of the safety of homebirth compared to hospital birth because of the sheer size of the project. In the UK, for example, it would apparently require more than 700,000 women to be able to include 176,000 in a randomised trial (NH&MRC 1994: 25). On a different tack, a sociologist of science (Richards 1991: 231–6) has argued against the scientific 'truths' yielded by randomised control trials on the grounds that objective assessment is impossible. The medical expert must be seen as a 'partisan participant' in the design, operation and evaluation of any research trial. It is also not adequate, she argues, that social and economic criteria simply be added onto the clinical trial, but that social values and needs must be injected into the design phase as well as the evaluative process.

In the case of randomised trials conducted on comparative safety levels, it is difficult to separate out the variables and hold each constant so that only one variable may be tested because all processes are related and accumulative. Also, it would be impossible to accord an appropriate weighting to phenomenological factors. Yet qualitative evidence gathered from my interviews with forty women (which are reported in this chapter) indicates the significance of their perceptions of the environment upon bodily functions and progress in labour and delivery[2]. From yet another perspective, an independent midwife believes that safety is significantly underpinned by continuity of care. On this view, getting to know the woman and her family over a period of time allows the midwife to assess her idiosyncratic desires and responses during the labour process. As she says. . . . 'Whatever you do, the woman must have ascendancy in the relationship' (McDonald 1992: 207).

It is worth considering Beck's thesis about the self-referential and closetted nature of medical science in relation to the debate about comparative PNMR levels. Tew's research was cited in the UK Government's Winterton Report (Health Committee 1992) as a more 'radical' set of findings. Campbell and McFarlane's more cautionary stance that hospital was not safer (as opposed to Tew's more positive finding that homebirth had been found to be safer at every level of risk status of the mother including high risk) appeared to find more favour with the investigating Committee. Moreover, it took fifteen years for mainstream orthodox medical journals to recognise and publish Tew's work.

The attribution of risk as a form of social control

In the case of childbirth, it is argued that the imposition of a risk category on all women acts as a form of micro-social regulation bringing about acquiesence to medical intervention. It is true that the majority of women are deemed medically low-risk cases, but the very term 'risk' implies the probability of mischance. Douglas (1990) is correct to point out that the term 'risk' has a forensic dimension. It is employed retrospectively to explain a mishap and it is used to forewarn of immanent disaster should the action be repeated. The rhetoric of risk is further augmented within maternity discourse. Adverse events are not only regarded as inevitable, but their timing is seen to be capricious and unpredictable. By deduction, therefore, all women are subject to obstetric control and surveillance because all women are regarded as 'at risk'. For example, the obstetric team at the Royal Women's Hospital, Melbourne believes that:

> Despite careful selection of a low-risk population there remains a persistent incidence of potential serious complications and a continuing need for obstetric intervention (Permezel *et al.* 1987: 22).

This statement pertained to a study of 1,794 low-risk women selected for delivery in a birth unit, of whom only 68.4% remained to deliver there. In other words, 34.4% were transferred to a hospital labour ward. Other Australian studies reported the same pattern. Morris *et al* (1986) found that 37.6% were transferred from a birth centre to a high-technology labour ward and Linder-Pelz *et al* (1990) found that 30% of women transferred from birth centre to labour ward. By contrast, Australian studies of homebirth show lower rates. Woodcock *et al* (1990) reported a transfer rate of 24.6% and Crotty *et al* (1990) reported a 17% rate of transfer. In the UK, a study by Shearer (1985) recorded a transfer rate of 11.9% and a Dutch study by Damstra-Wijmenga (1984) reported a 15.6% transfer rate.

It is substantially on the grounds of this kind of evidence, collected with regard to medically-defined low-risk women, that obstetricians claim that all women are potentially at risk during childbirth. Medical criteria used to assess the risk status of individual women include age, parity (number of other live babies), previous history of post-partum haemorrhage, previous stillbirth, a history of caesarean section and adverse medical history. Although individual histories may furnish more precise details for assessment, even low-risk women so assessed are regarded as potentially at risk because of the generalised data on transfer rates and intervention levels in hospitals.

It should be noted that there are significant variations in childbirth procedures in hospitals in different countries and in different hospitals within the same country. Also many positive changes have occurred in more recent years. Yet a World Health Organisation survey of 23 countries revealed that women's choices are substantially circumscribed with regard to shaving, birth method, birth position, anaesthesia/analgesia, people present, choice of doctor, holding a dead newborn, electronic fetal monitoring and episiotomy (WHO 1985: 25). An Australian midwife (McDonald 1992: 151–2) who gathered qualitative evidence from women's experiences of hospital birth has described a fairly typical regime. The woman is asked to remove her clothes, don a gown and get onto a bed to be examined. Various tests are completed and questions asked. The mother lies on her back while the abdomen is examined and the baby's heartbeat is checked. The woman lies there until some time later the doctor comes in and repeats what the midwife did and asks her the same questions. He also feels her abdomen and wants to do an internal examination to verify that she is in labour. This would be amusing, says McDonald, except that 'disoriented submission' has already set in since the woman has been in this position for over half an hour while enduring contractions and longing to roll over. The doctor comforts her by saying that he will make sure she gets some pain relief when he is finished.

Risk communities

The imposition of a risk category also involves a moral dimension (Douglas 1990). Women may be categorised into those who are voluntarily risk-inducing because of their 'irresponsible' actions, as opposed to those who are voluntarily risk-avoiding because of their adherence to medical norms. Women who report to a doctor that they intend to birth at home, for example, may find themselves admonished for irresponsible behaviour. The following is a typical account from an Australian woman:

Caroline: My sister was also planning a homebirth . . . so we both fronted up together [at the public hospital] to book as public patients, just in case. I spoke to the sister in charge . . . who said 'Well don't worry about booking, we won't refuse you care but just don't mention the home birth or just come in – come into the clinic and just go through the motions and make your booking and it's best if you just don't mention the homebirth.'

British women have reported similar responses from their GPs in the 1980s, although not all GPs in Britain have been antipathetic to homebirth. More recently the Winterton recommendations (Department of Health 1992) demanded that GPs respect women's choices to birth at home. The following is an account by a British woman:

Janet: The first GP I went to was Dr Smith . . . and she tore strips off me and said I was irresponsible and she wouldn't have anything to do with such an irresponsible act. I was putting myself and the baby at risk and so on, and so forth. I said 'Well, I was only sort of enquiring about it, but OK get off me'. And my husband thought it would be horribly risky and we would need a lot of medical assistance around.

And then by chance I had to go to the GP because I had awful flu when I was pregnant . . . and then mentioned 'Well I know you're not terribly keen on homebirth'. And he said 'Well, who said I wasn't . . . no, on the contrary I'm very supportive of homebirth'.

Women's perceptions of the social and physical environment

It is argued here that women's interpretations of their social and physical environment are determining factors in the progress of the labour. Affective states should therefore be included in risk assessment. Yet women's emotional and subjective responses are regarded as either secondary or insignificant by obstetric staff. This suppression of women's emotional responses follows from a medical theory which embraces a reductionist and mechanistic view of the birthing process. In the medical model, birthing is conceptualised as a set of discrete internal, muscular and chemical reactions unrelated to external (social, historical and personal) factors. When the body fails, it is logical under this philosophy for an external agent to correct the internal malfunction. Immediate contextual factors, including positive and negative social exchanges and emotional responses to physical surroundings, are rarely examined or considered in the causal framework of the medical model. However, these contextual factors are the primary social determinants of risk precipitating medical intervention.

This chapter has already cited the substantial number of cases which are transferred from birth centre to labour ward and the assumption made by the medical model that women are inherently at risk because of the pending failure of their bodies. Little research has appeared on the question of why women fail to progress, yet over one third of hospital deliveries in Victorian hospitals in Australia cited 'lack of progress in labour' as the reason for transfer (Health Department, Victoria 1990: 93). This umbrella term incorporates uterine inertia, lack of dilatation of the cervix and maternal exhaustion. It is argued here that these terms merely describe an already existing state. They are not reasons, but states of being. These states of being may seem legitimate reasons for medical intervention, but they do not provide a causal explanation. It is suggested here that the social context is a crucial determining influence, among others, in the progress of labour. For example, the following evidence was given by Australian women who have been deterred from satisfactory progress because of their negative perceptions of social relations surrounding the birth, or the childbirth regimes:

Meredith: The birth was going well. It was the people around me who didn't make it any easier and I basically stopped it from fear then.

They really upset me and I stopped contracting and I didn't start till 5 o'clock the next morning. [This delay was sustained for approximately 12 hours].

Francis: Actually I enjoyed the first part at the hospital because that was very low key and I was in a bath a lot. In fact when I was just with the midwives I was fine. It was when the doctors got involved that things became more negative for me because I think the midwives do treat you as if you're a person, the doctors do treat you as if you're a case. [Francis was 9 cm dilated before she decided to enter hospital. After entering hospital her contractions stopped until oxytocin was administered]:

Women's negative perceptions of hospitalised birthing are also demonstrated dramatically in the sequence which is called the 'cascade of intervention' (Health Department Victoria 1990: 90, World Health Organisation 1985: 98). It is common for women to enter hospital in 'good' labour but to find that their progress deteriorates over time. The following account from a woman who delivered in a British hospital in 1991 describes such a case:

Mona: By that time [on entry to the maternity ward at 1 p.m.], I was already 3 cm dilated, it was very quick . . . The room itself was very stark and not particularly comfortable, and they did offer me the option of a bean bag, but I ended up finding that lying on my side was comfortable. Then there was all this panic over not being able to find the baby's heartbeat that started fairly early on in the first stage. They kept making me lie down to find the baby's heartbeat. I asked for Pethidine an hour before the end of the first stage, when things were getting really tense and the contractions were very painful. . . . And then they wouldn't let me get into that position where I was upright. [Because she was asked to lie down the urge to push receded]. Once or twice I actually persuaded them to let me come up and they put the back of the bed into a sitting position. I lent forward over it and that was really comfortable but they were fumbling around with this monitor around my stomach. At this stage the urge was beginning to come back and then they said 'No, no, we can't trace the baby's heart, this is no good, you'll have to lie down'. So I did. . . . Really I didn't have the urge . . . so I was having to really work and that was up here in my head. It was such hard work and I can remember towards the last few hours I was really, every time I pushed I was shouting out. I remember the midwife saying 'If you put more energy into the pushing and not through your vocal cords you'd get there a lot quicker'. They said that to me and I thought that was miserable. . . . They wouldn't let me do what I wanted, which was to sit up. They seemed to be overly panicky tracing the baby's heartbeat and they wouldn't actually let me sit up. . . . Then because I just got so tired and his head was coming and going, coming and going, they gave me whatever the drug is that helps you to push. And then they gave me an episiotomy, because I just couldn't push him out and I was tearing and I tore all the way to the anal canal. I needed 26 stitches and what was worse was my GP went and left it to the sister, who didn't realise how deep the tear was. The next day the whole lot broke down and I had to have it all done again. Despite the anaesthetic I could feel every stitch and they were giving me gas and air and I was just sobbing as every stitch went in. I can just remember feeling uncontrolled, I just had no pride any more, I just sobbed and sobbed.

It is not claimed here that there is a direct, causal effect between entering hospital and intervention. What follows is a 'cascade of intervention' – a situation where a minor, initial intervention is followed by a further intervention and where the accumulative effect is a catalogue of treatments which deny autonomy, choice and satisfaction for most women. Medical personnel appear impervious to the huge gap between women's desires for 'natural' birth and the high levels of intervention because they assume that intervention is normal and necessary. Thus, a circular logic takes place. Women are told, and some believe, that they needed to have intervention and that failure to intervene would have resulted in death or injury. It is never examined whether it was women's perception of the nature of the environment and their reactions to the minor, initial intervention which precipitated major invasionary procedures. Kennell et al. .(1991) have provided evidence of the importance of phenomenological factors during birth by showing that there is less need for augmentation of labour and delivery by caesarean section when women are supported by a trained birth companion or if a neutral observer is present in the hospital delivery room.

In summary, the assumption of general and inevitable risk might be considered a risk-inducing factor. A contrasting set of data is available from women who booked to give birth at home in Australia (around 0.1% of the total who gave birth during 1988–90). Of the 2,372 women who intended to give birth at home, only 12.9% were transferred to hospital, and only 5.6% were transferred due to lack of progress in labour. Only 7.2% of these required augmentation, assisted vaginal birth or caesarean section (Bastian and Lancaster 1992: 32–3). Not all of these women were medically-defined as low-risk, although a precise breakdown of previous obstetric and gynaecological histories was not published[3]. The woman's perception of her own competence to birth without intervention is dependent upon the nature of the setting, the relations between the mother and those surrounding the birth, and the mother's perceptions of the immediate physical and social environment. Of particular importance to women is their sense of maintaining control over all events (Lane 1993, 1994).

Hospital rules are designed to rationalise the birthing process in the interests of medical and hospital planning, to guard against any unforseen adversity, and to protect doctors against litigation procedures on the grounds of neglect or mismanagement (Katz-Rothman 1982). In many cases, intervention occurs precipitously and defensively 'just in case something goes wrong'. It is now conventional for medical staff to state that a safe birth can only be judged in retrospect. As one obstetrician is recorded as saying 'Nature is a lousy midwife' (The Australian College of Midwives retaliated with the reply that 'Nature could equally be a lousy obstetrician') (cited in Bundy 1993: 3). The effect of the medicalisation of birth is to incite varying degrees of anxiety, irritation, humiliation, pain and fear, rather than comfort, confidence and security[4]. Yet confidence in her body is probably the greatest asset to the mother during labour and delivery. Conversely, fear is the most decisive element in the erosion of safety and ease of delivery.

Has the risk vocabulary colonised the debate?

Debates about childbirth have been colonised around the notion of 'risk'. My argument is that obstetricians have pursued the issue of mortality rather than the quality of the woman's experience. For obstetricians, a birth has been successful if both the mother and the baby remain alive after the birth. The birth of a 'perfect baby' from a medical point of view does not involve any reference to a patient's experience. As one obstetrician reported:

> It was what we were all trained to always go after – the perfect baby. That's what we were trained to produce. The quality of the mother's experience – we rarely thought about that (Davis-Floyd 1990: 277).

Many studies of consumer preferences indicate that women employ a far greater range of criteria in addition to mortality to assess the conditions pertaining to positive birth. On the issue of maternal satisfaction, Australian women found little to recommend hospital-clinic care with its lack of continuity, low staff-client ratios, and lack of respect for individuality and intimacy (Health Department Victoria 1990). One study found that 40% of respondents who gave birth in hospitals would prefer another place of birth, usually a birth centre (Health Department Victoria 1990). A study conducted at Westmead Hospital, Sydney supports the view that women preferred a midwifery-run clinic to a normal labour ward (Giles et al., 1992). Also, the great majority of women who have experienced homebirth would choose that option again (National Childbirth Trust 1991, Goldthorp and Richman 1974, O'Brien 1978).

A joint study by women's health units in Monash and Melbourne universities found that women experienced a greater degree of dissatisfaction and an increased risk of being depressed after major obstetric intervention during birth (Brown et al 1992). A randomised controlled trial conducted by Giles (1992) at the antenatal clinic at Westmead Hospital, University of Sydney, indicated that the group cared for by midwives showed significantly greater appreciation of the continuity of care and information given than the group cared for by obstetricians. (Salary cost savings of between 28%–68% were also achieved). Elliott (1992) reported a high degree of maternal satisfaction with midwifery-only care at Boothville maternity hospital. A study on planned homebirth in New Zealand (Abel and Kearns 1991) reported that midwifery-only care afforded three dimensions of experience unavailable in a hospital context: control, continuity of care and the familiarity of setting.

Chamberlain et al (1991) found from a survey of 1,109 Canadian women that those who had experienced a homebirth would make the same choice again. Schlatter (1990) evaluated the responses of one hundred and fifteen women who delivered at Illinois Masonic Medical Centre in Chicago. Those who delivered in the Alternative Birthing Centre reported more involvement in decision-making and higher levels of satisfaction than women who attended the conventional labour ward. Flint et al (1989) found that the 'Know Your Midwife' Scheme was associated with greater continuity in all phases of maternity care, higher levels of satisfaction, and less obstetric intervention, particularly in augmentation of labour and intrapartum analgesia. Skibsted and Lange (1989) in Denmark found that women preferred the physical surroundings, personal attention and friendly environment of the (maternity-run) birth centre and that their positive outlook expedited delivery.

Conclusion

Oakley (1986) and Tew (1990) have argued that, although childbirth involves a risk to life and health for a minority of women and babies, the major risks are associated with factors which exist socially and historically. Risk is, therefore, both general and systemic. Major risks to women include: i) medical interventions, ii) generalised historical factors which produce poor health including low income, poor diet and smoking, and factors which are associated with the manual social class, and iii) women's negative perceptions of the social and physical environment (Lane 1993, 1994).

Studies of comparative models of care show that midwifery care has been associated with higher consumer participation in decision-making; a greater degree of control experienced by women over conditions and procedures; and higher levels of emotional satisfaction, which in turn contribute to the ease, efficiency and safety of labour and delivery. These conditions in turn discourage intervention. The conclusion is that the moral high-ground traditionally occupied by orthodox obstetrics has no rational or scientific basis. It is evidence of their political power that, until recent years, little pressure has been exerted by governments to exhort obstetricians to explain the inordinate and unjustifiably high intervention rates and depressed levels of maternal satisfaction associated with hospital birth. Further, since hospitals are said to be safer because of rapid access to high-technology and superior medical knowledge, it is logical to assume that hospital PNMRs should be lower than homebirth mortality levels. Tew (1990) and Campbell and Macfarlane (1987) have shown that this has not been the case in Britain, especially for the vast majority of low-risk cases, but also for high-risk infants.

Beck (1992) is partially correct to argue that the self-referential nature of medical science discourages autocritique, even in the face of mounting evidence to show its narrow and mechanistic fallibility. However, his thesis asserts a hermetically-sealed professional closure. This is why he calls it 'the extreme case of sub-politics'.

Some qualification needs to be made. It is not the case that obstetric power is impregnable from consumer criticism. Medical litigation in Australia in relation to obstetrics represented 30% of the total sum that was awarded for all payments between 1984–7 and obstetricians feel themselves to be increasingly under attack (Sweet, 1989). Forde found that 'there is a degree of paraonoia among some doctors that their patients and/or lawyers are out to get them' (1989: 6). In addition, Bastian (1990) has argued that for those obstetricians who feel the outcome of birth is their total responsibility, a damaged baby may be seen as a personal failure as well as grounds by consumers for financial compensation. Policy-makers have identified one solution in the expansion of birth centres staffed by midwives, who will care for women in all stages of maternity – antenatal, delivery and postnatal phases. It is also worth noting that governments have favoured alternative models of midwifery care partly because of the cost savings associated with lower intervention levels – lower wages, lower theatre costs, lower pharmaceutical costs and reduction in days spent in hospital proceeding the birth (Health Department, Victoria 1990).

In cases where a woman-centred model of care is adopted as birth-centre policy (and this may not always be the case), the problem of litigation may be alleviated. Women will be encouraged to exercise agency at all stages of labour, and a policy of non-intervention may be institutionalised except in extraordinary cases. Women will maintain control over procedures and they will experience continuity of care – two of the most important criteria identified in the study reported elsewhere in this chapter as germane to positive birthing. The other criteria are peace and security of the birth place. In terms of risk discourse, the criteria of risk assessment will be expanded from purely medical and obstetric criteria to include social and environmental factors. These changes could be a progressive step for women giving birth so long as the new model is not used repressively. That is, so long as the new model does not set a specific standard which must be reached in order to avoid being labelled a failure. For example, it would be repressive for childbirth reformers to suggest that women should only birth at home, in a birth centre or without any medical or obstetric intervention (such as analgesia, or caesarean section). Such a proposition would only introduce a new set of social controls. Women may perceive themselves to have exercised full control where they participated in the decision to have an epidural or a caesarean section, or where they agreed to transfer from home to hospital for whatever reason. The issue is to what extent women are consulted and informed of possible options and outcomes.

It is unlikely that the expansion of birth centres will be recognised in terms of expanding the set of risk criteria, or as an arrangement which recognises the equal importance of women's experiences in the assessment of a 'good' outcome. Obstetricians are not trained to address the emotional and affective determinants of physiological efficiency. However, they may reasonably accept that 'patients' in hospitals feel resentment at perceiving themselves simply 'as numbers in the system' (Sweet 1989). The social outcome of medical changes may be the same – to facilitate greater participation by women in the events surrounding their delivery. Increased participation may well induce a greater responsibility on the part of women where there is an unexpected and adverse outcome and less consumer resentment towards medical professionals. Studies cited above show that an alternative model may render childbirth a more satisfactory event for women and their families. The more general point to be made is that consumer resistance is growing. This is in response to individual experience of unsatisfactory treatment and because the popular literature offering women alternative views of birthing is expanding significantly. As I argued earlier, government policies in Britain and Australia are also changing, although at a much slower place in Australia.

'Risk society' is an insightful description of one of the negative legacies of the Enlightenment. However, whereas Habermas (1992) pessimistically sought the apogee of the Enlightenment in a perfection yet to come with an illuminated form of communicative rationality, Beck has characterised the risk society as perfection realised. Science and industry are now held accountable for the production of risk. Beck's (1992) only reservation is applied to medical science because medicine's self-referentiality has histor-ically protected it from democratic intervention and consumer criticism. In addition, the insatiable appetite for medicine in the risk society means that medicine creates a permanently expanding market for itself.

Beck used *in vitro* fertilisation to argue his case for medical science as an extreme case of sub-politics, that is, one which was substantially immune from external criticism. In the case of obstetrics, Beck's thesis is substantially supported. For example, until more recently, obstetricians have successfully colonised the debate on childbirth by directing attention specifically and narrowly to the question of mortality, despite an expanded range of criteria applied by women to assess a successful birth. However, obstetrics is not immune from general and growing consumer criticism which is itself substantially reflexive. Most consumer lobbying groups systematically carry out their own research and amass critical lit-erature regarding the long-term risks to infants associated with a range of 'routine' medical procedures. This critical literature has not escaped the notice of governments, committees of inquiry and policymakers. The case of obstetrics shows that the power of the medical lobby is immense, but that it is not impenetrable. Beck's thesis regarding medical sub-politics refers to a very broad and largely undifferentiated range of medical insti-tutions and industries. Beck does not investigate a range of specific med-ical activities and/or interactions between practitioners and patients. It is at this level that his thesis cannot be supported. Many studies have been cited in this paper which show a sustained critique of medical science. Governments have more recently been persuaded by these critiques and subsequent policy changes indicate that medical power has been chal-lenged.

Notes

1 These quotations were derived from interviews with women who gave birth in South Australian hospitals in 1991. The interviews were lodged in the J. D. Somerville Oral History Collection, Mortlock Library of South Australiana: No. OH153/3.
2 These arguments draw upon qualitative evidence gathered between 1990 and 1994 from 40 interviews conducted with British and Australian women who gave birth at home (10 in Britain and 10 in Australia) and in hospital (10 in Britain and 10 in Australia). In Britain, the hospital-birth respondents were recruited from independent childbirth educators (NCT). In Australia the hospital-birth respondents were also recruited from separate classes run by independent child-birth educators (at a Community Health Centre). Homebirth respondents were recruited via independent childbirth educators and homebirth groups.
3 Personal communication with P. Lancaster, author of *Homebirths in Australia: 1988–90*.

4 Women who gave birth in hospitals almost universally reported some negative
   assessments of procedures and relations. Women who gave birth at home in
   this study reported no negative experiences. This finding is supported by a
   study conducted by Bastian (1992) of 552 women who planned to give birth at
   home. In that study, 98.9% of women said they would choose homebirth in
   the future.

References

Abel, S. and Kearns, R.A. (1991) Birth places: a geographical perspective on
planned home birth in New Zealand, *Social Science and Medicine*, 33, 825–34.

Albers, L.L. and Katz, V.L. (1991) Birth setting for low-risk pregnancies: analysis
of the current literature, *Journal of Nurse-Midwifery*, 36, 215–20.

Bastian, H. (1992) *Who Gives Birth at Home and Why? A Survey of 552
Australian Women Who Planned to Give Birth at Home.* Canberra: Homebirth
Australia Inc.

Bastian, H. and Lancaster, P.A.L. (1992) *Home Births in Australia 1988–1990.*
Sydney: Australian Institute of Health and Welfare, National Perinatal
Statistics Unit.

Beck, U. (1992) *Risk Society: Towards a New Modernity.* London: Sage
Publications.

Biro, M. and Lumley, J. (1991) The safety of team midwifery: the first decade of
the Monash Birth Centre, *The Medical Journal of Australia*, 155, 478–80.

Brown, S., Lumley, J., Small, R., and Astbury, J. (1992) The social costs of intervention in childbirth. Paper presented at Public Health Association 24th
Annual Conference: 'Choice and change: Ethics, politics and economics of public health', 27–30 September.

Bundy, J. (1993) *Home Birth – Why Not?* Adelaide: John Bundy.

Campbell, R., Davies, I.M., Macfarlane, A., and Beral, V. (1984) Home births in
England and Wales, 1979: perinatal mortality according to intended place of
delivery, *British Medical Journal of Clinical and Residential Education*, 289,
6447, 721–4.

Campbell, R. and Macfarlane, A. (1987) *Where to be Born: The Debate and the
Evidence.* Oxford: National Perinatal Epidemiology Unit.

Cavero, C.M., Fullerton, J.T., and Bartlome, J.A. (1991) Assessment of the
process and outcomes of the first 1,000 births of a nurse-midwifery service,
Journal of Nurse-Midwifery, 36, 104–10.

Chamberlain, M., Soderstrom, B., Kaitell, C., and Stewart, P. (1991) Consumer
interest in alternatives to physician-centred hospital birth in Ottawa, *Midwifery*,
7, 74–81.

Crotty, M., Ramsay, A. T., Smart, R. and Chan, A. (1990) Planned homebirths
in South Australia 1976–1987, *The Medical Journal of Australia*, 153, 664–67.

Damastra-Wijmenga, S. (1984) Home confinement: the positive results in
Holland, *Journal of the Royal College of General Practitioners*, 34, 425–30.

Davis-Floyd, R.E. (1990) Ritual in the hospital: giving birth the American way.
In Hunter, D.E.K. and Whitten, P. (eds), *Anthropology: Contemporary
Perspectives* (Sixth Edition). Glenview: Scott Foreman.

Declercq, E.R. (1984) Out-of-hospital births, U.S. 1978: birth weight and Apgar scores as measures of outcome, *Public Health Report*, 99, 63–73.

Department of Health (Great Britain) (1992) *Maternity Services: Government Response to the Second Report from the Health Committee*, Session 1991–2. London: HMSO.

Department of Health (Great Britain) (1994) *Changing Childbirth*. London: HMSO.

Douglas, M. (1990) Risk as a forensic resource, *Daedalus*, 119, 1–16.

Duran, A.M. (1992) The safety of home birth: the farm study, *American Journal of Public Health*, 82, 450–3.

Elliott, C.E. (1992) Obstetrics in a small maternity hospital, *Australian Family Physician*, 21, 613–9.

Flint, C., Poulengeris, P., and Grant, A. (1989) The 'Know Your Midwife' Scheme – randomised trial of continuity of care by a team of midwives, *Midwifery*, 5, 11–16.

Ford, C., Iliffe, S., and Franklin, O. (1991) Outcome of planned home births in an inner city practice, *British Medical Journal*, 303, 1517–9.

Forde, K. (1989) Reducing the risks of being sued, *Australian Practical Management*, 1, 6–11.

Foucault, M. (1973) *The Birth of the Clinic*. London: Tavistock.

Giles, W., Collins, J., Ong, G., and MacDonald, R. (1992) Antenatal care of low risk obstetric patients by midwives. A randomised controlled trial, *Medical Journal of Australia*, 156, 158–61.

Goldthorp, W.O. and Richman, J. (1974) A case study of the effects of the hospital strike upon domiciliary confinement, *The Practitioner*, 212, 845–53.

Habermas, J. (1992) *The Structural Transformation of the Public Sphere: An Inquiry into a Category of Bourgeois Society*. Cambridge: Polity Press.

Haire, D.B. and Elsberry, C.C. (1991) Maternity care and outcomes in a high-risk service: the North Central Bronx Hospital experience, *Birth*, 18, 33–7.

Health Department, Victoria (1990) *Final Report of the Ministerial Review of Birthing Services in Victoria: Having a Baby in Victoria*. Victoria: Health Department (referred to as the Birthing Services Review).

Health Committee (House of Commons, Great Britain) (1992) *Maternity Services: Second Report*, Vol. 1. London: HMSO (The Winterton Committee Report).

Hemminki, E., Kojo-Austin, H., Malin, M., and Koponen, P. (1992) Variation in obstetric interventions by midwife, *Scandinavian Journal of Caring Sciences*, 6, 81–6.

Katz-Rothman, B. (1982) *In Labour: Women and Power in the Birthplace*. London: Junction Books.

Kennell, J., Klaus, M., McGrath, S., Robertson, S., Hinkley, C. (1991) Continuous emotional support during labor in a US hospital, *Journal of the American Medical Association*, 265, 17.

Lane, K. (1993) The Politics of homebirth. In Mills, M. (ed) *Prevention, Health and British Politics*. Avebury: Aldershot.

Lane, K. (1994) Birth as euphoria: the social meaning of birth. In Colquhoun, D. and Kellehear, A. (eds) *Health Research in Practice, Volume Two – Recent Changes and Ongoing Issues*. London: Chapman and Hall.

Linder-Pelz, S., Webster, M.A., Martins, J. and Greenwell, J. (1990) Obstetric risks and outcomes: birth centre compared with conventional labour ward, *Community Health Studies*, 14, 39–46.

Marsden, W. (1994) *Pursuing the Birth Machine: The Search for Appropriate Birth Technology*. New South Wales: ACE Graphics.

McDonald, V. (1992) *Speaking of Birth*. Newham: Scribe Publications.

Monash Medical Centre (1993) *Midwives Community Birth Centre 1993 Statistics*. Monash: Monash Medical Centre.

Morris, N., Campbell, J., Biro, M-A., Lumley, J., Rao, J., and Spensley, J. (1986) Birth centre confinement at the Queen Victoria Medical Centre: four years' experience, *The Medical Journal of Australia*, 144, 628–30.

National Childbirth Trust (1991) *NCT Maternity Services Survey*. London: National Childbirth Trust.

National Health and Medical Research Council (NH&MRC) (1994), *Draft Report: Options for Effective Care in Childbirth*. Canberra: Health Care Committee.

Oakley, A. (1986) *The Captured Womb: A History of the Medical Care of Pregnant Women*. Oxford: Basil Blackwell.

O'Brien, M. (1978) Home and hospital confinement: a comparison of the experiences of mothers having home and hospital confinements, *Journal Royal College General Practitioners*, 28, 460–6.

Permezel, J.M.H., Pepperel, R.J. and Kloss, M. (1987) Unexpected problems in patients selected for birthing unit delivery, *Australian and New Zealand Journal of Obstetrics and Gynaecology*, 27, 21–3.

Richards, E. (1991) *Vitamin C and Cancer: Medicine or Politics?* South Melbourne: Macmillan.

Schlatter, B.L. (1990) Control and satisfaction with the birth experience, unpublished PhD. Chicago: University of Illinois.

Shearer, J.M.L. (1985) Five year prospective survey of risk of booking for a home birth, *British Medical Journal*, 291, 1477–80.

Skibsted, L. and Lange, A.P. (1992) The need for pain relief in uncomplicated deliveries in an alternative birth centre compared to an obstetric delivery ward, *Pain*, 48, 1230–4.

Street, D., Gannon, M.J. and Holt, E.M. (1991) Community obstetric care in West Berkshire, *British Medical Journal*, 302, 1082.

Sweet, R. (1989) The obstetrician's dilemma, *The Medical Journal of Australia*, 150, 545–6.

Tew, M. (1990), *Safer Childbirth? A Critical History of Maternity Care*. London: Chapman and Hall.

Tew, M. and Damstra-Wijmenga, S.M.I. (1991) Safest birth attendants; recent Duth evidence, *Midwifery*, 7, 55–63.

Turner, B.S. (1994), *Orientalism, Postmodernism and Globalism*. London: Routledge.

Tyson, H. (1991) Outcomes of 1001 midwife-attended home births in Toronto, 1983–88, *Birth*, 18, 14–19.

Woodcock, H.C., Read, A.W., Moore, D.J., Stanley, F.J. and Bower, C. (1990) Planned homebirths in Western Australia 1981–1987: a descriptive study, *The Medical Journal of Australia*, 153, 672–8.

World Health Organization (1985), *Having a Baby in Europe: Report on a Study, Public Health in Europe No. 26*. Copenhagen: World Health Organization.

4. The risk of resistance: perspectives on the mass childhood immunisation programme

Anne Rogers and David Pilgrim

Introduction

The policy of mass childhood immunisation (MCI) enjoys the support of medical professionals and government health agencies worldwide. In 1977, the World Health Organisation and UNICEF proposed that there should be a 90 per cent immunisation coverage of children in all countries (Egan *et al.* 1994). This aim has been met already in Britain and *The Health of the Nation* (DoH 1992a) sets a higher target of 95 per cent coverage for 1995. MCI is deemed to be an effective health promotion strategy for two reasons: it has a direct impact on individuals immunised, by stimulating resistance to infectious disease; and an indirect impact, by reducing the circulation of pathogenic micro-organisms within a population. The latter effect is technically called 'herd immunity'.

In Britain, since 1990, when a new general practitioner (GP) contract was introduced, a cash payment of £1,800 has been given to each doctor reaching the 90 per cent target for their infant patients. The introduction of this financial inducement signalled that spontaneous parental compliance was not considered sufficient, in itself, to ensure targets being met. As well as this market mechanism, the government has continued to fund a multi-media Health Education Authority (HEA) campaign to persuade parents that vaccination is safe and effective. It has also introduced local immunisation co-ordinators into health authorities. In Britain MCI remains a voluntary scheme, although mandatory measures to ensure targets have been mooted (Leese and Bosanquet 1992). These might include linking it to school entry (as in the USA, parts of Germany and some states in Australia). In France proof of immunisation is a pre-requisite of receiving child benefit payments.

Using documentary and interview data, this chapter will examine the views of four communities about MCI: health promoters; medical scientists; primary health care workers; and dissenting parents. This is not an exhaustive list of interest groups and the groups contain individuals who may share more than one role. For example, general practitioners are often also parents. The four groups have been chosen because they illuminate the main perspectives on the disputes about the benefits and risks of MCI.

Assessing and communicating risk

Whilst calculations made by official risk assessors are often accepted uncritically by lay people, an alternative view to expert orthodoxy is also evident. Opposition to an official doctrine like MCI reflects a wider phenomenon in which lay people challenge scientific knowledge or re-assemble it in order to resist a government policy (cf Brown 1992, Balshem 1991, Davison *et al.* 1991). At times lay people develop their own dissenting view of disease etiology and a different assessment of risk. This constitutes a challenge to the authority of expert knowledge and the way in which professionals define a problem (Giddens 1991, Williams and Popay 1994). Moreover, they tend to assess risk at the personal or famil-ial level, whereas medical experts tend to be more concerned with popula-tion level risk. It has been noted that we live at a time when a tension exists between one cultural tendency to allow risk assessment to be man-aged by experts and another in which the taking of risk and avoidance of danger is deemed to be a personal responsibility (Beck 1991, Giddens 1991, Douglas 1992). Douglas (1992) points out that modern expert risk assessors claim to bracket off 'the grime and heat of politics', that the issue of risk involves. Accordingly, they assume that ordinary people lack the capacity to reason probabilistically. However, as she points out, lay people have always made calculations about risks and chances based on many factors in the environment. These may include, but they are not limited to, scientific information provided by experts. Giddens, too, makes the point that:

. . . risk profiles do not remain the special preserve of the experts. The general population is aware of them, even if often it is only in a rough and ready way, and indeed the medical profession and other agencies are concerned to make their findings widely available to lay people . . . (1991: 120)

These observations from commentators of the sociology of risk are per-tinent when the views of different social groups with an interest in MCI are examined. Expert risk assessment is not sealed off from public obser-vation. Public health experts, because of their acquired responsibility for population level risk of infection, obscure or ignore the views of individu-als in assessing and communicating about risk. Similarly, epidemiologists may treat the question of infection risk as if it is merely a mathematical or technical puzzle and lose sight of the citizen's view of their task. These stances of medical experts – guardians of risk in the population or decoders of a technical puzzle – are challenged by some lay people, who carry out their own separate risk assessment exercise of infectious disease and immunisation.

The case of MCI also entails two peculiarities. Firstly, the attention paid by public health experts to the risks of, and eradication of, childhood infectious diseases does not reflect their degree of threat, compared to other contemporary hazards. In comparison to AIDS, environmental pollution, violence and accidents in advanced capitalist societies, the dangers posed by childhood infectious diseases are actually quite small. (For pertussis (Whooping Cough) there were 15,286 notifications and 7 deaths in 1990 and 5,201 notifications with no deaths in 1991 (Leese and Bosanquet 1992). There are currently less than five cases a year each for Diphtheria and Polio (Egan *et al.* 1994). There were no deaths associated with mumps in either 1990 or 1991 (Egan *et al.* 1994). In 1991 there was only one death associated with measles (Egan *et al.* 1994)). Despite this, MCI retains a privileged position in public health policy. Secondly, the latter now overwhelmingly emphasises 'lifestyle' and 'health behaviour' factors. Thus, MCI is anomalous, as it remains fixed on the issue of contagion and 'the spaces between people'. By contrast, the dissenting lay view on MCI appears to be commensurate with most other health promotion policies reflecting the cultural tendency for people to see their bodies in isolation from society.

In the rest of this chapter we set out the positions and perceptions of risk of four social groups interested in MCI and then discuss them in their social context. This entails questions about the ways that different social groups and individuals in society understand the risk of infection and the potential impact this has for the policy arena. After presenting the views of the different groups, we will return to these questions in a discussion section.

The perspectives of the four groups are assembled from different types of data. The first two (health promoters and medical scientists) are gleaned from medical and health promotion literature. The other two (primary health care workers and dissenting parents) are derived from a study about non-compliance with immunisation conducted by the authors (Rogers and Pilgrim 1994).

Health promoters

The Department of Health (DoH) produces an annual guidance book to health workers in Britain, entitled *Immunisation Against Infectious Disease*. This book, known in the trade as the 'green book', contains information about schedules, the individual vaccines and their contraindications. Sometimes this is augmented by pointed advice or directives from the government's Chief Medical Officer. These letters or memoranda are circulated to all medical practitioners and health personnel responsible for encouraging and monitoring uptake.

In addition to this dissemination of guidance to local agencies, there is a mass circulation of DoH and HEA leaflets to parents through libraries, surgeries and health centres. One DoH leaflet points out, under the heading 'Vaccination of infants – the facts' that:

Vaccines are amongst the safest and most effective medicines there are. Every year they prevent countless serious illnesses and many deaths . . . Vaccines like other medicines can cause reactions. These are usually mild and brief. Very rarely, they are serious. For this reason, vaccines should be given only by doctors, or nurses, who are qualified to give them and who are in a position to advise where there is any indication against their use . . . (1990: 1).

Similarly, in the more elaborate leaflet *Immunisation – Information for Parents* the HEA advises that:

Immunisation protects most children completely. Very rarely, an immunised child catches one of the diseases, but it is then usually very much milder and far less dangerous than if the child had not been immunised . . . [I]mmunisation is quick, simple, effective – and free. But for a small number of children, immunisation may carry some risks. You need to know about these and about the risks of the diseases themselves so that you can feel confident about having your child immunised. For almost all children the risks of the diseases are far greater than any risk involved in immunisations . . . (1993: 1)

In this leaflet the rationale of herd immunity is explained and each disease is considered individually to explain why it is serious and why immunisation is needed to induce individual immunity. One disease, whooping cough, is singled out for special attention in order to counter the 'worries' arising from 'publicity' . . . 'which "can easily get out of proportion . . ." ' At the end of the DoH pamphlet is the message in large letters and bold type: 'These facts will help you to make your decision – but your doctor is there to advise you' (1990: 10). GPs are thus assigned as the final authority figures in the negotiation.

The official promotional literature emphasises: the scarcity of iatrogenic risk; effectiveness of vaccines in protecting individuals and in reducing infection outbreaks; rarity of vaccine failure; reliability and authority of primary health care workers as sources of risk assessment on behalf of parents; and the irrationality of parental doubts about immunisation.

Together these points reflect the strong affective and moral character of promotional literature. Despite the recurrent use of the term 'facts' (which implies the transmission of neutral information), the literature clearly sets out to induce anxiety and guilt in those parents responsible for children who are not immunised. A formula to immediately reverse this induced distress is then prescribed – 'immunise your child'. This directive implies that the costs and benefits of immunisation have been weighed up authoritatively, in advance, for parents and the latter are to be assured by this process. For example, in the HEA leaflet there is, 'To sum up these facts, it is safer to have the measles immunisation than not' (1993: 10). The affective tone of other promotional material is even more unambiguous. For instance, when the (Haemophilus influenzae type B) Hib vaccine was introduced, the HEA commissioned television and magazine advertisements which showed a nursery in which a toy box was transformed into a coffin.

The literature also has its relevant silences about the factors which determine risk of infection and its possible lasting consequences. There is nothing on the role of poverty, low social class, poor diet or inadequate sanitation – even though these determinants of risk are well known within public health (McKeown 1979). Nothing is mentioned about the uncertainty surrounding the natural history of the virulence of micro-organisms. Scarlet fever, syphilitic psychosis and rheumatic fever all increased and then declined in incidence in the absence of vaccine use. This was officially recognised by the DHSS in the 1970s (DHSS 1976) but health promoters today do not put this knowledge into the public domain. State payments to vaccine damaged children, which between 1987 and 1993 amounted to £780,000 (Hansard 1994), are not mentioned, nor is the GP contract, with its financial inducement.

In the health promoters' campaign is a righteous commitment to the view that MCI is safe and effective. Parents are there to be persuaded. Their views of contraindications are reported in studies by public health doctors as being 'mythical' (Klein *et al.* 1981), 'parentally perceived' or 'false' (Barlow and Walker 1990). Essentially, the defaulting parent is either neglectful or neurotically wrong-headed. For health promoters the problem of MCI is only the problem of parental non-compliance. MCI is about 'uptake' not consent – the right to access a service not the right to refuse a medical intervention – and still less is it to do with making alternative interpretations about the balance of risks between vaccination and contracting an infection.

Medical scientists

The views of epidemiologists studying the relationship between MCI and disease transmission are not as clear cut as the above position, but more cautious. Risk is viewed as the probability of an event, combined with the extent of the gains and losses it will entail, and risk assessment is an all round estimation of probable outcomes. For example, in relation to the notion of herd immunity, some epidemiologists have expressed doubts about the simple mathematical rule of 90 per cent coverage:

There is increasing evidence that the concept of herd immunity may not be applicable to measles transmission. Human and in particular urban populations are not homogenous herds; they consist of sub-groups whose members associate in a non-random way so that the presence of any under-vaccinated sub-group in the larger population permits measles transmission and the occurrence of outbursts (Levy and Bridges-Webb 1990: 490).

Researchers studying the impact of MCI have drawn attention to three perverse or contradictory features of the policy. First, the higher the immunisation coverage the higher is the average age of those who do become infected. This has particularly threatening consequences for females in relation to rubella, who are pushed nearer to child bearing age. With mumps and measles, later ages of infection bring with them more serious symptoms and complications. Second, the greater the coverage, the higher the risk ratio becomes between the iatrogenic effects from vaccines and complications from contracting the disease, as the proportion of those infected becomes smaller and the number immunised becomes higher. Third, certain vaccine types may be high on efficacy but low on safety. This can lead to the contradiction that the greatest benefit at the population level is associated with the greatest risk at the individual level:

> Ultimately if an infectious disease has been nearly eradicated, the risks associated with the vaccination are expected to exceed those of infection. Hence there is a conflict of interest between the individual (risk associated with the vaccine) and the group (benefits of herd immunity) (Nokes and Anderson 1991: 1312).

These authors go on to point out that the best vaccine for mumps protection for a population is the Urabe strain. This was withdrawn in Britain in 1992 because of it being a source of aseptic meningitis. Only the safer strain (Jeryl Lynn) is used now, but this gives weaker population level protection.

The medical researchers above who made these points still support MCI. For example, they suggest 100 per cent immunisation of cohorts of 2 year olds against rubella and a double dose regime of measles vaccine to reduce the probability of vaccine failures. But the dogmatism of the health promoters is replaced by a set of cost-benefit analyses and mathematical models which concede the risks as well as the benefits of MCI. Some examples of the immediate risks of vaccines reported in the medical research literature and noted by Nokes and Anderson are: anaphylaxis; convulsions; encephalitis; meningitis; and arthritis.

Despite the identification of vaccine risk, the cost-benefit analysis leads to the conclusion that MCI remains a sound policy. Support for MCI is based on an assessment of its population level benefit; it is not denied, indeed the evidence is supplied, that some individuals may be iatrogenic casualties of the policy. However, what is left unacknowledged in the 'neutral' calculations of risk and subsequent support for MCI are the underlying interests of medical practitioners as a group working in the field of epidemiology or public health. Epidemiologists have access to knowledge which suggests that 90 per cent of the decline in infectious disease levels occurred before the introduction of MCI (McKeown 1979). However, today, in the face of health promotion and prevention strategies which implicate changes in individual behaviour, vaccines still offer the hope to medical practitioners of them retaining a role by placing a technocentric tweak on the global downward trend of infection levels during this century.

Primary health care workers

GPs and health visitors are the recipients, mediators and executors of advice and directives from health promoters and the DoH. By deploying a variety of strategies they are in a position to alter compliance levels. In addition to passing on DoH and HEA literature, they can use computer records to trigger follow up letters to uncooperative parents. When faced with parents and their infants in the surgery, they can remind them about immunisation and then offer the vaccination on the spot.

In the study conducted by the authors (Rogers and Pilgrim ibid) the ten primary health care workers interviewed (7 GPs and 3 health visitors selected via a local medical committee of GPs in South East London) varied in their negotiating position with doubting parents. At one extreme there was the GP who told defaulters that they were being selfish in putting their child and other children at risk by not complying with immunisation. At the other extreme was a health visitor who set up meetings between groups of parents and a local homeopath to discuss an alternative viewpoint about MCI. She saw defaulting as a civil right and complained that dissenting parents were regularly harassed by GPs and health visitors. She was also concerned that a preoccupation with increasing uptake in high risk groups might lead to the selective surveillance and targeting of those who were already vulnerable and oppressed (like poor Asian families in inner city areas).

In between were those who enacted the paternalistic role set for them by health promoters as an authoritative advisor. They gave time to parents to air their anxieties and then offered them advice about potential risks and benefits. However, GPs did not always share the same assumptions about vaccine risk. For example, two doctors in different practices only a few miles apart spoke of the potential danger of arthritic problems linked to the rubella component of the Mumps, Measles and Rubella Vaccine (MMR). The first commented about this iatrogenic effect:

> I've not seen it. Its one of those things that all these American books address. I've had one parent mention it who has read the (sic) book, but it doesn't seem to be a general concern . . .

The second doctor, in contrast, said:

> I would be very surprised if it [the rubella vaccine] didn't cause some problems. I mean rubella itself causes problems, particularly in adults . . .

This GP chaired his local immunisation committee and was committed to MCI but was also respectful of those who disagreed with him. His ambivalent attitude and his personal experience as a parent himself are captured by the following two quotes:

> I've . . . quite a few colleagues who were convinced that the MMR is the new wonder jab, but then saw children with a rather nebulous malaise for a month afterwards. I mean you expect a slight tempera-ture or even a measles rash or a mumps swelling. I warn parents about these but the ones that go on for quite a while, I do get worried about them.

The respondent then goes on to talk of his own children:

> My three were immunised by my colleague down the road. My wife took them and had all three done together. She walked out of the surgery and half way up the road 'Janet' collapsed. She ran back with her into the surgery and the GP rang me, then stuck her into his car and ran her to the hospital. She had stopped breathing and was white and floppy and wheezy-like with asthma. When I got there half an hour later she was still non-responsive, unconscious. She was two hours before she started to recover normally . . .

Despite this personal incident, the GP remained committed to his sup-port of MCI for his own and other children. Next, another GP discusses the ambivalent views on the risk-benefit dilemma, following the whooping cough scare in the late 1970s, which led to Government payments for vaccine damage:

> I'm sure that we were getting the story right about the safety of the whooping cough vaccine, but the picture was very confused at the time. I now think that it is remarkably safe but I have this idea in my head that safety and efficacy are inversely related. So I also felt that we should respond honestly if people raised legitimate doubts. But this is a complicated question about all the studies for and against both stan-

dard and alternative medicine . . . The question of protecting the community runs through my mind . . . but I think that it is wrong to put it into the foreground when you are talking to doubting parents . . . Instead I would emphasise that whilst we do not know everything about the risk of vaccination, we do know that the risks are tiny. Comparatively, the risks associated with suffering from the after effects of the actual disease are much greater. That's how I put it because that is what I believe . . .

The allusion to 'getting the story right' reflects a central feature of risk assessment, a shifting official position about vaccine safety. For instance, during the 1980s, following the whooping cough controversy in the late 1970s, the government made compensation payments to vaccine damaged children, whilst altering their account of the safety of the vaccine over time. As time progressed, the 'green book' offered fewer and fewer contraindications – allergic children and those with a family history of fits were no longer deemed to be vulnerable to adverse reactions.

Data collected from the primary care workers suggest that the constraints of dealing with people face to face under conditions of knowledge uncertainty often lead them to fall short of the zealous campaigning expected by the health promotion position. It is unsurprising that health promoters remain frustrated with GPs (not just with parents) for being 'over-cautious' in their negotiations (Barlow and Walker 1990). Health promoters are concerned with population-level calculations of risk and benefit. By contrast, primary health care workers are dealing with individuals who they have an ongoing relationship with as both parents and patients. The sense of personal involvement is captured in the following quotation from a health visitor who had her own children fully immunised, except for one in the late 1970s who was not given the whooping cough vaccine. The child became very ill with the disease and the worker now regrets her omission:

I mean any vaccine has a slight risk attached to it. So you can give people the facts and the figures but you must respect their right to refuse. As a parent myself I think that it would be wrong to make immunisation mandatory. It would make my life easier in one way if I was not responsible for negotiating compliance because the state imposed it, but I still think that it would be wrong. Even if there is a one in five million chance of a child becoming brain damaged, say, what of the poor parents with that child who were denied the right to refuse?

Thus the dilemma for primary health care workers about MCI is how to negotiate a population level driven policy with individual parents. The dilemma also illuminates something of the ambiguity of self-identity that primary health care workers face. They identify both with being parents *and* the 'rational' scientific knowledge that forms the core of their secondary socialisation as primary health care workers. Doubt is reinforced by the position that primary health workers occupy at the interface between official, state endorsed, immunisation policy and the immediacy of the reactions of the dissenting recipients of such a policy.

Dissenting parents

The study by the authors also included interviews with nineteen mothers who had refused immunisation for their children. Parents interviewed were mainly over 30 years of age from a middle class 'professional' background (*e.g.* journalism, social work, special needs teaching). Accounts from parents indicated that becoming a 'non-complier' with childhood immunisation tends to develop over time and is influenced by a number of intricate factors and processes. Only five parents decided at the outset not to have their children immunised. It was generally the case that dissenting parents began as compliers with the traditional medical regimens and became non-compliers over time.

These parents articulated a complex rationale which was derived from a mixture of world views held about the environment, healing, holism and the roles and responsibilities of parenting, and a critical reading of the scientific and alternative literature discussed above. The balance between these varied across accounts. For example, one mother, who was a research psychologist, focused her comments almost exclusively around methodological problems and uncertainties of research reports and the lack of knowledge she perceived her GP to have both about infectious diseases and vaccine side-effects. Another parent (a choreographer and artist) described her reasons for becoming a non-complier in relation to her views about fate. When faced with the rationalistic argument put forward by some health professionals that the risk of damage from vaccine was far less than crossing the road – she responded by saying that if her child was killed or injured by a car she could accept this as an inevitability – something that she had no control over. She felt she could not 'forgive herself' if something happened to her child as the result of her decision to introduce deliberately something she viewed as toxic into her child's body. Generally, however, the doubts about immunisation were initiated by a maternal 'instinct', or intuition, which were confirmed and solidified into a coherent anti-immunisation position by finding out more from the medical and alternative literature.

The question of risk assessment for these parents was essentially in conflict with the types of knowledge claim common in the health promotion literature outlined earlier. The data elicited suggest that this risk assessment involves a combination of some of the following: medical opinion on vaccine risk is misleading; host health status, not immunisation status, is the best predictor of healthy recovery from naturally contracted infections (in those committed to homeopathy); immunisation debilitates a child's immune system, making him or her prone in later life to auto-immune disorders; naturally acquired immunity is permanent, whereas vaccine induced immunity may wear off or even fail to provoke anti-body activity at all; and vaccines provoke a far greater level of serious iatrogenic effects than are officially conceded and recorded.

Some of these ideas were arrived at intuitively, but often they were shaped and reinforced by access to anti-immunisation arguments in their social network, or by reading critiques of MCI from alternative medicine and social medicine literature. One of the paradoxes about this group of mothers, in their challenge to the official health promotion position, is that they were paragons of virtue, if not zealots, about reducing potential risks to their children's health in every respect apart from their opposition to immunisation. They adhered slavishly to long periods of breast feeding. They also emphasised healthy eating, mental and physical well being.

In rejecting the passive acceptance of expert interventions, like immunisation, they were acting consistently with the overarching rationale of modern health promotion – that health is maintained by attending to personal responsibility, action and lifestyle duties. Immunisation represented an anomaly within this rationale. It is vaccination which is at odds with the general policy of health promotion not those who refuse it.

These points are brought out in the following quotes starting with one response to the question 'what do you think of the literature advocating mass immunisation?':

Immunisation for some children is perhaps not the best thing, especially if you have got catarrhy, asthmatic or highly allergic children

The second describes her child's adverse reaction to the polio vaccine:

I took her in and they said 'oh it is uvelitis. It is an extremely dangerous condition because when it is that swollen (the eye) it can cut the blood supply off to the optic nerve and then she will lose her sight and she could get meningitis through the inflammation to the brain'. Lucy has always been prone to eye infections. Well I believe it and feel very strongly about it, that the polio immunisation knocked her reserve just enough, so should couldn't fight that very local little infection and then it blew up like that . . .

Next a respondent expresses sarcastic frustration at the reluctance of professionals to concede a cause and effect relationship between immunisation and an adverse reaction:

I mean, if I hit my child over the head with a hammer and took it down to the clinic because it had a bloody great lump on its head, somebody would make a connection between me hitting it on the head with a hammer and having a bloody great lump on its head. But they vaccinate the child and 24 hours later its got a bloody great swelling and they are saying 'Oh well, it's not down to us John' and the cause and the effect is just so obvious. I think that my attitude to conventional medicine from then on was that I would just make use of it when it suited me and they couldn't be trusted to really make proper judgements . . .

A distrust of the ability of medical experts to make neutral risk assessments was compounded by respondents' views about the introduction of financial incentives in the GP contract:

What I was really concerned about was that they were in no position to give an unbiased view because they are paid a lump sum and they have to get a percentage of children vaccinated, and I thought that was crazy. She couldn't possibly be objective about it. Certainly none of her advice was geared to me personally. It was just geared to money.

Whilst some of the mothers were opposed to immunisation as an overall philosophy, others were prepared to be selective according to the risk apparent in a particular situation. One mother who travelled a lot was asked 'what about tetanus?':

You have to be open-minded. Every situation is different. When my son badly cut his head I rushed him to hospital and I agreed that he should have a tetanus jab.

The attitude of the respondents to the question of herd immunity was dealt with in two ways. First, as one mother put it in response to the topic being raised:

. . . Well if they (other children) have been immunised they shouldn't be vulnerable to it, should they? No, I don't see that we are putting everybody else at risk. . . .

The second way was to argue that catching diseases was desirable to procure natural, life-long immunity:

. . . You do have to ensure the health of your children in other ways, and to maintain a good level of health before that, of hygiene . . . but it is important to have children who catch these diseases naturally and get over them naturally . . .

This last response illustrates the gap which exists between dissenting parents and health promoters about the risk of infection. The medical consensus about the legitimacy of MCI is brought into question by these representatives of an alternative culture. The latter is individualistic, stresses holism and is compatible with ecological approaches to understanding health.

Discussion

The difference in understanding between the positions taken up highlight two central questions: are unvaccinated children a health risk to themselves and others and are vaccines a health risk to individual children? From the data and literature examined here the health promoters and dissenting parents have expressed diametrically opposed positions in answering these questions, and the primary health care workers have given a variety of answers. It would seem that the position of dissenting parents and that of the health promoters are incommensurable. The state endorsed public health position assumes that MCI possesses a self-evident trans-cultural legitimacy. This confidence, which rationalism often inspires, is without reference to cultural diversity in ways of understanding the meaning of infectious disease which may clash with the risk assessments made by 'experts'. These ways of understanding extend beyond the 'healthism' philosophy of the dissenting parental group reported here. For example, in the Netherlands in the 1970s, of those failing to comply with polio immunisation prior to a brief epidemic, a sixth (70,000 people) refused on religious grounds (Veenman and Jansma 1980). Such a position was taken up by many in Britain when the smallpox vaccine was introduced (Clark Nelson and Rogers 1992). Recently (October 1994) there has been another vivid example of the continuing opposition to MCI based upon religious beliefs when some Catholics objected to the development of a vaccine from aborted foetal tissue.

Douglas (1975) has pointed out that competing views emerge between tribes about pollution and those responsible for it. Once individuals become committed to a tribal view they are part of a moral community and they will be highly resistant to persuasion from those in another tribe. Whilst this analysis most accurately reflects the positions of the health promotion and dissenting parent groups, there is a more complex picture of individual risk versus community benefit in the medical scientific literature and a range of views amongst primary health care workers. Whereas the medical researchers have tended to ally themselves to the position taken by health promoters (swayed perhaps by the lure of the 'technical fix'), primary health care workers do not have a fixed self-identity in relation to MCI. They are at the interface between the state-endorsed position on MCI and that of doubting or dissenting parents. Often they are parents themselves and they have to maintain workable personal relationships with their patients. Faced with apparently contradictory evidence and pressures in the face of uncertainty, they employ a variety of risk communication strategies ranging from authoritarianism to libertarianism.

Armstrong (1993) notes that the recent 'new public health', with its emphasis on environmental hazards, was preceded at the turn of the century by an emphasis on personal hygiene. The rationale of MCI is an indication of inertia about this earlier and environmentally unattended phase of bio-medical authority, which itself had routinised even earlier concerns with sanitary measures (clean air, water and food). The personal hygiene rationale saw individual bodies as the source of disease, which implied the need for surveillance and control over their boundaries. Through self-surveillance individuals were expected to take seriously their responsibility for reducing the risk of disease – by removing themselves from contact when infected and keeping themselves clean. Vaccination can be seen as an intervention following on a confluence of both self and external surveillance – the individual's skin or mouth was to accept a state-prescribed intrusion for the sake of public hygiene, the collective reduction of risk and the greater good. The non-immunised were to be seen, henceforth, as threats to their peers, in the way that those actually infected were in the past.

Where self-surveillance now fails to stimulate public duty, then older techniques may be deployed which reimpose a form of quarantine (*e.g.* links to school attendance). Compared to other health promotion strategies with their diffuse and difficult to measure impact (Palmer and Short 1989) immunisation is a form of intervention which can be readily monitored and quantified. The top down approach of MCI necessitates the production of techniques of persuasion and propaganda. Guilt and anxiety induction are emphasised within the latter, and in some parts of the world (*e.g.* France) coercion is added, usually by linking MCI to school entry and child benefit payments. Notions of service user empowerment or civil liberties are outside of the strategic ambit of global MCI.

A feature of recent times has been the ongoing fears of catastrophic social disruption exemplified by public concerns about AIDS – the new plague. Strong (1990) discusses this in terms of 'epidemic psychology'. It is clear that the fear of epidemics retains a strong resonance in the minds of people everywhere. Fear, then, is a source of motivation to prevent individual and collective disaster. Triggering this association in parents is central to all of the literature on health promotion for MCI. For those too young to remember, health promoters re-record past catastrophes by reference to the mortality and morbidity toll for a disease in a particular year or period. Those with non-immunised children are confronted with images suggestive of death (as in the media campaigns launched by the HEA and DoH discussed earlier).

In order to sustain a consensual moral view, the dangers associated with rule violation are accentuated within society. Sanctions are then justified against those deemed to be dangerous rule breakers (Douglas 1975). In the case of immunisation the source of danger is attributed to parents who fail to have their children immunised. This focus on non-immunisers diverts attention from the responsibilities of those with the power to make this attribution of dangerousness. The latter (governments and their public health agencies) then are not held accountable for their own inaction about reducing infection risk via political measures (*e.g.* improving housing conditions and poverty). Once MCI is adopted as the optimal political response to the fear of epidemics, then its promoters necessarily become zealots. This is seen in the righteousness which characterises the medical advocacy of MCI. For their part, dissenting parents, with their mixture of cynicism about bio-medicine and anger about their rights as citizen consumers, exude their own version of outrage and indignation. They render their civil disobedience a form of honourable, responsible activity rather than child neglect.

MCI also fits poorly with the wider shift from dependence on medical experts to self-reliance in British health promotion policy. Two contradictions in particular are apparent in this regard. First, MCI, with its assumptions of 'doctor knows best' and blind population compliance, is not about the surveillance or promotion of healthy behaviour, except in the narrow sense of parents 'presenting' their children for immunisation. MCI is incompatible with the notion of the health promoting patient – an informed agent actively involved in taking responsibility for their health. The connotations of the term 'herd immunity' fit poorly with those of human agency. One implies groups of animals to be manipulated by a higher authority, the other suggests that patienthood is about choice, responsibility and partnership.

Secondly, as the MCI strategy becomes more and more successful, as judged by population target levels being met, then the 'prevention paradox' is encountered (Davison *et al.* 1991) – the greater the success at the population level, the less and less health relevance there is at the individual level. Davison *et al.* discussed this phenomenon in relation to 'coronary candidacy'. In the case of MCI, this can be thought of more extremely as a prevention *contradiction*. As was noted earlier, the risk ratio gradually tilts in the direction of vaccines being dangerous to individual recipients, as ever higher population level immunisation targets are met and the more that infection outbreaks decline. Dissenting parents then quite rationally opt to protect their children optimally from risk via non-compliance.

Currently, MCI is hegemonic. However, its predominance is sustained only by the constant updating and publication of health promotion literature, financial inducements and other forms of carrot and stick policy, deployed by government health agencies. Aspects of the current policy context suggest that this predominance is precarious and time limited. In advanced Western capitalist societies, increasing expectations of consumer rights in service transactions have led to the need for greater availability of information and the citizen's right to accept or reject a product. The MCI programme fits poorly with these expectations, leading to a conflict of values and interests between state/medical paternalism and citizen consumerism. More specifically, within the current British health policy context, there has been the introduction of the Patient's Charter (DoH 1992b) and consumerism in the NHS. These emphasise the need for information and informed consent and give less credence to professional interests. This could put the authority of public health experts about vaccine risk under new pressures.

Wider cultural and social influences are also likely to strengthen these trends. The willingness of the media to give voice to parental concerns about vaccine risk is likely to reinforce rather than detract from concerns about risk. Short (1984) notes that public awareness of risk is heavily influenced by media coverage. The increasing tendency for various social groups to consult with what Giddens (1991) terms 'guides to living' (manuals, guides, books on self-help) may mean that the knowledge accumulated at the moment by a small group of dissenting parents about vaccine versus infection risk may become more widespread at the expense of more orthodox literature.

The tendency for late modernity to engender the creation of 'new' social movements concerned with challenging expert risk assessments may also present a problem for the traditional public health view of MCI. The traditional pattern of authority and deference between expert and non expert is breaking down. Traditional authority enjoys less deference from non experts than in the past. The lay person is now faced with a range of experts who disagree with one another on a topic like vaccination. Doctors, alternative therapists, lawyers, campaigning journalists, public health specialists and primary care workers may all offer authoritative advice to be assessed by lay people. As Giddens (1991) points out, this range of expert views leads to lay people now consulting other sources of information such as self-help manuals. The recent formation of campaigning groups (such as 'The Informed Parent' and JABS) which are critical of the current immunisation policy has started to expose medical knowledge to debate in the public sphere. These groups question the legitimacy of public health policy in relation to MCI and take direct action (a further example of public suspicion of experts entrusted with protecting ordinary people's interests is addressed by Phil Brown in this volume). Campaigning has included: setting up forums where advice and information on MCI are given by 'non expert' parents; giving publicity to alternative discourses on disease prevention from alternative medicine;

lobbying parliament over the current criteria for awarding financial compensation for children who have been vaccine damaged; and suing multinational drug companies for compensation for brain damage caused by vaccines.

Thus the inherited tension between the medical rationale of the early twentieth century and the tradition of questioning state interference is now amplified by consumerism and the loss of trust in expert systems (Giddens 1991). Consequently, it is not surprising that MCI is surfacing as a controversial policy. This controversy is made more likely by other emerging cultural emphases about health, such as self-responsibility and holism and the emergence of new social movements.

Acknowledgements

We are grateful to the respondents who took part in the Health Education Authority funded study for their time and interest in the project. We would also like to thank Jonathan Gabe, Maggie Pearson and the two anonymous reviewers for their helpful and constructive comments on an earlier draft of this chapter.

References

Armstrong, D. (1993) Public health spaces and the fabrication of identity, *Sociology*, 27, 393–410.

Balshem, M. (1991) Cancer, control and causality – talking about cancer in a working-class community, *American Ethnologist*, 18, 152–72.

Barlow, H. and Walker, D. (1990) Immunisation in Fife Part II – Failure to immunise against whooping cough – reasons given by parents, *Health Education Journal*, 49, 103–5.

Beck, U. (1992) *Risk Society: Towards A New Modernity*. London: Sage.

Brown, P. (1992) Popular epidemiology and toxic waste contamination: lay and professional ways of knowing, *Journal of Health and Social Behaviour*, 33, 267–81.

Clark Nelson, M. and Rogers, J. (1992) The right to die? Anti-vaccination activity and the 1874 smallpox epidemic in Stockholm, *The Society for the Social History of Medicine*, 23, 369–88.

Davison, C., Davey Smith, G. and Frankel, S. (1991) Lay epidemiology and the prevention paradox: the implications of coronary candidacy for health education, *Sociology of Health and Illness*, 13, 1–19.

DHSS (1976) *Prevention and Health: Everybody's Business*. London: HMSO.

DoH (1990) *Vaccination Protects*. London: HMSO.

DoH (1992a) *Health of the Nation*. London: HMSO.

DoH (1992b) *The Patient's Charter*. London: HMSO.

Douglas, M. (1975) *Implicit Meanings: Essays in Anthropology*. London: Routledge.

Douglas, M. (1992) *Risk and Blame: Essays in Cultural Theory*. London: Routledge.

Egan, S., Logan, G., and Bedford, H. (1994) *Low Uptake of Immunisation. Associated Factors and the Role of Health Education Initiatives in Uptake of Immunisation. Issues for Health Educators*. London: Health Education Authority.

Giddens, A. (1991) *Modernity and Self-Identity*. London: Polity.

Hansard (1994) Vaccine damage payment scheme. Written answer to Mr Ian McCartney MP, Monday 27 June, PQ2080.

Health Education Authority (1993) *Immunisation: Information for Parents*. London: HEA.

Klein, N., Morgan, K. and Washborough-Jones, M.H. (1981) Parents' beliefs about vaccination – the continuing propagation of false contraindications, *British Medical Journal*, 283, 1231–3.

Leese, B. and Bosanquet, N. (1992) Immunization in the UK: policy review and the future economic options, *Vaccine*, 10, 491–9.

Levy, M.H. and Bridges-Webb, C. (1990) Just one shot is not enough – measles control and eradication, *Medical Journal of Australia*, 152, 489–91.

McKeown, T. (1979) *The Role of Medicine*. Oxford: Blackwell.

Nokes, D.J. and Anderson, R.M. (1991) Vaccine safety versus vaccine efficacy in mass immunisation programmes, *The Lancet*, 338, 1309–12.

Palmer, G. and Short, S. (1989) *Health Care and Public Policy; An Australian Analysis*. Melbourne: MacMillan.

Rogers, A. and Pilgrim, D. (1994) Rational non-compliance with childhood immunisation: personal accounts of parents and primary health care professionals. In Health Education Authority (eds) *Uptake of Immunisation: Issues for Health Education*. London: Health Education Authority.

Short, J. (1984) The social fabric of risk: toward the social transformation of risk analysis, *American Sociological Review*, 49, 711–25.

Strong, P. (1990) Epidemic psychology: a model, *Sociology of Health and Illness*, 12, 249–59.

Veenman, J. and Jansma, L.G. (1980) The 1978 Dutch polio epidemic: a sociological study of the motives for accepting or refusing vaccination, *The Netherlands Journal of Sociology*, 16, 21–48.

Williams, G. and Popay, J. (1994) Lay knowledge and the privilege of experience. In Gabe, J., Kelleher, D. and Williams, G., (eds) *Challenging Medicine*. London: Routledge.

5. Popular epidemiology, toxic waste and social movements

Phil Brown

Introduction

Epidemiology has changed dramatically from the original shoe-leather epidemiology of John Snow, a committed and passionate discoverer of the causes of human suffering and death. In recent decades epidemiology has been shaped on a laboratory science model, often more concerned with protecting the increasingly rigid standards of scientific procedures than with safeguarding public health. At present, there is a countervailing approach – that of popular epidemiology – which returns to the roots laid down by Snow. By examining popular epidemiology, I intend to illustrate the changing nature of discovery involving environmental hazards and diseases.

In particular, I want to show that the current efforts of laypeople and certain scientists represent a significant contribution to both human health and scientific endeavour. These people are discovering disease clusters, agents which cause those diseases, and vectors by which the agents reach humans. They are also discovering a variety of social structural features: corporate dumping and cover-up, governmental complicity or at least failure to act appropriately, and local boosterism which pits co-residents against the lay investigators. And, they are engaging in self-discovery: finding the strength to carry out incredibly difficult and lengthy researches, learning to work collectively and cooperatively, and for some, redefining themselves as social activists with a larger political awareness.

Origins of epidemiological discovery

Shoe-leather epidemiology

Epidemiology begins for most of us with John Snow's 1854 discovery of the relationship between water contamination and a cholera epidemic in Soho, London. Snow listened to other people's anecdotal evidence about connections between water and cholera, and then made his own observations of such connections. He determined a localised area where the epidemic was most severe, and then surmised that the water pump at Broad Street was the cause (Goldstein and Goldstein 1986).

Snow conducted a health survey which showed him that mortality among people living further from the well occurred only when they specifically used that well. Mortality away from the well was at the pre-epidemic rate. To account for cholera among two groups of people who were believed to have not drunk contaminated water, Snow tracked down the indirect sources of water intake. To account for lack of cholera, he found that workhouse residents had their own water supply, and that brewery workers were drinking beer instead of water. Snow determined the source of the water as being one of two companies, identifiable by pipes and further confirmed by chloride concentration. The tabulation of cholera rate by water company provided proof of the source. Snow's famous removal of the handle from the Broad Street pump actually occurred after the epidemic had peaked, though that by no means diminishes the significance of his action (Goldstein and Goldstein 1986).

Note how advanced Snow was in his recommendations: 'The communicability of cholera ought not to be disguised from the people, under the idea that the knowledge of it would cause a panic, or occasion the sick to be deserted.' Such withholding of information is today one of the major problems in present-day relations between contaminated communities and government (Goldstein and Goldstein 1986).

Withholding stems from the highly political and economic nature of epidemiological investigations. In his 1882 play, *An Enemy of the People*, Henrik Ibsen (1951) portrays a remarkably modern perspective on epidemiological discovery. Dr. Stockmann, physician of the town's famous and profitable minerals baths, discovers toxic contamination from nearby tanneries. The good doctor refuses town leaders' demands that he hide the evidence. For his public health investigation and his refusal to cover up the data, Stockmann is fired, evicted, beaten, stoned, stigmatised as an enemy of the people, driven to mental breakdown, and his children attacked and thrown out of school. Still, he vows to fight on for justice.

Stockmann's struggles are the same kind that modern-day popular epidemiologists engage in. With this in mind I now turn my attention to those current efforts. I begin with a stages model derived from my research on the Woburn, Massachusetts leukemia cluster and other toxic waste sites in the United States. From this I move to a discussion of the various areas where lay perspectives come into conflict with scientific and official perspectives. Then I examine the social movement of toxic activists which surrounds this popular epidemiology phenomenon.

Popular epidemiology
Traditional epidemiology studies the distribution of a disease, and the factors that influence this distribution, in order to explain the etiology, and to provide preventive, public health, and clinical practices. Popular epidemiology is a broader process whereby lay persons gather data, and

also collaborate with experts. To some degree, popular epidemiology parallels scientific epidemiology, such as when laypeople conduct community health surveys. Yet it is more than public participation in traditional epidemiology, since it usually emphasises social structural factors as part of the causal disease chain. Further, it involves social movements, utilises political and judicial approaches to remedies, and challenges basic assumptions of traditional epidemiology, risk assessment, and public health regulation.

Popular epidemiology efforts do not *require* epidemiological health studies, even though these may occur. Indeed, activists generally want the hazards avoided and remediated. If the government and/or corporations involved would admit the problem and take appropriate action, activists would have no need for or interest in health studies. But the activists experience much resistance to their claims, and require the kind of public, political and scientific support that often presses for more concrete evidence of causation.

Popular epidemiology is similar to other lay advocacy for health care, in that lay perspectives counter professional ones and a social movement guides this alternative perspective. Some lay health advocacy acts to obtain more resources for the prevention and treatment of already recognised diseases (e.g. sickle cell anemia, AIDS), while others seek to win government and medical recognition of unrecognised or under-recognised diseases (e.g. black lung, post-traumatic stress disorder). Still others seek to affirm the knowledge of yet-unknown etiological factors in already recognised diseases (e.g. diethylstilbestrol [DES] and vaginal cancer, asbestos and mesothelioma). Popular epidemiology is most similar to the latter approach, since original research is necessary both to document the prevalence of the disease and the putative causation.

This leads us to consider popular epidemiology as having two elements. The first is a general description of the phenomenon of lay discovery of disease. This is often environmental or occupational, though it need not be. The second is the more specific participation of activists in epidemiological studies. It is important to note, however, that laypeople who embark on a process of social discovery of toxic contamination do not typically have any idea of the extent of their future involvement. Hence, the more 'routine' popular epidemiology (general discovery) cannot be so easily distinguished from the more 'formal' type (involvement in health studies).

From studying contaminated communities where well-organised citizens' groups have discovered toxic contamination, we observe a typical set of stages. My chief model is the Woburn, Massachusetts case, where citizens discovered a leukemia cluster, pushed for government action, collaborated with scientists to conduct a health study on leukemia, reproductive disorders, and birth defects, and also filed suit against the companies they believed to be responsible.[1] These stages may vary in different locations, and may overlap each other:

1. *Lay observations of health effects and pollutants.* Many people who live at risk of toxic hazards have access to data otherwise inaccessible to scientists. Their experiential knowledge usually precedes official and scientific awareness.

2. *Hypothesising connections.* Activists often make assumptions about what contaminants have caused health and ecological outcomes.

3. *Creating a common perspective.* Activists begin to piece together the extent of the problem, and to organise it coherently. 'Lay mapping' of disease clusters is a typical feature of this stage. Citizens also make discoveries of actual pollution sources.

4. *Looking for answers from government and science.* Activists expect government health agencies and their scientific colleagues to investigate the problem. Citizens are often given little or no support from officials and scientists. In-depth epidemiological studies are rarely done. Rather, officials may merely make statements about the relationship of rates in the toxic community to state or national rates.

5. *Organising a community group.* Citizens formalise their social action by setting up an organisation to provide social support and information for toxic victims, deal with local, state, and federal agencies to attract media attention, and often enough to make connections with other toxic waste groups.

6. *Official studies are conducted by experts.* Additional pressure leads to more detailed studies, but these tend to continue the denial of toxic waste-induced disease.

7. *Activists bring in their own experts.* Here is where the more 'formal' popular epidemiology efforts begin. With official support for their claims of toxic contamination, citizens find sympathetic scientists who are willing to help them in health studies. There are differing degrees of lay involvement in these studies.

8. *Litigation and confrontation.* Often, citizens file suit against corporations they believe are responsible for the contamination. They may also take other political action, such as picketing, boycotting, and lobbying.

9. *Pressing for official corroboration.* When lay-supported or lay-involved health studies are completed, citizens attempt to use that data to confirm their claim. They typically meet even more resistance, often from a growing number of national actors such as professional organisations, federal agencies, and disease philanthropies.

10. *Continued vigilance.* Whether or not activists have been successful in making their case, they find the need to be continually involved in cleanups, additional official surveillance, media attention, and overall coordination of efforts.

Throughout these stages, lay and professional disputes occur. I now turn to the main elements of those disputes: lay participation, standards of proof, constraints on professional practice, disputes over the nature of risks and hazards, quality of official studies, and professional autonomy.

Struggles over scientific discovery

Popular participation and the critique of value-neutrality
Popular epidemiology practitioners disagree that epidemiology is a value-neutral scientific enterprise. Traditional epidemiologists criticise health studies where citizens play a role, as in the case of Woburn where activists worked with biostatisticians to conduct a large health survey. That study determined that exposure to contaminated well water was associated with increased childhood leukemia and a variety of birth defects and reproductive problems (Lagakos *et al.* 1984). The critics who argued that the study was biased upheld the notion of a value-free science in which knowledge, theories, techniques, and applications are devoid of self interest or bias. Sociological and other social scientific studies of science dispute such claims, arguing that scientific knowledge is not absolute, but rather the subject of debate among scientists. As well, scientific knowledge is shaped by media influence, economic interest, political pressure, and social movement activism (Dickson 1984). On a more practical level, science is limited by financial and personnel resources; lay involvement often supplies the labour power needed to document health hazards. Science is also limited in how it identifies problems worthy of study. It does not typically take its direction from the lay public, but from established professional and organisational routines.

Toxic activists see themselves as working to correct problems not dealt with by the established scientific community. The centrality of popular involvement is evident in the history of the women's health and occupational health movements which have been major forces in pointing to often unidentified problems and working to abolish their causes. Among the hazards and diseases thus uncovered are DES, Agent Orange, asbestos, pesticides, unnecessary hysterectomies, sterilisation abuse, and black lung.

Some epidemiologists who support lay efforts to uncover environmental health effects put forth a distinctively value laden epidemiology. Wing (1994) best exemplifies this alternative conceptualisation of epidemiology:

1. It would ask not what is good or bad for health overall, but for what sectors of the population.
2. It would look for connections between many diseases and exposures, rather than looking at merely single exposure-disease pairs.
3. It would examine unintended consequences of interventions.
4. It would utilise people's personal illness narratives.

5. It would include in research reporting the explicit discussion of assumptions, values, and the social construction of scientific knowledge.

6. It would recognise that the problem of controlling confounding factors comes from a reductionist approach that looks only for individual relations rather than a larger set of social relations. Hence, what are nuisance factors in traditional epidemiology become essential context in a new ecological epidemiology.

7. It would involve humility about scientific research, combined with a commitment to supporting broad efforts to reform society and health.

Standards of proof

Many scientists and public health officials emphasise various problems in standards of proof, ranging from initial detection and investigation to the final interpretation of data. Scientists focus on problems such as inadequate history of the site, the unclarity of the route of contaminants, determining appropriate water sampling locations, small numbers of cases, bias in self-reporting of symptoms, getting appropriate control groups, lack of knowledge about characteristics and effects of certain chemicals, and unknown latency periods for carcinogens. Epidemiologists often believe that they are not choosing the research questions they think are amenable to study, but rather are responding to a crisis situation. Traditional approaches also tend to look askance at innovative perspectives favoured by activists, such as the importance of genetic mutations, immune disregulation markers, and non-fatal health effects such as rashes and persistent respiratory problems.

Some problems in adequate research stem from the newness of environmental epidemiology. Yet activists believe that scientists are too concerned with having each element of scientific study as perfect as possible. Residents are convinced that there is disease, clear evidence of contamination, and strong indications that these two are related. From their point of view, the officials and scientists are hindering a proper study, or are hiding incriminating knowledge.

The level of statistical significance required for intervention is a frequent source of contention. Many communities that wish to document hazards and disease are stymied by insufficient numbers of cases to achieve statistical significance. Some community oriented professionals adhere to accepted significance levels, while others argue that such levels are often inappropriate to environmental risk. This latter group distinguishes statistical significance from public health significance, since an increased disease rate may be of great public health significance even if statistical probabilities are not met. They believe that epidemiology should mirror clinical medicine more than laboratory science, by erring on the safe side of false positives (Ozonoff and Boden 1987).

But epidemiologists prefer false negatives to false positives, yielding a burden of proof which usually exceeds the level required to argue for intervention. Supporters of the popular epidemiology approach disagree with this burden of proof. As Couto observes from his study of Yellow Creek,

The important political test is not the findings of epidemiologists on the probability of nonrandomness of an incidence of illness but the likelihood that a reasonable person . . . would take up residence with the community at risk and drink from and bathe in water from the Yellow Creek area or buy a house along Love Canal (1985: 60).

Indeed, these questions are presented to public health officials wherever there is dispute between the citizen and official perceptions. Beverly Paigen, who worked with laypeople in Love Canal, makes it clear that standards of evidence are value-laden:

Before Love Canal, I also needed a 95 percent certainty before I was convinced of a result. But seeing this rigorously applied in a situation where the consequences of an error meant that pregnancies were resulting in miscarriages, stillbirths, and children with medical problems, I realized I was making a value judgment . . . whether to make errors on the side of protecting human health or on the side of conserving state resources (1982: 34).

Lay-professional differences concerning risks and hazards
Scientists have been professionally socialised to believe that science and technology are best left to scientists and engineers. Growing public fears of toxic wastes – quite often realistic – have encountered much epidemiological disagreement. Communities which believe themselves to be contaminated or at risk have found that the epidemiological response is often defensive and hostile, based on a view that alternative hypotheses are threats to scientific inquiry. In particular, scientists often cite what they view as erroneous public beliefs concerning increases in cancer rates, the extent of environmental causes of cancer, and the existence of cancer clusters. Scientists often charge laypeople with being 'anti-scientific', when in fact citizens may simply work at science in a nontraditional manner, or else are critical of official practices. Indeed, surveys of toxic activists show that they express support for scientists as important sources of knowledge (Freudenberg 1984).

Professionalist practices of excluding the public are particularly ironic in the case of epidemiology, since the original 'shoe-leather' epidemiological work that founded the field is quite similar to popular epidemiology. Yet modern epidemiology has come far from its origins, turning into a laboratory science with no room for lay input. Along the way, the passionate discovery has been transformed into a routinised science establishment.

This clash of rationalities discussed above is particularly evident in risk assessment. Langdon Winner (1986) views the rise of risk assessment in the 1970s as a backfire against environmentalism, with 'health hazards' redefined as 'health risks'. Thus, he notes, 'What otherwise might be seen as a fairly obvious link between cause and effect, for example, air pollution and cancer, now becomes something fraught with uncertainty.'

The early approaches to risk, which continue to dominate, came from engineers and cognitive psychologists. These risk assessment experts employed questionnaires, in tandem with actual hazard rates, to argue that respondents overestimate 'flashy' causes of death and those which receive more media coverage. At the same time respondents underestimate less 'flashy' ones. Scholars explained this by noting that people rely on anecdotal evidence, have an emotional involvement in the issue, have deep distrust of social authorities, are overconfident in their personal ability to actively avoid hazards, have difficulty imagining low probability/ high consequence events happening to them, and have trouble taking in new information, and often stick with past judgements. Lay people are more likely to assess high risk when the activity is seen as involuntary, catastrophic, not personally controllable, inequitable in distribution of risks and benefits, unfamiliar, and highly complex. The risk assessors calculated these dimensions of risk as falling into three factors: their familiarity with the hazard, the conceptual 'dread' associated with it, and number of people exposed to the hazard (Fischoff et al. 1982).

Tversky and Kahneman (1974) believe people generally use heuristics, inferential or judgement rules, rather than relying on actual hazard rates. These are similar to heuristics used to judge size and distance of objects. However, we should note that these comparative concerns of size and distance may have little or no dangerous outcomes, and hence may not apply well as analogs for environmental hazard perception. For Tversky and Kahneman, there is an ideal optimal rationality for all people. The risk assessors' task is to explain how lay perceptions deviate from professional rationality, and to educate laypeople in order to 'bring them onto the curve.'

Starr and Whipple (1980) were puzzled by the fact that people are concerned more with multiple-death accidents than a series of individual accidents reaching the same total. They called this a 'preoccupation' but, from a sociological perspective, multiple death events pose a danger to community structure and survival that is quite different to discrete deaths. This classic risk assessment approach writes off collective social meaning.

Starr and Whipple (1980), like Fischoff and his colleagues, were surprised by the lack of linearity in risk perception and actual risk. This stems from a positivist assumption that all risks have been identified, and that they fit into a logical model. Why, however, assume linearity in the world? Despite its attempts to put forth a positivist worldview, the actual measurement of much of this research was flawed. Covello (1983) notes that many of the findings were based on surveys of small, highly specialised, unrepresentative groups. Little or no effort was made to analyse organisational and structural variables, *e.g.* ethnicity, religion, sex, region, age, occupation, education, income or marital status. Further, there are well known response biases in survey research, such as giving answers even when one has no opinion, and responding with the first thing that comes to mind. This seems very likely when laypeople are asked about scientific rates of hazard occurrences and the resultant mortality.

Rayner and Cantor (1987) turn around the underlying logic of risk assessment, arguing that risk perception stems from the social context, and cannot be studied as an atomised concept. Indeed, risk perception is an attribute of a culture not of an individual. Similarly, Short (1984) writes that risk analysis rarely deals with risk to the social fabric overall. The social fabric involves such components as fairness, confidence, trust, fiduciary responsibility, moral responsibility, competence, and legitimacy. Like Krimsky and Plough (1988), Short emphasises the distinction between 'social rationality' and 'scientific rationality.' Freudenburg (1988) offers a 'social rational model,' in contrast to a supposedly individual rational model. It relies on assuming that different social groups and institutions have differential interests. Social institutions emphasise some risks more and others less. They select and manipulate facts, symbolic meanings, and the agenda for discourse.

When we look sociologically at the rise of risk assessment we must ask the question: why does a form of knowledge come into being at a particular time? The classic risk assessment studies began with nuclear power issues. As late as 1983, Covello's (1983) review of the literature showed that most risk perception research dealt with nuclear power. Risk perception research continued during a period of environmental crisis. There was a receptive audience in corporate and government leaders who faced many challenges from a growing social movement. The need to push risk perception toward the rational logic of risk measurement meant that it would be useful to find flaws in public perception and to let experts teach them how to think better. This may be seen as a response to the questioning of scientific superiority. This approach realises that people may be critical of science and technology, and therefore professionals are needed to steer laypeople in the right direction. This is an inherently anti-democratic approach since it proposes that people accept scientific leadership without having democratic input into science policy.

Intellectually and practically, risk assessment models combined the engineering model (tinkering toward perfection) with the economic model, especially the cost-benefit approach in which rational individuals make up a social agglomeration. Chauncy Starr, the originator of cost-benefit approaches to risk perception and risk assessment, converts all social benefit into dollar equivalents. For example, the benefits of air travel were calculated as dollars saved compared to auto travel; benefits from the Vietnam War were calculated on the assumption that all citizens benefited intangibly from war expenditures, determined as per capita spending on war effort. The social biases here are quite apparent.

When applied to environmental hazards, traditional risk assessment frequently is used to argue against the significance of environmental hazards. Although different social groups have structurally different beliefs about the nature of risks, risk assessment scientists and the public officials who use risk assessment fail to adequately grasp these social differences (Vaughan and Seifert 1992). Activists have no interest in applying risk assessment models to their efforts, even though they are sometimes willing to attempt epidemiological studies. From their point of view, risk assessment is an approach thoroughly loaded against the interest of citizens.

It is important, especially when studying race and class differences, to add another concern – the population studied. Risk assessment, as well as epidemiological research, typically treat race and class burdens as variables to be controlled, rather than as special features of populations. Yet populations are not random; they are stratified according to social structural features such as race and class. The context of this stratification means that the hazard exposures are not random, and hence we cannot accurately find universal dose-response relationships (Wing 1994). Because of the stratification of society, hazards are inequitably grouped together and people experience them as collective assaults rather than as individual probabilities.

These contextual issues can be seen in Martha Balshem's (1993) study of how a Philadelphia cancer prevention project clashed with the white, working-class neighbourhood's belief system. The project identified excess cancer in this area, a fact widely known by the residents and the media. The medicalised approach of the health educators focused on individual habits, especially smoking, drinking, and diet. Tannerstown residents countered this worldview with their belief that the local chemical plant and other sources of contamination were responsible.

The professionals approached the working class as a monolithic mass of people with many unhealthy behaviors and nonscientific attitudes. What professionals call working class 'fatalism' appears more sensible as a response to economic insecurity in the face of Philadelphia's declining industrial workforce. The health educators medicalised working class fatalism as a 'disease' that prevents people from complying with cancer prevention experts' prescriptions. To change lifestyles appeared merely to be what Balshem (1993: 57) notes is 'to adapt to life in the "cancer zone".'

Balshem recounts one woman's tale of agony over her husband's death from pancreatic cancer. Jennifer fights for the right to see John's medical record. When she finds a line about his smoking and drinking, she asks the doctor, 'What's this on here?' He responds 'That's not important.' Jennifer retorts, 'It's important to me. You're going to take this report saying he's an alcoholic and he smokes and this is what causes cancer. Then you wonder why we get upset because the statistics are wrong.' Jennifer struggles to get his medical record rewritten, and she demands and autopsy to show that he didn't die of lung cancer, but of metastatic pancreatic cancer, and hence is not blamed for smoking-inducer cancer. Jennifer, like toxic waste activists, wants justice and fairness, and will use science if it can be of help. But they do not desire a science 'above' ethics and morality. That is a contradiction in terms for them.

Scientific contributions of popular epidemiology

Lay epidemiological approaches have changed the nature of scientific inquiry in various ways.

1. Lay involvement identifies the many cases of 'bad science,' *e.g.* poor studies, secret investigations, failure to inform local health officials, fraud and coverup.

2. Lay involvement points out that 'normal science' (Kuhn 1963) has drawbacks, *e.g.* automatically opposing lay participation in health surveys, demanding standards of proof that may be unobtainable or inappropriate, being slow to accept new concepts of toxic causality.

3. The combination of the above two points leads to a general public distrust of official science, thus pushing laypeople to seek alternate routes of information and analysis.

4. Popular epidemiology yields valuable data that often would be unavailable to scientists. If scientists and government fail to solicit such data, and especially if they consciously oppose and devalue it, then such data may be lost. This goes against the grain of traditional scientific method.

5. Popular epidemiology has pioneered innovative approaches. For example, the Environmental Health Network is testing a new way to ascertain quickly the relationship between disease clusters and toxic wastes by using the Environmental Protection Agency's (EPA's) Toxic Release Inventory, a computerised database accessible to all citizens in public libraries.

These five elements have been common to many contaminated communities, but in Woburn the lay contribution to scientific endeavour has been dramatic. The Woburn case was the major impetus for the establishment of the state cancer registry. Of particular value is the discovery of a trichloroethylene (TCE) syndrome involving three major body systems – immune, cardiovascular, and neurological – which is increasingly showing up in other TCE sites.

Activism has also contributed to increasing research on Woburn: the Department of Public Health (DPH) and Centers for Disease Conrol (CDC) are conducting a major five year reproductive outcome study of the city, utilising both prospective and retrospective data, and citizens have a large role in this process. The DPH is conducting a case-control study of leukemia. Toxic waste activism in Woburn has also led to several Massachusetts Institute of Technology (MIT) studies. One group of projects, totalling $3.33 million in federal support, will produce a complete hydrogeological study; a history of the tanning industry, a major polluter; and an innovative genetic toxicology study based on human cell mutation assays, which will endeavour to produce a 'unique chemical fingerprint' of a large number of known and suspected toxic substances (Massachusetts Institute of Technology 1990). A second MIT effort is a three year study funded by the Agency for Toxic Substances and Disease Registry and the National Institute for Occupational Safety and Health. It will examine the scientific, ethical, and legal issues in monitoring residents and clean-up workers in three Superfund sites, one of which is Woburn. It is significant that both public officials and university scientists attribute the strength and innovativeness of this variety of research to the strong community involvement.

How do we know if lay investigations provide correct knowledge?
Toxic activists are not anti-scientific. In many cases, popular epidemiology findings are the result of scientific studies involving trained professionals, even if they begin as 'lay mapping' of disease clusters without attention to base rates or controls. This lay mapping phenomenon is almost an instinctual reaction. Patricia Nonnon did it when she noticed high rates of leukemia in the Pelham Bay section of the Bronx in New York City (Lorch 1989). In Staten Island, another New York City borough, a landfill worker tracked down the health status of his workmates when he discerned an elevation in cancer and other diseases. A Coeur d'Alene, Idaho woman tracked down several entire high school graduating classes when she noticed a huge cancer increase. Leon and Juanita Andrewjeski kept what they termed a 'death map' of cancer deaths and illness and of early heart attacks among farmers downwind of the Hanford, Washington nuclear reservation (Kaplan 1991). In Leominster, Massachusetts, a doctor told a woman, 'You do so well with your [autistic] children, you should talk with other parents on your block who have autistic children.' This led to lay mapping of 35 cases in a small area (Lang 1994).

At the scientific level lay-involved surveys are sometimes well-crafted researches with defendable data. Laypeople may initiate action, and even direct the formulation of hypotheses, but they work *with* scientists, not in place of them. Thus, the end results can be judged by the same criteria as any study. But since all scientific judgements involve social factors, there are no simple algorithms for ascertaining truth. Scientific inquiry is always full of controversy; what is different here is that laypeople are entering that controversy.

To err on the side of caution

Toxic activists believe that epidemiology needs to return to its roots. One central part of that is the elevation of public health over abstract canons of science. Doing that means, among other things, to err on the side of caution. A society more concerned with overall well-being will conduct research differently, and act on it differently. When the Swedish government found a connection between power lines and childhood leukemia, the government immediately made plans to alter power lines. The alternative in the US would be, at best, to appoint a National Cancer Institute or Department of Energy panel to study this question for several years, with a host of lobbying efforts to make sure the utility companies received adequate representation. That would be similar to the situation in 1992 when the tobacco industry got the EPA to throw certain scientists off a second-hand smoke panel because they were considered too vocal in their beliefs that tobacco caused lung cancer.

The elevation of public health concerns also means a more powerful role for social activists in setting the health agenda. We remember the importance of veterans' organisations in confronting Agent Orange. Women's health activists were central in showing links between DES and vaginal cancer. Recently, activists won a large federal research effort to study excess breast cancer in Long Island, New York, and forced President Clinton to publicly support more funding.

Sociologically, we may situate research silences and scientific/governmental resistance in a large context of professional resistance to controversial discoveries concerning such problems as drug side effects, unnecessary surgery, and environmentally induced diseases. Normal science and its supporters do not like to challenge political, economic, and intellectual sources of power. Nor do they want to change the theories and methods to which they are accustomed. They do not want alterations in their professional and institutional arrangements which might threaten funding, power, influence, and tradition. They most certainly do not like lay input, and lay input is pervasive in the discussions of environmentally caused disease.

Toxic waste activism and environmental justice

My definition of popular epidemiology early in this chapter included the centrality of political action and social movements. Many local toxic action groups do not initially view themselves as part of a national or international movement. Rather, they are only dealing with what they perceive as local problems. But the initial groups, such as the Love Canal activists, set in motion a new movement. As well, the subsequent prevalence of these groups contributes to an already existing movement which has some more consciously political centres of activity. While most of these groups would not style themselves as popular epidemiology practitioners, this is what they are doing in their lay efforts to uncover disease and act on that discovery. The toxic waste movement represents a solidification into broader social action of popular epidemiology's critique of traditional science.

A new type of social movement
The toxic waste movement has been a dramatic force in US society in the last two decades. Unlike other social movements, this one is not characterised by national organisations. The toxic waste movement is highly decentralised, composed of thousands of small community-level groups. Its few national organisations, such the Citizen's Clearinghouse Against Hazardous Waste and the Environmental Health Network, are sources of inspiration and resources, rather than officials and organisations exerting influence over local groups. There are also some statewide toxic activist coalitions that play similar roles.

Some local organisers have become highly politicised, such as Lois Gibbs, whose experiences at Love Canal inspired her to form a national group. Patty Frase, without prior political experience, started as a local organiser in her home town of Jacksonville, Arkansas, site of the Vertac Chemical Corporation which produced herbicides and pesticides. She moved on to organise a statewide toxic waste coalition (Capek 1993). Some local activists have become somewhat professionalised – two staff members of Woburn's For a Cleaner Environment (FACE) group later worked for a national non-profit organisation that provides consultation to local groups engaged in lay epidemiology. Even when local activists lose their political naivety, they still may cease their activism when they attain their goals. Yet while many groups have a short life, their large number guarantees increasing strength to the overall movement.

There are several reasons for the lack of national participation. Without a history of radical political action, local activists do not automatically see the benefits of a national organisation. Local activists have often suffered family injury or death directly, and they spend enormous time on arranging health care and organising their lives around a debilitating or fatal disease. Local groups are bogged down in lengthy and difficult efforts at discovery, remediation, litigation, and organising. For example, Woburn's Ann Anderson began her 'shoe-leather epidemiology' in 1973. As of 1994, the two Woburn Superfund sites are still not cleaned up, and the litigation appeal only ended in late 1990. In the Velsicol case in Hardeman County, Tennessee, a state regulatory agency brought the problem to light in 1964; in 1966 the United States Geological Survey got involved; in 1972 Velsicol was ordered to close the dump; in 1977 residents began to organise, and in 1988 the final appeal of the case was heard (Brown and Mikkelsen 1990: 71–2). Such lengthy processes diminish groups' potential for broader activism.

Some critics argue that the toxic waste movement is too motivated by narrow self-interest – protection of one's own 'backyard' rather than the larger common good. It is true that toxic waste activists are not usually motivated by global environmental concerns, although a good number quickly come to understand their local problems in that larger context. As Lois Gibbs (1991) points out, 'NIMBY has now become NIABY, Not in Anyone's Backyard.' In other words, these groups seek the protection of all people against toxic waste hazards through minimal environmental discharge, on-site mobile disposal, and the banning of entire dangerous categories of chemicals and metals. As the 'NIABY' approach becomes more dominant, local activists grasp their role as one of many groups which have altered the national political life (Freudenberg and Steinsapir 1992). In Lois Gibbs' (1991) words, 'We're working locally and affecting national policy.' Local toxic waste activist groups have been mistrustful of the global emphasis of mainstream environmentalism, since those national organisations have taken up global issues at the expense of local matters of human health.

New sources of activism
Because toxic waste activists start out from personal experience, rather than political ideology, they differ from participants in the broader environmental movement in several ways: their generally lower class background, lower levels of education, a predominance of women members and leaders, and a higher level of participation by minorities than in the environmental movement. Overall, activists have less overall political ideology or experience than do mainstream environmentalists.

Toxic waste activists are typically working class and lower middle class people who are politicised by actual or feared harm to their families (Milbrath 1984). The toxic activists who have made their mark in American politics organised in response to known contamination, or at least to perceived potential contamination from actual sites. There are also groups which oppose LULUs (locally unwanted land uses) such as potential sitings of landfills and incinerators. These rarely stem from direct experience of illness, though in other respects they are similar to toxic waste activists in that they struggle for democratic control of their local environment, in which they come into conflict with corporations, government and scientists.

Women play central roles in the toxic waste movement (Brown and Ferguson 1995). Women are the most frequent organisers of lay detection, partly because they are the chief health arrangers for their families (Levine 1982), and partly because their child care role makes them more concerned than men with local environmental issues (Blocker and Eckberg 1989). Women approach the problem of toxic contamination and official response with a notion of fairness, equity and collective protection. They centre their worldview more on relationships than on abstract rights, and on their roles as the primary caretakers of the family. These roles lead women to be more aware of the real and potential health effects of toxic waste, and to take a more skeptical view of traditional science. They often undergo a transformation of self, based on changes noted by Belenky *et al.* (1986) in their concept of 'women's ways of knowing.' That perspective traces the ways that women come to know things, beginning with either silence or the acceptance of established authority, progressing to a trust in subjective knowledge, and then to a synthesis of external and subjective knowledge (Brown and Ferguson 1995).

Toxic waste activists are very often inexperienced in political action and do not start from a politicised view of the world. The ideology underlying the movement is largely based on democratic principles which activists perceive as subverted by government and corporate actions. Unlike the more highly educated members of the environmental movement, these people do not generally start from a cynical approach to government; they tend to have faith in the established order. Community contamination and the official response to it comes as a revelation. While citizens are basically aware that business is self-serving, they have assumed that the democratic system protects the public from excesses and abuses. Corporate denial of responsibility and government opposition to lay detection demonstrate that the government acts in an undemocratic fashion. The discovery that public safety does not necessarily take precedence over profit is a deep shock, since it is so unexpected (Krauss 1989). So these activists face the betrayal of two cornerstones of modern culture: science and democratic government. This makes them especially sharp critics of both the official social construction of scientific knowledge and the political-economic machinations of the dominant society.

Environmental health and environmental justice
Environmental justice has become the leading approach within the toxic waste movement, centring on the race, class, and to a lesser extent gender

differences in environmental burden. To some extent, the environmental justice movement is a subset of the broader toxic waste movement, yet it also pushes that broader movement to take up its viewpoint – even some largely white organisations have adopted the environmental justice framework. The Citizens' Clearinghouse for Hazardous Wastes, led by Love Canal leader Lois Gibbs, has defined itself as an organisation dedicated to environmental justice. And the Environmental Health Network, another national activist group, leans strongly in that direction.

Unlike the broader toxic waste movement, whose primarily working class and lower middle class activists generally have little prior political background, the largely minority environmental justice movement stems from a civil rights tradition. The environmental justice framework probably can be best dated to the 1978 protests by residents of Warren County, North Carolina over a polychlorinated biphenyl (PCB) dump. Through the 1980s more minority groups developed, though keeping to their own localities. Research findings increasingly showed excess minority environmental burden, particularly the 1987 United Church of Christ report (United Church of Christ 1987). Conferences in the late 1980s and early 1990s provided a more well defined national presence that pressured the EPA to establish an Office of Environmental Equity.

Bullard (1992a) argues that the 'dominant environmental protection paradigm' focuses on hard-to-document fatalities, rather than on illnesses. This dominant paradigm 'exists to manage, regulate, and distribute risks.' It has institutionalised unequal reinforcement, traded human health for profit, placed the burden of proof on victims, legitimated human exposure to harmful substances, promoted risky technologies such as incinerators, exploited the vulnerability of disenfranchised communities, subsidised ecological destruction, created a risk assessment industry, delayed clean up programs, and failed to develop preventive measures.

Environmental justice advocates define themselves in opposition to that legacy, and put forth a comprehensive social ecology program. Environmental justice includes the rights of all people to be protected from environmental degradation; adopts a public health prevention model; shifts the burden of proof to polluters who do harm, discriminate, or do not give equal protection to minorities; and redresses disproportionate burden through targeted action and resources (Bullard 1992b).

Minority activists have made much of empirical research, but not usually epidemiological studies. Instead, they have focused on demonstrating the geographical distribution of environmental hazards on the basis of race and class. In a majority of cases, race appears more significant than class; in others class is more dominant than race. Different areas show different minority groups (blacks, Hispanics) to be affected, though blacks are the most typically over-exposed to hazards. Studies have examined a variety of geographic units (zip codes, census tracts, cities, metropolitan statistical areas) and a variety of hazards (Superfund toxic sites mandated by the federal government for clean up, toxic emissions, existing waste facilities). As Mohai and Bryant (1992) noted in their review of 15 studies, the wide range of geographical areas (local, regional, national) provides a combined body of knowledge which finds race and class, especially race, to be large factors in exposure to environmental hazards. Those, along with subsequent studies, provide extensive evidence for excess exposure of minorities (especially blacks), and substantial excess exposure by class, in the following categories: i) presence of hazardous waste sites and facilities (landfills, incinerators, Superfund sites; ii) air pollution; iii) exposure to various environmental hazards, *e.g.*, hazards in pesticides and foods, toxic releases measured by the EPA's Toxic Release Inventory; iv) actual and planned clean ups at Superfund sites; v) fines for environmental pollution; vi) specific health statuses which are related to environmental burden (*e.g.* blood lead); and vii) siting decisions for incinerators, hazardous waste sites and nuclear storage sites (Brown 1994).

Successes of the toxic waste movement
Toxic waste organising has had considerable success. Toxic activist organisations have provided desperately needed support and encouragement to their own members and to activists in other locations. Groups have catalysed clean ups of hazardous waste sites, blocked hazardous facilities, halted pesticide spraying, and forced companies to upgrade pollution management technology. Through these successes, the movement has forced corporations to consider the environmental effects of their production and disposal practices, resulting in source reduction. At the government level, groups have won legislation, as well as the right-to-know about local hazards and the right-to-participate in decision making. For the overall public, the toxic waste movement has increased public support for environmental protection (Freudenberg and Steinsapir 1992).

Activists observe science in practice as being a servant of corporate and governmental interests, and thus seek a lay, democratic science which we see in popular epidemiology. As with other social movements in health, the toxic waste movement alters accepted scientific definitions of the problem, and leads to significant advances in scientific knowledge. In doing so, it challenges normal routines of corporate power, political authority and professionalism.

The toxic waste movement, especially under the influence of the environmental justice perspective, helps steer the environmental movement clear of an emphasis on personal solutions and recycling; it emphasises the well-being of humans as a crucial issue, as opposed to wildlife and wilderness; it forces awareness of the Third World ramifications of toxic waste dumping; it introduces a different class and racial awareness based on the groups most affected; it places gender in a central role, due to the predominance of women activists and their particular approaches to social problems; it offers political participation to many who would otherwise not be recruited, especially minorities and working class people (Dunlap and Mertig 1992, Brown and Masterson-Allen 1994).

Conclusion: causes and implications of popular epidemiology

Dramatically increasing scientific, as well as lay attention to environmental degradation, may make it easier for many to accept causal linkages previously considered too novel. Similarly, many more disease clusters are being identified as a result of this expanding attention and its related social movements. Growing numbers of similar cases containing small sample sizes and/or low base-rate phenomena may allow for more generalisability. These increasing cases also produce more anomalies, allowing for a paradigm shift.

Causal explanations from outside of science also play a role. Legal definitions of causality, developed in an expanding toxic tort repertoire, are initially determined by judicial interpretation of scientific testimony. Once constructed, they can take on a life of their own, setting standards by which scientific investigations will be applied to social life, for example, court-ordered guidelines on claims for disease caused by asbestos, nuclear testing, DES, and radiation experimentation.

Popular epidemiology stems from the legacy of health activism, growing public recognition of problems in science and technology, and the democratic upsurge regarding science policy. Communities face difficulties in environmental risk assessment due to differing conceptions of risk, lack of scientific resources, poor access to official information, and government policies which oppose or hinder public participation. In popular epidemiology, as in other health-related movements, activism by those affected is necessary to make progress in health care and health policy. In this process there is a powerful reciprocal relationship between the social movement and new views of science. The striking awareness of new scientific knowledge, coupled with government and professional resistance to that knowledge, leads people to form social movement organisations to pursue their claims-making. In turn, the further development of social movement organisations leads to further challenges to scientific canons. The socially constructed approach of popular epidemiology is thus a result of both a social movement and a new scientific paradigm, with both continually reinforcing the other.

Notes

1 Details are from Brown (1992) and Brown and Mikkelsen (1990).

References

Balshem, M. (1993) *Cancer in the Community: Class and Medical Authority*. Washington D.C.: Smithsonian Institution Press.

Belenky, M.F., Clinchy, B.M., Goldberger, N.R., and Tarule, J.M. (1986) *Women's Ways of Knowing: The Development of Self, Voice, and Mind.* New York: Basic Books.

Blocker, T.J. and Eckberg, D.L. (1987) Environmental issues as women's issues: general concerns and local hazards, *Social Science Quarterly*, 70, 586–93.

Brown, P. (1992) Toxic waste contamination and popular epidemiology: lay and professional ways of knowing, *Journal of Health and Social Behavior*, 33, 267–81.

Brown, P. (1994) Race, Class, and Environmental Health. Working Paper Series from the Working Group in Society and Health. Boston: Working Group in Society and Health.

Brown, P. and Mikkelsen, E.J. (1990) *No Safe Place: Toxic Waste, Leukemia, And Community Action.* Berkeley: University of California Press.

Brown, P. and Masterson-Allen, S. (1994) Citizen action on toxic waste contamination: a new type of social movement, *Society and Natural Resources*, 7, 269–86.

Brown, P. and Ferguson, F. (1995) 'Making a big stink': women's work, women's relationships, and toxic waste activism. *Gender & Society* 9, 145–72.

Bullard, R. (1992a) Anatomy of environmental racism and the environmental justice movement. In Bullard, R. (ed) *Confronting Environmental Racism: Voices from the Grassroots*, Boston: South End Press.

Bullard, R. (1992b). Conclusion: environmentalism with justice. In Bullard, R. (ed) *Confronting Environmental Racism: Voices from the Grassroots.* Boston: South End Press.

Capek, S.M. (1993) The environmental justice frame: a conceptual discussion and an application, *Social Problems*, 40, 5–24.

Couto, R.A. (1985) Failing health and new prescriptions: community-based approaches to environmental risks. In Hill, C.E. (ed) *Current Health Policy Issues and Alternatives: An Applied Social Science Perspective.* Athens: University of Georgia Press.

Covello, V.T. (1983) The perceptions of technological risks: a literature review, *Technology Forecasting and Social Change*, 23, 285–97.

Dickson, D. (1984) *The New Politics of Science.* New York: Pantheon.

Dunlap, R.E. and Mertig, A. (1992) The evolution of the U.S. environmental movement from 1970 to 1990: An overview. In Dunlap, R.E. and Mertig, A. (eds) *American Environmentalism: The U.S. Environmental Movement, 1970–1990.* Philadelphia: Taylor and Francis.

Fischoff, B., Slovic, P., and Lichtenstein, S. (1982) Lay foibles and expert fables in judgments about risk, *The American Statistician*, 36, 240–55.

Freudenberg, N. (1984) Citizen action for environmental health: report on a survey of community organizations, *American Journal of Public Health*, 74, 444–48.

Freudenberg, N. and Steinsapir, C. (1992) Not in our backyards: the grassroots environmental movement. In Dunlap, R.E. and Mertig, A. (eds) *American Environmentalism: The U.S. Environmental Movement, 1970–1990*. Philadelphia: Taylor and Francis.

Freudenburg, W.R. (1988) Perceived risk, real risk: social science and the art of probabilistic risk assessment, *Science*, 242, 44–9.

Gibbs, L. (1991) Keynote address. 1991 conference of Massachusetts Campaign to Clean up Hazardous Waste. Boston, Massachusetts, April 13.

Goldstein, I. and Goldstein, M. (1986) The Broad Street pump. In Goldsmith, J.R. (ed) *Environmental Epidemiology*. Boca Raton, Florida: CRC Press.

Ibsen, H. (1951) *Six Plays*. New York: Modern Library.

Kaplan, L. (1991). 'No more than an ordinary X-Ray': a study of the Hanford Nuclear Reservation and the emergence of the health effects of radiation as a public problem. Ph.D. Dissertation. Heller School, Brandeis University, Waltham, MA.

Krauss, C. (1989) Community struggles and the shaping of democratic consciousness, *Sociological Forum*, 4, 227–39.

Krimsky, S. and Plough, A. (1988) *Environmental Hazards: Communicating Risks as a Social Process*. Boston: Auburn House.

Kuhn, T. (1963) *The Structure of Scientific Revolutions*. Chicago: University of Chicago Press.

Lagakos, S.W., Wessen, B.J., and Zelen, M. (1984). An analysis of contaminated well water and health effects in Woburn, Massachusetts, *Journal of the American Statistical Association*, 81, 583–96.

Lang, M. (1994) 'Welcome to the Plastic City': Community responses to the Leominster, Massachusetts autism cluster. Presentation at American Sociological Association, Los Angeles. August 8.

Levine, A.G. (1982) *Love Canal: Science, Politics, and People*. Lexington, Mass.: Heath.

Lorch, D. (1989) Residents force start of cleanup at Bronx dump, *New York Times*, Nov. 14.

Massachusetts Institute of Technology (1990) Center for environmental health sciences at MIT. Cambridge: Massachusetts Institute of Technology.

Milbrath, L. (1984) *Environmentalists: Vanguard for a New Society*. Albany: State University of New York Press.

Mohai, P. and Bryant, B. (1992) Environmental racism: reviewing the evidence. In Bryant, B. and Mohai, R. (eds) *Race and the Incidence of Environmental Hazards*. Boulder, CO: Westview.

Ozonoff, D. and Boden, L.I. (1987) Truth and consequences: health agency responses to environmental health problems, *Science, Technology, and Human Values*, 12, 70–7.

Paigen, B. (1982) Controversy at Love Canal. *Hastings Center Report*, 12, 29–37.

Rayner, S. and Cantor, R. (1987) How fair is safe enough? the cultural approach to social technology choice, *Risk Analysis*, 7, 3–9.

Short, J.F. (1984) The social fabric at risk: toward the social transformation of risk analysis, *American Sociological Review*, 49, 711–25.

Starr, C. and Whipple, C. (1980) Risks of risk decisions, *Science*, 208, 1114–19.

Tverksy, A. and Kahnemann, D. (1974) Judgement under uncertainty: heuristics and biases, *Science*, 185, 1124–31.

United Church of Christ, Commission for Racial Justice (1981) *Toxic Waste and Race in the United States: A National Report on the Racial and Socioeconomic Characteristics of Communities with Hazardous Waste Sites*. New York: United Church of Christ.

Vaughan, E. and Seifert, M. (1992) Variability in the framing of risk issues, *Journal of Social Issues*, 48, 119–35.

Wing, S. (1994) Limits of epidemiology, *Medicine and Global Survival*, 1, 74–86.

Winner, L. (1986) *The Whale and the Reactor: A Search for Limits in an Age of High Technology*. Chicago: University of Chicago Press.

6. Public health risks in the material world: barriers to social movements in health

Gareth Williams, Jennie Popay and Paul Bissell

Introduction

Over the last two decades western societies have experienced significant transformations in the relationships between the state, civil society, and capital or what is nowadays referred to as 'the market'. This ideological and cultural transformation has reverberated across many sectors of public life: education, social services, housing, health, prisons, and the police. The precise nature of the transformation is the subject of considerable discussion in academic journals and newspapers, on television, and in government. However, notwithstanding the very real complexities involved, in simple terms what we have seen is the intrusion of market forces into the public sphere – those areas of life which were previously not subject to the dictates of the market. The political consensus over the propriety of publicly owned and controlled utilities, services, and goods has disappeared, supplanted by a belief in consumer choice and the free market as the guiding principles of social and economic life (Edgell *et al.* 1994).

One important dimension of this transformation is the fragmentation of political alliances based on class divisions and the increasing visibility of a different form of political action. These 'new social movements' and 'new politics' have mobilised around a wide range of issues. However, concerns about health damaging aspects of the physical environment – particularly the problems posed by the dumping of toxic waste or the hazards of inner city living – are at the heart of many of the activities of new social movements documented in the literature (Brown, P. 1992, Williams and Popay 1994, Burningham and O'Brien 1994). Moreover, these protests are part of a general social milieu in which everyone seems to be an environmentalist of some sort (Yearley 1992).

In this chapter we consider the relationship between public health problems and the development of social movements from a perspective somewhat different from that generally evident within the literature. It has been suggested that most sociological analysis of public protest and social movements focuses on one or other of two factors: either the activities and claims of the groups or organizations involved, or the structural conditions facilitating the emergence of certain groups making particular claims (Allen *et al.* 1992). This chapter concerns the second of these factors. However, rather than seeking to understand the structural origin of such movements by studying one or more cases in detail, we consider why, in the face of significant hazards to health, some communities do not protest, organise or mobilise for change. In particular we focus on the role of lay knowledge or awareness of risk in the development of social movements in the public health field.

In the first section we consider the literature on the nature of social movements in contemporary western societies. This is followed by a discussion of selected issues from the literature on perceptions of and responses to risk. Using data from a recent qualitative study we then briefly explore lay perspectives on public health risks in an inner city area in the north of England where there has been no significant collective action for change. We suggest that although the nature and extent of these risks was clearly understood, and attitudes to professional experts were healthily sceptical, structural and cultural forces prevented collective action from finding a way onto the agenda. In the final section of the chapter we argue that if due status is given to lay knowledge as 'essential datum on the identification and management of risk' this would have profound implications for the development of policy and practice in the public health field (Royal Society 1992).

The nature of contemporary social movements

Notwithstanding the continuing salience of 'class differences' in wealth and health in contemporary western societies (Davey Smith and Egger 1993, Phillimore et al. 1994), there is much evidence that political affiliations have undergone 'class dealignment' during the past two decades. In relation to national voting patterns, for example, it has been argued that population groups have been increasingly voting against what would appear to be their class interests (Edgell 1993). In the past, debates within the social sciences over the relationship between citizenship and capitalism, have been dominated by the notions of social class and class conflict (Turner 1986). However, according to some commentators, many western societies are now characterised by '. . . the progressive fragmentation of class structures and class consciousness' (Edgell 1993: 120), and the disempowerment of labour as a force for change. As Habermas argues:

> The utopian idea of a society based on social labour has lost its persuasive power . . . because that utopia has lost its point of reference in reality: the power of abstract labour to create structure and give form to society (1989: 53).

The only class left is the underclass; those who fall outside all our formal definitions and measures of social position. The welfare state, which developed in response to the deprivation and despair caused by capitalist development, has itself become part of the problem, intervening through the surveillance and control of the everyday lives of ordinary people (Habermas 1989). At the same time it is seen to be responsible for producing a lumpen-class whose economic, political, psychological, and ethical profile marks it out as a class apart.

In response to the tendency towards the bureaucratisation and corporatisation of everyday life, new forms of politics have come into being, with the public sphere being regarded as a sphere consisting of many publics and distinguished by social pluralism (Thompson 1992). These politics have been characterised as value-oriented, universalistic, anti-centralist, anti-formalist, anti-statist and, above all, anti-bureaucratic (Crook *et al.* 1992). While the novelty of these politics of rebellion is debatable (Isaac 1992), it is true that political activity organised around locality, lifestyle, and identity – 'non class movements' – have become more visible in recent years (Jameson 1984, Harvey 1989, Brown, D. 1992). It has been argued by some that these developments represent a retreat from politics into culture because of the focus on values and life-styles, something reflected in recent debates within the British Labour Party (White 1994, Gray 1994). Elsewhere, the smell in the air surrounding the radical university campuses of the United States is no longer tear gas but fresh braised garlic and ginger (Ehrenreich 1994). Others argue that these new movements should be seen, in contrast, as a vital politicisation of areas of inequality and injustice – associated for example with gender, sexuality, ethnicity, age and disability – that were previously excluded from the sphere of legitimate political debate because they did not fit orthodox class interests (Scott 1990).

Whatever interpretation is placed upon these developments, there has undoubtedly been a proliferation of '. . . movements of opposition to the disruptions of home, community, territory, and nation' (Harvey 1989: 238). These movements spread beyond the confines of class struggle, to encompass a rainbow of religious, sexual and social interests (Giddens 1994). The Freedom Network, for example, a 'non-organization' which has emerged in response to the perceived threats to autonomy posed by the British Home Secretary's Criminal Justice Bill, includes '. . . the No M11 (motorway) Campaign, the Rainbow Tribe, Road Alert, the Exodus collective, the Donga tribe, SQUALL the squatters' magazine, the pagan Dragon Environmental Group and many others' (Travis 1994: 5).

For many, therefore, the object is less one of resistance to capitalist exploitation on a grand scale, and more one of revolt against certain ways in which the technocratic state marginalises or abuses local knowledge and community values; or stigmatizes different ways of life within the cultural sphere (Scott 1990). From this viewpoint, the problems of distribution characteristic of class conflict are not the primary shaping force within these new forms of confrontation. Rather, as Habermas has argued, they '. . . concern the *grammar of forms of life*' and '. . . arise at the seam between system and life-world' (1981: 33, 36).

Contemporary public protests and new social movements are about the mobilisation of the sentiments of individuals to resist threats to some aspect of their personal autonomy through the development of solidarity and mutual aid (Scott 1990). It might be possible to perceive commonalities in this '. . . infinitely varied texture of oppositions (Harvey 1989: 238), but they are undoubtedly diverse, in some instances internally divided, and many have limited life expectancy. For these reasons their political influence has sometimes been restricted. For example, during the 1980s in Britain the impact of the developing 'community health movement' was limited by the lack of shared imperatives, common goals, or clear strategies for their achievement (Watt 1987).

In some ways the concept of 'social movements' is like that of the 'underclass'. Both attempt conceptually to account for groups of people who fall outside our conventional categories of social analysis. Analysis of the statistics of social movements of culture and life-style suggest that they find stronger support in '. . . the new middle classes, among the younger generation, and in groups with more formal education' (Habermas 1987: 392). One example of this is the environmental or green movement in Germany which has had striking success (and some recent failure) in not only mobilizing large sections of civil society, but in forming political parties based on the green agenda. Interestingly, this example also indicates how unwise it is to define social movements as cultural *rather than* political, and indeed some ecosocialists argue that the politics of the environment has replaced the politics of class as the bearer of universal values (Gorz 1982, 1994, Jamison *et al.* 1990).

However, class is far from irrelevant to an understanding of environmental movements. While the membership of environmental movements has been largely middle class, those whose health is most at risk of damage from 'the environment', are working class. Indeed, something akin to an inverse care law (Hart 1971) appears to exist in both the development and to some extent the focus of social movements in the public health sphere. Those who most need something done to improve the physical environment in which they live are least able to mobilise the resources necessary to do so, and the hazards they face rarely sit centre-stage in contemporary social action. For example, traditionally the ecological movement, although often local in its initial organisation, has focused less on specific examples of toxic environments, and more on global concerns about ozone depletion, global warming and oil spillage.

Serious as many of these problems are, they do not relate easily to the problems of individuals living on low incomes, in poor housing, in congested and unsafe inner-city neighbourhoods. Indeed, it is argued that one of the powers of social movements such as eco-populism is that they are linked to 'global issues and general values' (Crook *et al.* 1992: 156), but it is also suggested that the political clout of such value frameworks can only be examined within local contexts of action (Burningham and O'Brien 1994). Additionally, in some specific instances the action of the ecological movement may represent a threat to the living conditions of poor communities, in the short term at least, when the cry is for the closure of nuclear or other industrial plants in which members of the local communities are employed.

Recent interest in the USA in the Toxic Waste Movement (TWM) has arisen, in part, in response to the distance of the ecology movement from the everyday concerns of working class people (see Brown in this volume). A number of instances have been described of groups of people becoming concerned about the effects of certain local pollutants on their health. In one survey of organisations in the USA, 153 potential environmental hazards were identified, the most common of which were toxic dumps, pesticide or herbicide spraying, and air pollution. The most commonly cited health effects were cancer, respiratory problems, and birth defects (Freudenberg 1984). While an increased incidence of cancer, particularly among children, has often been the focal point of the mobilisation of sentiment and protest, some protests have been concerned with less clear cut symptoms and morbidity felt to be related in some way to the physical environment.

Social movements, public health and expert knowledge

Questioning of the role of professional experts has been an important feature of many social movements including those focused on toxic environmental waste (Wynne 1987). This has most frequently taken the form of a challenge to the use of 'scientific' evidence in support of the argument that a risk does not exist or is merely the product of community anxiety amplified by the prurient attention of the mass media (Williams and Popay 1994). In the face of expert resistance to their claims of risk, some local groups have undertaken their own research to establish the validity of their case (Popay and Williams 1994, Williams and Popay 1994); an activity similar to the worker epidemiology and social research that has struggled to inform debates over health and safety in industry (Watterson 1993).

These doubts about established expertise, and the subversion of the role of experts in society, are illustrations of the more general changes in civil society described above. Within the public sphere three particular concerns about the role of professional scientific experts have been voiced. First that science and scientific expertise in technological development are responsible for many of the problems of contemporary civilisation. Secondly, that there is a tendency for technical expertise to move beyond its traditional spheres of influence to 'colonise' large areas of social and political life. And finally, there is concern about the gulf between the specialised languages of scientific expertise, and the ordinary language in which social and political issues are discussed (Irwin 1994, Crook *et al.* 1992).

This problem of language is not simply one of the impenetrability or transparency of vocabulary and syntax, it is a reflection of the incompatible, if not incommensurable, frames of reference with which people construct their worlds (Goffman 1975). Without effective 'translation' between expert and public languages or discourses, it is argued, effective democratic participation in technical decisions is impossible (Habermas 1971, 1972, Hayes 1992, Irwin 1994). It is perhaps worth noting that this questioning of the relevance of scientific expertise in the context of local concerns bears marked similarities to grassroots environmental action for sustainable development in the Third World (Ghai and Vivian 1992). In both cases, scientific knowledge is imported into situations to 'solve' problems as if no prior, indigenous knowledge existed.

From the point of view of some scientific experts the problem is not their failure to communicate, but rather widespread public ignorance about what science has done and can do (Birke 1990). It was concern about this that led originally to the work which culminated in the Royal Society's report on the *Public Understanding of Science* (1985). The response of many in the professional scientific community to this report was to suggest that the public understanding of science needs to be improved, and that scientists are best placed to do this because of science's 'unnatural nature' (Wolpert 1992). However, it is not clear from the experts' viewpoint, what prevents the public understanding science; with a combination of ignorance, credulity, and hostility often being cited (Crook *et al.* 1992, Irwin 1994). In contrast to this condescending attitude to lay knowledge, some recent work in the public health field suggests that the break up of established social divisions, including divisions between different forms and contexts of knowledge, is requiring science to legitimate itself beyond the normal process of peer review by fellow experts (Beck 1992, Irwin in press). Nowhere is this more apparent than in relation to contemporary social movements in the health field.

Citizen involvement in public and environmental health

The development of public participation and citizen involvement in social movements about public health issues appears to be a complex and variable process. On the basis of his own work and an examination of research conducted elsewhere, Phil Brown (1992) argues that 'citizen involvement' in environmental health issues usually consists of a number of stages. First, a group of people in a contaminated area notice separately health problems and pollution, and they hypothesise something out of the ordinary connecting these apparently separate phenomena. On the basis of this insight local people begin to share information and build up a common perspective. Gradually they become more cohesive and talk to other people – officials and experts – about their observations and hypotheses, eventually forming groups to pursue their investigation. Official studies are conducted in response to pressure, and these typically find no association between the factors the community has identified. Discontented with this, local people bring in their own professional experts to investigate, engage in litigation and confrontation with official agencies, and finally press for corroboration of their findings by official experts and agencies.

Although models such as this describe retrospectively the 'natural history' of social movements, they do not necessarily help us to understand the triggers that move local people from one point to the next. One of the problems in explaining and accounting for the toxic waste movement in particular, and social movements in the public health field in general, is that in concentrating on cases in which mobilisation takes place, little is known about what prevents mobilisation and protest taking place in other neighbourhoods equally exposed to environmental hazards. It is likely that many factors will have a role. These will include the priority local people give to health issues, the level of awareness about local environmental hazards to health and the extent to which perceptions of risk are shared within a locality. Access to the mechanisms that would facilitate effective action and to relevant experts, such as the local health promotion department or environmental health experts, might also be influential. These 'experts' may share their definition of 'the environment' and its relationships to the ill-health experienced by people, though as we have discussed above, this is frequently not the case. Even where the experts' and the local people's views of the nature of ill-health and the environment coincide, it may be that the experts work in organisational settings in which the dominant ideology of public health prevents them from acting on their assessment of the evidence.

The growing number of surveys of health needs undertaken by health authorities in the UK strongly suggest that health is given high priority in many localities in which the physical environment is poor (Popay and White 1993, Ong 1993). There is also some evidence from the United States that 'community activation' as a health promotion strategy, is more common amongst higher income communities than lower income communities (Wickizer et al. 1993). Women appear to be key actors in mobilising people around public health issues, a feature which may well contribute to variations in local responses to hazards (Brown and Ferguson 1992). In the survey of community organisations referred to earlier, for example, members were most often aged between 26 and 40 and the single most common occupation for group leaders was 'home-maker' (41 per cent), though two-thirds of the groups reported leaders who were '. . . professionals of one sort or another' (Freudenberg 1984: 445). Perhaps the factor which might most obviously be related to the genesis of collective action against public health risks in local neighbour-hoods is the nature and level of knowledge about risks amongst residents.

Conceptualising risk in the health field

There is a burgeoning literature dealing with the concept of risk, and public perceptions of risks (British Medical Association (BMA) 1987, Cvetkovich and Earle 1992, Beck 1992, Roberts 1993). From this conven-tional perspective, 'risk analysis' can be said to involve '. . . the scientific elucidation of damage mechanisms from different natural or technical processes, and the quantification of probabilities and consequences' (Wynne 1987: 2). In this literature, which crosses many disciplines, the conceptualisation of risk shaping contemporary health policy and practice is the subject of much criticism.

Anderson (1984: 114), for example, argues that 'epidemiologists have typically considered a narrow band of 'risk behaviours' – linking struc-tured measurements of the frequencies and intensities of specific behav-iours to disease outcomes' whilst neglecting the wider social context of these behaviours. The profound impact of the material world remains something which many experts in risk find difficult to incorporate into their 'value frameworks'. The British Medical Association, for example, in its award winning guide to *Living with Risk* (BMA 1987), makes no reference to the material factors responsible for the unequal distribution of risks, except in relation to the behaviour patterns contributing to heart disease mortality. In the same vein, much contemporary practice within health education and health promotion has been argued to rest unduly on an individualistic behavioural framework. This, it is argued, frequently leads to the pathologising of typical conduct, the labelling of social behaviour according to stereotyped constructs of moral failure and per-sonal inadequacy (Nutbeam, 1984), and the fostering of a punitive victim-blaming approach to health policy (Scott and Williams 1992).

Alternative notions of risk and related models of policy and practice do strive to be heard within the health field. However, the dominance of lifestyle – drugs, smoking, diet and exercise – as the focus for national and local effort remains unassailable. In the face of this it has been argued that there is a growing mismatch between notions of risk underlying health policy and much health education and 'the health concerns, experiences and self-defined needs of the lay public' (Farrant and Russell 1986).

Like the fear of crime, public perceptions of risk often appear to bear no relationship to what some professional experts say about the 'actual' probability of certain kinds of events taking place (Vaughan and Seifert 1992, Dake 1992); and the assumption of the professional expert has often been that ignorance or some kind of anti-rationality underlies the divergence between lay views and technical calculations. However, it is increasingly recognised that lay populations and professional experts differ not only in the extent and sophistication of the calculations they make, but also in terms of the concepts or frames within which those calculations take place:

> When dissimilar frames are adopted, information, regardless of its quality, may do little to narrow differences because information compatible with one framework is judged to be of little use from another perspective (Vaughan and Seifert 1992: 124).

As one concerned resident of a south Wales town with a long history of dioxin pollution declared in a newspaper interview: 'However well-explained it is, it'll always be an abstract thing. You'll always worry. My son may not notice the effects, but his children may' (Vidal 1994: 27). On this view, the problem is not the absence of technical knowledge in lay people, but divergent perceptions and rationalities which are socially structured (Wynne 1987: 7). One of the most interesting lines of enquiry from the perspective of this chapter is that which attempts to locate lay perspectives on risk within the context of everyday social and material lives. According to this perspective, the 'frames' with which lay people operate in consideration of risks are politically negotiated and socio-culturally constructed (Dake 1992, Douglas 1992). The use of such frames can result in profound discontinuities between professional assessments of risk and those of lay people.

Graham's studies of smoking behaviour amongst women living in poverty (Graham 1987, 1994); Roberts and her colleagues' research on how working class women keep their children safe in unsafe environments (Roberts *et al.* 1992, 1993, Rice *et al.* 1994); Cornwell's research into knowledge about health and illness in the East End of London (Cornwell 1984): these and other studies highlight the same general messages – 'risky' health related behaviour is rarely explained by a lack of knowledge. They point to our incomplete understanding of the relationship between knowledge, attitudes and behaviour in the health field; and they also demonstrate that this understanding will only be strengthened if lay perceptions of risk and responses to risks are studied in the context of everyday lives and the social relationships and structures that shape them.

Public health risks in Salford

Evidence from a small scale qualitative study carried out in an inner city area of Salford in the North West of England (Bissell 1993) suggests that the level of knowledge about environmental risks does not explain the lack of political mobilisation in many disadvantaged areas of contemporary western societies. The study was conducted over six months in 1993 in the Blackfriars ward in inner city Salford. The overriding aim of the research was to enable people to talk widely about what it was like living in the area and to explore their perceptions of the health-related risks they faced within the context of their daily lives. This was not a study of collective responses to health-related risks. Rather it was an exploration through interviews with individuals of the nature of their perceptions of health risks, and an attempt to understand the absence of collective responses in situations in which they might have been expected and justified.

Salford is a city of contrasts, with areas of relative affluence lying adjacent to areas of extreme social deprivation. Salford has amongst the worst mortality rates in England and Wales. Standardised Mortality Ratios (SMRs) show that for every 100 deaths in England and Wales, there are 123 recorded in Salford. In Blackfriars 80% of households have no car, compared to the city average of 54.3%. Nearly 23% of the male population were officially unemployed in March 1992, and of these 47% were classified as long-term unemployed. The main estate from which our respondents were selected lies within half a mile of Manchester's commercial centre. Built in the 1960s it comprises a mixture of deck access maisonettes, three storey flats, and high-rise blocks. In the mid-1980s, Salford City Council entered into a partnership with Barretts, selling off two-thirds of the estate, but keeping the maisonettes which were later decapitated. Many of the local residents who were moved out during this period did not return.

Respondents were selected from a number of sampling points including health centres, baby clinics, community centres, public houses, tenants associations, community drugs team offices, social services offices, youth clubs, schools, along with 'snowballing' from other respondents. Some interviews were conducted on the spot. However, in many cases this was not possible, and the respondent was asked to meet the fieldworker, either in the respondent's own home or at some other location at an agreed time. Problems with respondents being unavailable for interview when the time came were considerable, and although many were re-contacted at a later date this was not always possible. However, in-depth, unstructured and semi-structured interviews were eventually carried out with 69 respondents, with approximately equal numbers of men and women. Almost two-thirds of the respondents were under 30, but the ages ranged from 14 to 58. The interviews typically lasted for about half-an-hour, but were often longer.

Living in the material world
Although conscious of the effects of individual/behavioural factors, such as smoking, drugs, drinking, diet and exercise, on their health status, respondents emphasised socio-economic factors as the most powerful influences on their health. In some accounts a range of specific problems were identified.

Health problems associated with poor housing, for example, were a persistent feature of people's experience of life in the area. Specifically, people talked about the relationship between living in damp housing in their childhood and the onset of chronic illness in later life. As one woman in her forties stated:

You would get green mould on the bedding because it was so damp, and the wallpaper would fall off. Very damp it was and I have rheumatism now . . . I certainly feel its got something to do with the damp in the homes.

People living in high-rise accommodation stressed the practical and psychological difficulties of bringing up children in this environment – feeling depressed and isolated, being unable physically to get in and out of the area because of faulty lifts; trying to negotiate the area with prams and shopping. Some respondents had found it difficult to obtain any stable and secure accommodation in the first place, being subject to numerous moves around the locality over relatively short periods of time.

Unemployment, poverty, economic decline and the experience of crime were frequently mentioned as having severe and debilitating effects on people's health. Some people found it difficult to identify specific factors damaging their health, but feeling generally 'stressed' was central to their experience. As one woman commented:

I think the biggest health risk is mentally . . . 'cause it's a lot of pressure and there's nothing really for you to do . . . you're sort of segregated all of the time.

There was also a concern amongst some of the people interviewed that this area had inherited a legacy of pollution from the heavy industry that used to be widespread, permeating the environment in which they live:

Up here we are lucky . . . but at Greengate [an adjacent area in the valley] . . . and over the years, how much of the pollution has gone into the pipes and the buildings still there . . . it's a big problem.

Some of the people interviewed presented a sophisticated understanding of the network of factors which may structure perceptions of health-related risks and associated behaviour:

> . . . there are reasons why people are smoking. If they don't have a smoke then they are going round the twist and ending up going to the doctor for their nerves . . . or having a drink. I put it down to the environment , . . you'll find that in areas where people are poor . . . what happens to these people when they are going on the dole is that they are living on nothing until their giro arrives and they are so depressed that they are going straight to the pub when the giro arrives and living on nothing until the next one arrives . . . then they are back to being depressed afterwards.

Health related risk: who knows best . . . ?
As we have already noted studies have frequently pointed to a questioning of the role of professional experts as an important feature of the 'new' social movements. Such questioning, however, is also not a sufficient condition for the formation of collective action. Despite the absence of activities which could be described as a movement, there was amongst this group of inner city residents many ways in which the knowledge and activities of 'professionals' were viewed with some scepticism. Public agency responses to the problems identified in the interviews were often considered to be inadequate:

> You can have all the community workers under the sun . . . but that's no good, neither are youth centres. People want work, that's what they want.

In other instances these agencies were described in stronger terms. Several respondents reported thinking about or actually instituting legal proceedings against the housing department for poor maintenance or for unfair eviction. Similarly, one angry respondent commenting on the poor health of people in the local area noted that '. . . to me it is sheer bloody neglect by social services, the council, the police, and everybody'.

The criticisms were not confined to the action of officials, but also represented a challenge to the official definition of the problems people faced. This was most evident in relation to accounts of damp problems in houses.

> Do you mean my place? It's a nightmare . . . it's just literally damp everywhere. We keep getting told that it is just condensation by the Council . . . but we've had other people round who have verified that it is damp.

A similar challenge was apparent with regard to interpretations about the health risks associated with the legacy of the industrial past. One resident suggested that whilst 'the Council seemed to think it was nothing

. . . over the years how many people . . . have died of so many diseases which is never brought forward'.

The expertise of individual professionals was also questioned. Doctors were challenged by a number of respondents, with accounts of misdiagnosis being prominent themes in some interviews. As one woman noted: 'I've got no faith in the medical profession'. Another respondent, himself a heroin addict, noted that whilst he would have listened to a brother or sister about the dangers of drugs he 'would never have trusted a teacher'. Similarly, for some people, popular health promotion messages were to be discounted. In relation to diet, for example, it was noted that '. . . they tell you so many things these days that you don't know what is and what isn't healthy any more'.

Knowledge and action: a tenuous link
There was, therefore, a perception shared by many of the people interviewed in this study that many aspects of the local 'environment' had a substantial negative impact on the health experience of people living in this inner city area. This 'environment' was sometimes defined in terms of the absence of material amenities, for example, employment prospects, adequate incomes, decent housing, recreational facilities, parks, playgrounds and daycare for children. On other occasions it was defined in terms of the presence of phenomena that were detrimental to health: crime, traffic accidents, chemical pollution, discarded syringes and drugs.

Professional 'expert' and local people may differ over their definition of the environment and its relationship to the experience of ill-health. This was, as we have argued, evident in this study. The respondents emphasised structural problems in relation to their conception of the environment rather than focusing on personal risk-taking behaviour such as drinking, smoking, diet and exercise. Where they were mentioned, individual 'risky' behaviours were frequently explained by reference to 'trying to cope' with some aspect of daily life. One young woman explained it thus:

Well, I do reach for a ciggy when the baby gets out of control and goes running off. And I've seen my friends lighting up when they get a big bill or something like that.

And, as another respondent vividly argued:

Smoking, and drinking and drug taking. I put it down to one thing . . . until money is spent on these areas . . . there doesn't seem much point in trying to stop people smoking and what else. As long as the environment is going down the pan people will go down with it.

In an important sense the people interviewed were 'going down together': for amongst this small sample of people there was to a considerable degree a shared understanding of the problems they faced in their everyday lives; of the harm that it could and was doing to their health and that of their children and neighbours; and of their lack of power to change things. A sense of powerlessness and the burden of simply coping with the social and material difficulties they faced in this locality was starkly evident in many accounts. Talking about the potential harm arising from a chemical explosion in the area, which is discussed in more detail below, one young man noted:

> That was a worry and when Vicki got pregnant we thought: 'well, could it be airborne?' But then we fairly quickly forgot about it . . . we have to live and work so. . . .

Another, older woman suggested that the new times have got back to 'poverty times' and:

> The . . . people are sticking close again at home . . . a lot of these people won't step out of line. A lot of them are frightened of doing anything wrong in case they have to get out . . . they live in fear of eviction.

The common ground shared by many of the respondents in this survey and the factors that militate against collective action to change things is illustrated in accounts of an industrial accident which occurred in the area some ten years previously.

The Silk Street chemical explosion

On the 25 September 1982, an explosion occurred at a factory on Silk Street, in the centre of Blackfriars. The blast was heard 15 miles away and over 700 residents were evacuated from their homes on the evening of the explosion. Nobody was killed, though 60 people were treated in hospital. This event received national and local newspaper coverage for a number of days and it emerged that the warehouse in question had contained over 2000 tons of flammable and explosive substances, including over 25 tons of sodium nitrate – a toxic chemical.

Dust from the blast was carried as far north as Bury and Radcliffe, and the Salford City Reporter (the local newspaper) of 30 September 1982 noted that '. . . people were warned not to touch the ash but to sweep it off cars and to wash their cars or any part of their body on which ash may have fallen'. The immediate area, as noted by the then Labour MP, Frank Allaun, was one of the most densely populated in Europe and was surrounded by 15–20 storey tower blocks. Although there was considerable local and national media coverage of the event, the explosion does not seem to have given rise to any concerted form of protest. Residents in the area certainly link it to a range of health problems. As one respondent noted:

I remember having a sore throat and running eyes for weeks after it
. . . and it completely destroyed my garden – killed everything in it.

Another couple, drinking in a local pub on the evening of the blast,
remember how dust from the blast settled on their car, destroying the
chrome and some of the paint work.

If it was doing that to cars, it makes you wonder what it was doing to
your lungs, doesn't it?

Alongside the view that it represented a substantial threat to health,
there was, however, also scepticism about the feasibility of establishing
whether there were any long-term health effects resulting from the explosion, given the diverse nature of the environmental risks in the area. In
any event, what could be done about it anyway?

We were told it was alright to move back after one night, even though
there was all this dust around, for weeks afterwards. But what with all
the old factories, and chemical works that used to be around here,
you'll never really know if it caused any real harm. There's so much
else around here that's bad for you.

The silencing of doubt, or the inability to express concern, could be
seen as acceptance of expert authority or apathy about health damage.
However, as Irwin (in press) has argued, for unprepared citizens it is very
difficult to challenge the authority of experts directly, especially where the
realistic view is that a connection would be very difficult to prove in any
case. Whatever anxieties may exist, daily life crowds them out:

I know two lads who went on to get cancer – they both moved out
though, after it happened. I know a lot of people at the time were
worried about it, but you can't just sit around worrying about it can
you?

Embedded in these accounts, therefore, is a partial explanation for the
lack of public protest or other action following the explosion. Although
residents felt that there were likely to have been negative health effects as
a result of the blast, daily exigencies demanded their full attention. In any
event, where could people go? And how would they survive if they left
the area?

Conclusion

In the past people living in the Blackfriars area of Salford would have
been defined as working class. Their history can be garnered from the
publications still held in the Working Class Movement Library, a mile or
so from where they live, and the harshness of this 'classic slum' comes

128   Gareth Williams, Jennie Popay and Paul Bissell

across even when it is recounted with humour and literary skill (Roberts 1973). Nowadays, many of the people living in this part of Salford would be dealt with, conceptually as well as economically, by consigning them to an 'underclass'. These are '. . . the long-term unemployed, the unskilled workers in erratic employment, and younger single mothers . . . long-term or frequent claimants of income support' (Willetts 1992: 49). Beyond such minimalist and seemingly innocuous economic descriptors, the explanations for these people's lives are charged with the same kind of moral disapproval meted out to the 'bookies' runners, idlers, part-time beggars and petty thieves' recalled by Robert Roberts (1973: 21). In Dahrendorf's disdainful prose:

> . . . the underclass is the living doubt in the prevailing values which will eat into the texture of the societies in which we are living (Dahrendorf 1992: 57).

The literature on the underclass is in many ways a mirror-image of that on social movements. Both begin with an economic hypothesis about changes in the social structure that affect the material basis of people's lives, but end with a set of moral decrees about appropriate attitudes and behaviour. While the underclass threatens the state because it is seen to foreshadow the collapse of civil society, social movements signify the menacing mobilisation of civil society against certain manifestations of state power. In reality, however they are labelled, both are highly political expressions of social inequality and cultural and political disenfranchisement (Fraser 1992).

Against the background of the dominant values and ideology in society, both those engaged in protest over environmental and public health risks, and those for whom the risks are so overwhelming that no protest seems worthwhile, can be defined as people whose perceptions are based on misapprehension or ignorance. Revolt and apathy are both regarded as forms of anti-rationality. However, the data presented here reveal a rather different picture. Our respondents clearly understood that certain things were making them ill. They also realised that their own behaviour, in interaction with the material environment, could play a part in the generation of morbidity. They recognised the risks. They also understood that both their behaviour and the environment were part of socially structured patterns of disadvantage and inequality which formed the material of risk. They comprehended the genesis of the risks they faced. However, the men and women who participated in our study were living in a situation in which risk is widespread and persistent. There seemed to them to be little point in removing or reducing one or two risks – where there was a theoretical possibility of doing so – when the 'odds' against them seemed so overwhelming. Moreover, although they saw clearly enough that their personal troubles were shared with their relatives, friends, and neighbours, there was no forum accessible to them, no public sphere, in which that talk could be carried into effective debate and action.

Douglas (1992) argues that studies of risk emanating from branches of cognitive psychology have weak explanatory power in relation to individual behaviour because of their disregard for social structures as a moral system. This argument might also be relevant to an understanding of the genesis of social movements. However, it needs further development to incorporate the equally important neglect of social structures *qua* social structures – the material basis of people's lives which shapes both perceptions of risk and behaviour in response to risks. What is required, we would suggest, is a 'critical realist' approach which:

> . . . implies the need both to take account of people's own perceptions of their circumstances and to draw on other evidence and hypotheses to explore, where possible, with the people concerned, causal mechanisms at work of which people might not be aware . . . (Wainwright 1994: 104).

Such an approach allows us to acknowledge the multitude of voices to be heard in the social movements of 'late modernity', while forcing us also to recognise that many voices remain unheard. This silence is not the product of ignorance or apathy, but rather the very real material barriers which limit participation in public life. If the expertise of both professional and lay experts is to be tapped, the validity of their different forms of knowledge has to be recognised and then carried into the public sphere for debate.

References

Allen, J., Braham, P. and Lewis, P. (eds) (1992) *Political and Economic Forms of Modernity*. Cambridge: Polity Press.

Anderson, R. (1984) Health promotion: an overview, *European Movements in Health Education Research*, 6, 114–19.

Beck, U. (1992) *Risk Society: Towards a New Modernity*. London: Sage.

Birke, L. (1990) Selling science to the public, *New Scientist*, 1730, 32–36.

Bissell, P. (1993) *Risk: An Exploration of Styles of Life and Structural Context. A Locality Study*. A Report to the Department of Health Promotion, Salford Health Authority.

Bottomore, T. (1979) *Political Sociology*. London: Hutchison.

British Medical Association (1987) *Living with Risk: the British Medical Association Guide*. Chichester: John Wiley and Sons.

Brown, D. (1992) Institutionalism and the postmodern politics of social change, *Journal of Economic Issues*, 26, 545–52.

Brown, P. (1992) Popular epidemiology and toxic waste contamination: lay and professional ways of knowing, *Journal of Health and Social Behaviour*, 33, 267–81.

Brown, P. and Ferguson, F. (1992) 'Making a big stink': women's work, women's relationships, and toxic waste activism, Paper presented at the 1992 Annual Meeting of the American Sociological Association, Pittsburgh, Pennsylvania.

Brown, P. and Mikkelsen, E. (1990) *No Safe Place: Toxic Waste, Leukemia and Community Action*. Berkeley: University of California Press.

Burningham, K. and O'Brien, M. (1994) Global environmental values and local contexts of action, *Sociology*, 28, 913–32.

Cornwell, J. (1984) *Hard-earned Lives: Accounts of Health and Illness from East London*. London: Tavistock.

Crook, S., Pakulski, J. and Waters, M. (1992) *Postmodernization: Change in Advanced Society*. London: Sage.

Cvetkovich, G. and Earle, T.C. (1992) Environmental hazards and the public, *Journal of Social Issues*, 48, 1–20.

Dahrendorf, R. (1992) Footnotes to the discussion, in Smith, D.J. (ed) *Understanding the Underclass*. London: Policy Studies Institute.

Dake, K. (1992) Myths of nature: culture and the social construction of risk, *Journal of Social Issues*, 48, 21–37.

Douglas, M. (1992) *Risk and Blame: Essays in Cultural Theory*. London: Routledge.

Davey Smith, G. and Egger, M. (1993) Socioeconomic differentials in wealth and health, *British Medical Journal*, 307, 1085–6.

Edgell, S. (1993) *Class*. London: Routledge.

Edgell, S., Walklate, S. and Williams, G. (eds) (1994) *Debating the Future of the Public Sphere: Transforming the Public and Private Domains in Free Market Societies*. Aldershot: Avebury.

Ehrenreich, B. (1994) The food that ate the left, *The Guardian*, 6 August.

Farrant, W., and Russell, J. (1986) Community initiatives in health education publications: a role for health education officers? In Rodmell, S. and Watt, A. (eds) *The Politics of Health Education*. London: Routledge and Kegan Paul.

Fraser, N. (1992) Rethinking the public sphere: a contribution to the critique of actually existing democracy. In Calhoun, C. (ed) *Habermas and the Public Sphere*. London: MIT Press.

Freudenberg, N. (1984) Citizen action for environmental health: report on a survey of community organizations, *American Journal of Public Health*, 74, 444–8.

Ghai, D. and Vivian, J.M. (eds) (1992) *Grassroots Environmental Action: People's Participation in Sustainable Development*. London: Routledge.

Giddens, A. (1994) *Beyond Left and Right: The Future of Radical Politics*. Cambridge: Polity Press.

Goffman, E. (1975) *Frame Analysis: An Essay on the Organization of Experience*. Harmondsworth: Penguin (Peregrine Books).

Gorz, A. (1982) *Farewell to the Working Class: An Essay on Post-Industrial Socialism*. London: Pluto Press.

Gorz, A. (1994) *Capitalism, Socialism, Ecology*. London: Verso.

Graham, H. (1987) Women's smoking and family health, *Social Science and Medicine*, 25, 47–56.

Graham, H. (1994) Gender and class as dimensions of smoking behaviour, *Social Science and Medicine*, 38, 691–8.

Gray, J. (1994) Setting course for the left, *The Guardian*, 20 June.

Habermas, J. (1971) *Toward a Rational Society*. London: Heinemann.

Habermas, J. (1972) *Knowledge and Human Interests*. London: Heinemann.

Habermas, J. (1981) New social movements, *Telos*, 49, 33–37.

Habermas, J. (1987) *The Theory of Communicative Action, Vol. 2: The Critique of Functionalist Reason*. Cambridge: Polity.

Habermas, J. (1989) *The New Conservatism: Cultural Criticism and the Historians' Debate*. Cambridge: Polity Press.

Hart, J.T. (1971) The inverse care law, *The Lancet*, i, 405–12.

Harvey, D. (1989) *The Condition of Postmodernity: An Enquiry into the Origins of Cultural Change*. Oxford: Blackwell.

Hayes, M.V. (1992) On the epistemology of risk: language, logic and social science, *Social Science and Medicine*, 35, 401–7.

Irwin, A. (1994) Science and its publics: continuity and change in the risk society, *Social Studies of Science*, 24, 168–84.

Irwin, A. (in press) *Citizen Science*. London: Routledge.

Isaac, J.C. (1992) *Arendt, Camus, and Modern Rebellion*. New Haven: Yale University Press.

Jameson, F. (1984) Postmodernism, or the cultural logic of late capitalism, *New Left Review*, 146, 53–92.

Jamison, A., Eyerman, R., Cramer, J. and Laessoe, J. (1990) *The Making of the New Environmental Consciousness: A Comparative Study of Environmental Movements in Sweden, Denmark and the Netherlands*. Edinburgh: Edinburgh University Press.

Nutbeam, D. (1984) Health education in the National Health Service: the differing perceptions of community physicians and health education officers, *Health Education Journal*, 43, 115–9.

Ong, B.N. (1993) *The Practice of Health Services Research*. London: Chapman and Hall.

Phillimore, P., Beattie, A. and Townsend, P. (1994) Widening inequality of health in northern England, 1981–91, *British Medical Journal*, 308, 1125–8.

Phillimore, P. and Moffatt, S. (1994) Discounted knowledge: local experience, environmental pollution, and health. In Popay, J. and Williams, G. (eds) *Researching the People's Health*. London: Routledge.

Popay, J. and White, M. (1993) *A Review of Survey Research and Related Training and Advice Needs in the NHS in England: The Final Report*. The Public Health Research and Resource Centre, Bolton, Salford, Trafford, and Wigan Health Authorities, and the University of Newcastle upon Tyne.

Popay, J. and Williams, G. (eds) (1994) *Researching the People's Health*. London: Routledge.

Popay, J. and Williams, G. (in press) Public health research and lay knowledge, *Social Science and Medicine*.

Rice, C., Roberts, H., Smith, S.J. and Bryce, C. (1994) 'It's like teaching your child to swim in a pool full of alligators': lay voices and professional research on child accidents. In Popay, J. and Williams, G. (eds) *Researching the People's Health*. London: Routledge.

Roberts, H. (1993) Taking risks, *Medical Sociology News*, 19, 17–26.

Roberts, H., Smith, S.J. and Lloyd, M. (1992) Safety as a social value: a community approach. In Scott, S., Williams, G., Platt, S. and Thomas, H. (eds) *Private Risks and Public Dangers*. Aldershot: Avebury.

Roberts, H., Smith, S.J. and Bryce, C. (1993) Prevention is better . . . , *Sociology of Health and Illness*, 15, 447–63.

Roberts, R. (1973) *The Classic Slum: Salford Life in the First Quarter of the Twentieth Century*, Harmondsworth: Penguin.

Royal Society (1985) *Report on the Public Understanding of Science*. London: The Royal Society.

Royal Society (1992) *Risk: Analysis, Perception and Management* (a report of a Royal Society Study Group). London: The Royal Society.

Scott, A. (1990) *Ideology and the New Social Movements*. London: Unwin Hyman.

Scott, S., and Williams, G. (1992) Introduction. In Scott, S., Williams, G., Platt, S. and Thomas, H. (eds) *Private Risks and Public Dangers*. Aldershot: Avebury.

Thompson, K. (1992) Social pluralism and post-modernity. In Hall, S., Held, D. and McGrew, T. (eds) *Modernity and its Futures*. Cambridge: Polity (in association with Open University).

Travis, A. (1994) Eco-warriors to step up battle against Howard's Bill, *The Guardian*, 6 August.

Turner, B. (1986) *Citizenship and Capitalism*. London: Allen and Unwin.

Vaughan, E. and Seifert, M. (1992) Variability in framing risk issues, *Journal of Social Issues*, 48, 119–35.

Vidal, J. (1994) No room for old toxins in New Inn, *The Guardian*, 24 September.

Wainwright, H. (1994) *Arguments for a New Left*. Oxford: Blackwell.

Watt, A. (1987) Room for movement? The community response to medical dominance, *Radical Community Medicine*, Spring, 40–5.

Watterson, A.E. (1993) Occupational health in the UK gas industry: a study of employer, medical, and worker knowledge and action on occupational health in the late nineteenth and early twentieth century. In: Platt, S., Thomas, H., Scott, S. and Williams, G. (eds) *Locating Health: Sociological and Historical Explorations*. Aldershot: Avebury.

White, M. (1994) Blair seeks new social settlement, *The Guardian*, 20 June.

Wickizer, T., Von Korff, M., Cheadle, A., Maeser, J., Wagner, E.H., Pearson, D., Berry, M.P.H. and Psaty, B.M. (1993) Activating communities for health promotion, *American Journal of Public Health*, 83, 561–7.

Willetts, D. (1992) Theories and explanations of the underclass. In Smith, D.J. (ed) *Understanding the Underclass*. London: Policy Studies Institute.

Williams, G. and Popay, J. (1994) Lay knowledge and the privilege of experience. In Gabe, J., Kelleher, D. and Williams, G. (eds), *Challenging Medicine*. London: Routledge.

Wynne, B. (1987) *Risk Management and Hazardous Waste: Implementation and the Dialectics of Credibility*. London: Springer-Verlag.

Wolpert, L. (1992) *The Unnatural Nature of Science*. London: Faber and Faber.

Yearley, S. (1992) Environmental challenges. In Hall, S., Held, D. and McGrew, T. (eds) *Modernity and Its Futures*. Cambridge: Polity Press (in association with the Open University).

7. Boundaries of danger and uncertainty: an analysis of the technological culture of risk assessment

Simon Carter

Introduction

Risk assessment emerged after the Second World War as a technique that was originally applied to limited and pragmatic ends. The methods of the risk assessor are now being extended into many areas of late modern life. Each examination brings into view new possible threats to human health. The list of perils we all face already seems endless. At one end of a risk spectrum we have those large scale hazards which may compromise the sustainable future of all human life. These include: environmental concerns over global warming; the depletion of the ozone layer; the continued expansion of energy use; the release of engineered, and long lived, pollutants; nuclear catastrophe; and even the impact of extra-terrestrial bodies onto the surface of the earth. At the other end of the spectrum we are warned about those perils arising from the immediate environment or 'lifestyle' of the individual. Included here would be: microscopic pathogens linked to fatal and chronic illnesses (*e.g.* the HIV virus); consumption of particular foodstuffs supposed to cause disease (cholesterol/ heart disease) or containing invisible toxins (vegetables/pesticides); and avoidance of agents previously associated with pleasure (alcohol, tobacco, coffee and even the sun).

That a particular type of professional expertise, charged with quantifying these hazards, has arisen would appear to be a good thing. Indeed, many would see it as a duty of a civilised society to become aware of the dangers it may face and avoid them. If the dangers of modern life can be measured then we may be able to take action to reduce harm. Yet the way in which danger is understood differs according to social context. In other words, the professional risk analyst's view is only one among many possible understandings of jeopardy. For instance, anthropological studies have shown us that different cultures have a variety of intricate techniques (some may say rituals) for dealing with danger (see Malinowski 1992, Douglas 1966, Evans-Prichard 1976). Studies of western societies have suggested that our everyday understandings of danger are just as complex as these (see Davison *et al.* 1991, Wynne 1990). But such is the authority of the risk analyst that these informal ways of approaching danger are often ignored (unless it is to point out their irrationality compared to the experts methods) – debate is then left with little more than a discussion of the measures of danger, provided by the experts.

I do not wish to imply by this that expert risk knowledge represents a unified understanding of danger. Indeed there are regular public disagreements between experts about both the likelihood and consequences of danger. This public discord is often brought about when experts, from differing institutional backgrounds, are forced into open debate via the mechanism of the courts, public inquiries or media interest. Yet despite these disagreements, the expert management of danger still occupies a weighty position in policy and decision-making. As such this is part of a more diffuse ideology which represents the expert methodology as a neutral and objective way of forming judgements about peril – a method for arriving at decisions that is above any political or vested interests.

In this chapter I wish to explore what the ramifications may be of using expert knowledge in order to make decisions about threats to health. However, I will not focus exclusively on a consideration of the adequacy of such knowledges. By this I simply mean the relationship between the idea of a material 'external' danger and the concept of risk, used as a discursively inscribed, 'theoretical' construct, to describe it. Other commentators have already closely examined this area by looking at various aspects of those techniques involved in risk analysis. For example, to name a few: Kates (1978) has pointed out that risk analysis often ignores issues of justice and equity; Slovic et al. (1978, 1981) have examined the validity of expert perceptions of risk, as opposed to those of the lay public; Perrow (1984) has suggested that the use of expert risk knowledge does not fully take account of the complexity of the systems it seeks to model (and that such a model may be unattainable); and Abraham (1993) has examined how the institutional interests of scientists bias carcinogenic risk assessment. So rather than looking only at the technical adequacy of risk analysis I would prefer to view the problem of risk from an additional angle. Though there has been an increasing interest in studying the social dimension of risk, there has been little attention paid to a critical review of the place of risk in late modern society.

Risk assessment and health

Before examining the place that risk occupies in late modern culture we must ask what we mean by it. One of the problems is that the word risk, even when restricted to expert usage, can mean very different things in different contexts. Yet certain common themes can be discerned in many of the ways the word risk is used. Douglas has argued that whereas risk was once a relatively neutral term, taking 'account of the probability of losses and gains' (Douglas, 1990: 2), it is now no more than a technological reification of the word 'danger'. I would dispute that risk can be semiotically reduced to anything as unified as the idea of 'danger'. As Bauman has pointed out, the term risk 'belongs to the discourse of *gambling*, that is, to a kind of discourse which does not sustain clear-cut opposition between success and failure, safety and danger' (Bauman 1993: 200). Whereas danger is an unambiguous state of peril, risk alerts us to uncertainties about whether the future is safe or dangerous. We could say that the idea of risk is multifaceted, or Janus-faced, because it simultaneously points to the possibilities of security and insecurity. Taking a definition of risk, from the risk assessment literature, we can see this:

> . . . if one adopts the axioms of rational choice under uncertainty, the evaluation of any decision alternative should consider the probability distribution over the consequences resulting from the alternative, which may be expressed in a space of several dimensions (Mandl and Lathrop 1981: 42).

It is not immediately obvious, but the above quote came from a paper on the siting of liquefied gas terminals. I draw attention to this because many of the techniques associated with risk analysis first emerged in the assessment of areas not directly related to health. Even though the idea of calculating the risk to health has had a long history in the reckoning of annuities and insurance premiums (see Hacking 1975, 1990), its more widespread use has only occurred since the Second World War. Since this time techniques of risk assessment have been used to assess the hazards associated with many new technologies and the public's perception of them.

The problem has been one of predicting the future when the past can no longer be relied on to provide a guide – there is simply not enough of it to serve as an adequate model for a world in which rapid technological development is the norm. In an attempt to measure the risks of proposed technologies a variety of novel methods have been tried,[1] but perhaps the most widespread has been *risk-benefit* or *cost-benefit* analysis. This involves assessing the societal cost of a new technology and balancing it against the 'benefits to be expected from its implementation, and then adopt[ing] it only if the anticipated benefits outweigh the anticipated costs' (Fischhoff 1977: 178). Benefits and costs are normally estimated by mathematically combining the expected value of a particular outcome with the probability of its occurrence. One way of doing this is to draw a relation between value and monetary worth. Thus, in the 1970s, the Ford Motor Company carried out a cost-benefit analysis on its new Pinto automobile. They decided not to carry out a safety modification on the Pinto's fuel tank because it was calculated that payments in compensation, to the victims or families of those burnt in accidents, would be less than the costs of re-tooling its production plant (see Wright 1980, Jacobson and Barnes 1978). However, monetary worth may be only one dimension in the estimation of value – attempts may be made to take other numerical values into account, such as the number of premature deaths resulting from pursuing a particular technology.

Despite the differences in the calculation of value most forms of risk assessment rely heavily on probabilistic reasoning. As Hacking has written 'probability has two aspects' (Hacking 1975: 1) and these are directly related to an understanding of risk. First, it is connected with an appraisal of degrees of belief and evidence; and second, it is the characteristic displayed by populations and events to 'produce stable relative frequencies' (Hacking 1975: 1). In other words probability has both a theoretical and an empirical aspect. For example, I can speculate about throwing a coin several times by carrying out a *prior* calculation about the chances of certain combinations of heads and tails coming up – even if I have never seen this particular coin before (assuming it is a *fair* coin). Alternatively, I could collect information about actual events that had already occurred, by throwing a coin many times and recording the results. Massumi, in his characteristically tentative style, sums up this aspect of probabilistic reasoning as the 'interpenetration of two mutually exclusive tenses. . . . It has always already happened, yet persists as a possibility' (Massumi 1992: 181). The idea of risk points simultaneously to the presence of and possibility of danger.

The history of risk assessment has therefore been an attempt to chart

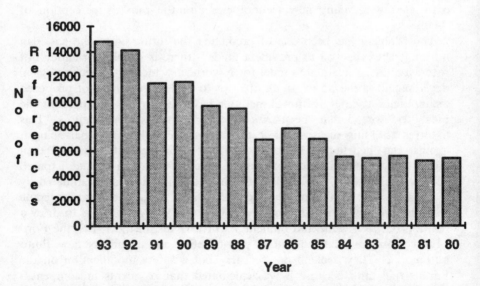

Fig. 1: References cited in Excerpta Medica containing the word 'risk', 1980–1993

the uncertainties of the future. Alternative courses of action are compared across the dimensions of probability and value so that a preferred outcome can be arrived at. Over the last 20 years these insights into the management of danger and uncertainty, gained from the analysis of technical hazards, have been increasingly applied to the problem of health. For instance, a search of the *Excerpta Medica* database for the word 'risk' reveals an increase from around 5,500 references in 1980, to just under 15,000 by 1993 (see Fig. 1)[2]. Of course, the word 'risk' is used in the medical literature in a wide variety of ways, some of which tend to slip into being simple replacements for the words 'hazard' or 'danger'. Be this as it may, I am going to concentrate on the distinctive usage of the word 'risk' – that is the attempt to calculate the uncertainties of future danger. Here the methods formerly used to assess new technologies have either been directly incorporated, or modified, in order to evaluate health care and policy interventions. One example of this is the increasing use of cost-benefit analysis in examining health care. Thus a 1993 paper in the *British Medical Journal* started with the following claim:

> Cost-benefit analysis is the most comprehensive and theoretically sound form of economic evaluation and it has been used as an aid to decision-making in many different areas of economic and social policy in the public sector during the last 50 years (Robinson 1993: 924).

The methods of cost-benefit analysis have been used in relation to health care evaluation at the societal level, by placing 'monetary values on both inputs (costs) and the outcomes (benefits) of health care' (Robinson 1993: 926). At a more individual level the method has been translated into health risk appraisal. As Hayes has observed, this is a 'method to help physicians practise preventative medicine by focusing prospectively on the avoidance of premature mortality' (Hayes 1992: 401). In such an appraisal various characteristics of the individual's biology and lifestyle are measured as factors in a danger/safety dichotomy. Items included may range from clinical measures (*e.g.* blood pressure, weight, levels of compounds found in blood) to socio-environmental factors (*e.g.* family history, gender, ethnicity, personal habits). In this way, traits of the individual are seen to contribute to some overall measure of risk. Here risk, as before, cannot be reduced to a simple representation of danger. Some of the traits measured are seen as altering the probability of premature death in a positive way. For example, eating high fibre foods, fresh vegetables and taking exercise are all seen as beneficial. On the other hand, different traits are seen as swinging the balance of probability against the individual. Thus smoking, eating high fat foods, sexual promiscuity and inactivity would normally be seen as unfavourable. As we shall now see, health risk appraisals of this type can then be used in two ways.

First, the information gained from an appraisal can be used to pass advice or health promotion on to the whole population. Expert knowledge is used to identify which particular habits may be enhancing, or diminishing, the future health of the individual. This knowledge is then passed on to the general public in an attempt to interpolate the individual into the expert knowledge frame. Once incorporated into this frame the individual has two choices: they either become responsible for managing their own health; or they become accountable for any sickness they may then experience. Some commentators have seen this passing of expert knowledge on to the lay public as an attempt to individualise the management of danger while ignoring possible structural impediments to ill-health (see Hansson 1989, Hayes 1992, Lupton 1993).

Expert knowledge is not, however, always passed on in a complete form. Much of this knowledge is constructed in the context of industrial or government establishments. These may be operating under conditions which come close to secrecy. For instance, O'Kelly (1989) has examined how, within the context of the UK, institutionalised decision-making about health and safety within industry functions under conditions of confidentiality whereby consensus is negotiated in an informal way between experts. Such procedures mean that expert authority is often absolved of any open and critical peer review (see Abraham 1994). If not operating under explicit conditions of confidentiality then expert knowledge is regularly passed on to the public in a partial form. Thus much health education advice, based on expert knowledge, minimises the inherent uncertainties in the concept risk while maximising the potential negative consequences.

Examples of risk assessment being used in this way would include recent health education programmes directed to ends such as modifying diet, reducing alcohol consumption, stopping smoking, reducing drug use and encouraging safer sexual behaviour. While these campaigns may provide information that allows us all to lead safer lives, it cannot shield the individual from the cultural meanings which become attached to various behaviours. Probabilistic reasoning identifies certain future states as possibilities, but possibilities which already exist, at least at the discursive level. Thus, should an individual fall prey to some form of ill-health the probabilistic reasoning can reverse – the cause of their personal tragedy existed all the time. This can lead to certain groups experiencing jeopardy becoming morally blamed for the danger they face. As Lupton has observed, 'the experience of a heart attack, a positive HIV test result, or the discovery of a cancerous lesion are evidence that the ill person has failed to comply with directives to reduce health risks and therefore is to blame for his or her predicament' (Lupton 1993: 430).

This raises the question of how far expert risk assessment can itself be implicated in the process of moral blame. It could be argued that risk assessment is simply a neutral tool and that the findings of expert risk assessors have been appropriated by a moral and political agenda that is not of their own making. However, the ascription of social meaning to the process of risk assessment cannot be divorced from its purely analytical role. In this respect risk assessment is similar to other forms of scientific knowledge. One of the understandings provided by the sociology of science has been that even apparently 'pure', non-policy oriented, scientific knowledge is permeated with wider social meanings that go beyond its analytical concerns (see Forman 1971), and that these social meanings cannot be entirely disentangled from the analytical-instrumental role of this knowledge (Wynne 1982). The relationship between expert risk assessment, health promotion campaigns and a more widespread cultural blame is a highly complex area. Expert risk assessment cannot be held to be exclusively accountable for individuals and groups being held to be morally culpable for their own ill health. Yet several commentators (Crawford 1977, Pill and Stott 1982) have identified the emergence of a preventive health ideology that focuses on individual responsibility while paying less attention to the social causation of disease. This focus on individual responsibility has a resonance with liberal political notions which tend to construct the subject as responsible for his or her own luck or misfortune (see Hall 1986).

This bring us to the second way in which expert knowledge, gained from health risk appraisals, may be applied. This is to identify those individuals with a high probability of ill-health and target them for specific interventions or treatment. This process operates in several stages: an initial health risk appraisal of a large population group is used to identify factors with an associated harm; next, the population is screened to find those individuals displaying these factors; and, finally, some technology must be made available to modify the individual's identified harm (technology may here mean anything from drug therapy to counselling).

Examples of this approach can be found in recent attempts to institute screening and intervention programmes. The case of cholesterol screening and lowering treatments provides a good example of risk assessment of this type. Here we can trace the different stages of the risk process. First, since the 1950s, high levels of cholesterol in blood have been identified by experts as one factor increasing the probability of coronary heart disease (see Moore 1989, Chapter 3). Second, a relatively simple and highly transportable test exists for measuring cholesterol levels in blood. Third, a variety of drug based interventions are available for lowering cholesterol levels in blood. It would appear that this was a situation in which a danger to health could be reduced by application of expert risk knowledge and medical technology. Yet this scenario disguises the full complexity of the debate over coronary heart disease. While the first stage of the assessment process (the link between cholesterol and coronary heart disease) may be relatively durable, stages two and three have been fundamentally challenged. Cholesterol testing kits may be inaccurate due to the inappropriate transportation of laboratory technology into a more general setting (see Sheldon *et al.* 1993). And cholesterol lowering drugs are of such a dubious benefit that Davey-Smith *et al.* (1993) claim that:

> Currently evaluated cholesterol lowering drugs seem to produce mortality benefits in only a small proportion of patients at very high risk of death from coronary heart disease. Population cholesterol screening could waste resources and even result in net harm in substantial groups of patients (Davey-Smith *et al.* 1993: 1367).

Danger boundaries

The case of cholesterol screening and intervention has parallels with a number of other medical circumstances, such as cervical screening, HIV testing and the new genetics. In particular, many of these programmes entail testing individuals who are exhibiting no outward sign of illness. The application of expert probabilistic reasoning manages to make the categories of health and illness ambiguous. Risk becomes a gamble about the significance of particular signs – revealed by the process of risk assessment. Does, for instance, an abnormal cervical smear represent a forewarning of a treatable or untreatable condition? Or, alternatively, was a negative result (*i.e.* a 'good' result) some artefact, or error, connected to the measurement process – the woman may 'really' be ill after all. All these simultaneously exist as future possibilities.

The advent of increasingly sophisticated screening programs, relying on specialist methods, has its own effects. They may allow the individual the opportunity to take remedial action to avoid danger. Yet, accompanying this, the power to define human health is increasingly removed from the lay public into the hands of experts. Posner (1991), in her ethnographic examination of women undergoing cervical screening, eloquently summarises the situation:

> In cervical cytology screening, medical assertion of the significance of a sign unavailable to women is an attempt to control uncertain future developments – to extend clinical control over risk. In the absence of acknowledgement of the uncertainty and a fuller sharing of information and language . . . medical aims prevail. Women's health status is defined for them in a way that is disempowering and unhealthy (Posner 1991: 186)

The power to make the distinction between safety and danger has been increasingly concentrated, over the last 30 years, in the hands of the risk assessor and a new speciality, risk assessment, which has 'spawned an interdisciplinary quasi-profession with new terminology, methodology, and literature' (Kates and Kasperson 1983: 7027). That the future may be perilously uncertain no longer matters because the business of risk assessment is 'concerned with trying to turn uncertainties into probabilities' (Douglas 1985: 42). Thus dangerous uncertainties are excluded by being made knowable. By measuring the likelihood of future peril, or benefit, risk assessment defines a separation between safety and danger. Such a separation then constitutes a *boundary* which defines a space of safety. I use the word boundary because it calls to mind both the idea of change occurring as it is crossed and that such boundaries are socially constructed (the boundaries used by countries, and in sports, illustrate both these points). That these boundaries are socially constructed does not mean that material effects do not follow from their being crossed. The boundaries around the space of safety may be crossed either by overtly taking certain actions, defined as hazardous, or by having some trait about self revealed as dangerous.

But perhaps more insidiously, the process of risk assessment refers to a Cartesian split between boundaries which define a space of safety, for the 'self', and those which define spaces of danger, occupied by the 'other'. An example of this can be found in many of the discourses surrounding the risks associated with HIV/AIDS. Despite the switch from the epidemiological classification of risk group to risk practices, much debate still tacitly defines people in terms of their position with regard to the 'general population'. Paula Treichler (1991), in her linguistic analysis of both scientific and more general narratives of AIDS, has observed that various understandings of risk intersect and expand existing definitions of the 'self' and the 'other':

> We inherit a series of discursive dichotomies; the discourse of AIDS attaches itself to these other systems of difference and plays itself out there: self and not-self; the one and the other; homosexual and heterosexual; homosexual and 'the general population'; active and passive, guilty and innocent, perpetrator and victim; vice and virtue, us and them, anus and vagina; sins of the parent and innocence of the child; love and death, sex and death, sex and money, death and money; science and not-science, knowledge and ignorance; doctor–patient, expert–patient, doctor and expert (Treichler 1991: 63–64).

Yet it should be remembered that risk assessment is not just the enactment of excluding a dangerous 'other' or even about the expulsion of those un-decidable and dangerous spaces from modernity. Instead, it is about governing and controlling transgressions to, and from, the spaces defined as dangerous and safe. On the one hand, risk assessment is used to make decisions about technological developments that attempt to legitimate particular levels of danger (see Beck 1992: 64–70). The formal goal of cost-benefit analysis is, after all, to discover a 'useful' level of danger. And these 'useful' dangers are often threats to health which may be collectively faced by us all (and future generations). One example of this would be the rhetorical justification of dumping radioactive waste back into 'nature' – a practice constructed as safe by lieu of the higher levels of 'natural' radiation found in the general environment. On the other hand, the same methods of risk assessment are used to define personal boundaries of safety, which individuals step over at their own peril.

The discourses of risk, within the modern period, have sought to *manage* the problem of danger by attempting to constitute boundaries that were then controllable. It is important here to stress management – danger was not to be simply excluded as 'other' but, instead, controlled, via the application of scientific rationality, as useful and beneficial to decision-making elites. This can be seen if we consider the management of the boundary between certainty and uncertainty. One example of this is the recent concern as to the effects of human activity on climatic change. While, at present, there is little agreement between the forecasts provided by different climatic modelling techniques, the consequences of such change could have severe implications for human health (Gable *et al.* 1991). Such genuine scientific uncertainty is taken by decision-making elites, at both national and international levels, as a defence of delaying action that may restrict western industrial and economic activity (Dale 1994, Kolstad 1994, Norse 1994, Luhmann 1993).

If, as with the above example, decision-making elites play down the significance of the dangers posed by powerful institutions, the same does not hold true of the danger in our private lives. Here the understanding of danger is presented as certain and knowable. When danger is represented as knowable, risk knowledge is made useful by controlling connections between safety and danger. This can be interpreted in two ways. First, several writers have pointed out that risk assessments help to construct economic needs that may be virtually infinite (Beck 1992, Bauman 1993). 'To keep the wheels of the consumer market well lubricated, a constant supply of new, well-publicised dangers is needed' (Bauman 1993: 204). This is certainly the case with cholesterol screening and lowering. The current market for cholesterol lowering drugs is growing by 27% per annum and the market was valued at US $ 1.7 billion in 1989 (Davey-Smith and Sheldon 1993: 256). If this is put in the context of a more general marketing of low-fat products, and 'common sense' breakfast cereals, we can see that the potential for the marketing of risk modifying products may be enormous.

The second sense in which risk is made useful concerns the way in which the boundaries of the danger/safety dichotomy are drawn. As Frankenberg (1992) has pointed out, those groups facing danger which can become defined as 'other' often face controls which work in the interests of the powerful 'same'. Thus a range of social practices exist, connected with risk assessment, which, historically, have often targeted specific groups. Whether the target group refers to those eating fatty foods, people engaging in particular sexual practices, or those found to be carrying a coded genetic 'taint', the effect is to push the group into a space of danger – the place of the 'other'. Here they become a useful repository for our cultural ideas of danger. As long as we are 'good', as defined by the expert risk assessor, then danger is elsewhere, not part of the 'self'.

At a figurative level this way of thinking about risk implies that the 'other' can be controlled. Yet the 'other', here, should not be thought of as some passive entity. Part of the danger that the 'other' represents is the threat (even if it is imaginary) that it may colonise the self (rather than vice-a-versa). This, it could be argued, stems from the insecurity of the self and further necessitates that access to the 'other' is controlled. However, the ambivalence surrounding the terms of the 'other' (which is 'unknowable' by definition) allows a struggle to occur between oppositional and dominant discourses over the nature of risk. Here we could point towards environmental pressure groups who have challenged the capacity of industry to pollute with impunity, or campaigns in the 1980s from within the gay community to put the subject of HIV/AIDS on the political agenda. To retain its dominant position the expert discourse of risk must colonise these local and oppositional discourses. Thus we have seen the advent of 'green' consumer products or the appropriation of community sex education programmes by medical and health education discourses (see Crimp 1991).

However, this is not a totally one way process. Allowing risk assessment to occupy such a culturally hegemonic position creates a tenacious and forceful space for the dangers of which it speaks. And while risk assessment shares a number of common methods and procedures across disparate disciplines, the experts often profoundly fail to agree on safe or acceptable levels of danger (see Wynne 1989). Thus the modernist impulse to completeness is problematised in as much as attention is drawn to an understanding of knowledge in which there is no decisive, 'once and for all', narrative of safety. Doubt creeps back into the project of the risk assessor and the transition from uncertainty to probability is inverted.

A parallel can be drawn here to Michael and Still's (1992) use of the terms *freezing* and *liquefaction*. Michael and Still employ these expressions to explore the Cartesian metaphor. Thus freezing is the process whereby empirical data that is static and disorganised is made coherent through the application of scientific reason. Yet it is also pointed out, by drawing on post-structuralist theorists (*e.g.* Deleuze, Guattari, and Foucault), that though freezing 'proceeds through the imposition of categories' (ibid 1992: 873), these are *never* decisive. The possibility of resistance allows for a process of liquefaction in which 'categories and the relationships between categories are loosened and the hard-won objects begin to lose clarity as they melt away . . . the processes of freezing and liquefaction thus move in unison, tumbling over one another as the object is grasped, then escapes' (ibid 1992: 873).

Nevertheless, this doubt does not necessarily result in an oppositional discourse. The hesitancy in the status of knowledge can be used to stage a rhetorical display of uncertainty and ambivalence to the benefit of powerful groups. An example of this can be found in the strategies employed by the tobacco industry to counter evidence from the medical profession as to the harmful effects of smoking. This industry has sought to cultivate ambivalence in order to mount a medical defence of smoking. As Taylor (1984) says, in his account of the tobacco industry's stand against anti-smoking campaigns:

> The medical defence was that the case against cigarettes was not proven; the evidence was purely statistical; the precise causal mechanism by which cigarettes were alleged to produce cancer had never been identified; that no one knows the cause of cancer and only unbiased scientific inquiry will provide the answers (Taylor 1984: 12).

We can thus see that the process of risk assessment operates by establishing boundaries between the social spaces of danger and safety. The control of transitions or connections between these boundaries then become the domain of risk assessment. However, as Massumi points out, the connections which flow between these boundaries are socially repressed so that a 'bounded space' may still be conceived – a space of 'safety' for the self. Fluidity (connection) and boundary-setting (freezing) are not oppositional and contradictory for two reasons: first, as debates over levels of risk acceptability have shown (see Otway and Cohen 1975, Beck 1992: 64), boundaries are themselves fluid and socially constituted; and second, singularity is not defined by its limits but 'more by boundaries it crosses' (Massumi 1992: 203). Or, the boundaries are constituted in the moment that the possibility of their transgression is realised. However, the idea of 'risk' as the control of movement between boundaries (principally represented as safety and danger) has political implications which have been well summed up by Massumi (1992):

> For having boundaries that are actualised by being crossed is a very precarious way to run a world. It leaves little space for a negotiated crisis management. Either the crossing trips established regulatory power mechanisms into operation as it actualises the boundary, and the traditional imbalance of power holds; or the crossing eludes or overwhelms regulatory mechanisms and the only response to the threat

to the privilege of the traditional advantaged groups is 'offering' the enemy a 'choice' between unconditional surrender and maximum force . . . (Massumi 1992: 205–6).

The use of expert risk assessment prefaces the idea of the boundary over the idea of connection. The boundaries of safety, arrived at by the use of expert knowledges, are made publicly visible. Crossing these boundaries actualises a shift from safety to danger, from 'self' to 'other'. Yet the connections between these spaces remain socially obscured by their being placed in the control of the expert risk assessor. This has the effect of forging a discreteness between the subject, or self, and the social space which he or she occupies.

Conclusions

If it is accepted that societies need to avoid danger, then my account could be viewed as somewhat negative. In some senses I feel that no defence of this position is needed, as one of the duties of the social researcher should be to provide criticism – particularly of those discursive forms which may regarded as oppressive to individuals and groups already facing danger. Nevertheless my analysis may also provide some positive clues as to how we may approach the dangers written into modernity.

Despite misgivings about risk assessment it is important to point out that it can often act as a 'double edged sword'. On the one hand, the techniques often reveal dangers that challenge populations or localities. It may help explain ill-health that local or community groups have long suspected are far from random. This knowledge can then be used by groups, who may be in oppositional or subordinate positions, to campaign on their own behalf to reduce the danger they may be facing. A recent example of this would be the campaign conducted by families living around Sellafield, in light of epidemiological analysis suggesting a link between childhood leukaemia and low levels of radiation (see Gardner et al. 1987). On the other hand, the discourses of risk are themselves instances of 'risk production' in that they construct boundaries and connections to define spaces of safety and danger. As we have seen, this is often not a neutral, or even democratic, production but instead a discourse which uses the 'other' as a 'useful' source of danger.

The very way in which expert knowledge defines risk suggests that danger can be objectively defined and managed. Understandings of this type represent themselves as based on a scientific methodology in which an external entity, risk could be objectively measured, known and hence managed. The term objectivity here refers simply to the idea of disinterest

– that a statement's durability is independent of the person or group making it and, as such, it is opposed to the term subjectivity. Often disputes over risk focus on this objective/subjective duality. One example of this would be the debates over pesticide use in the 1980s. Toxicologists working for the British government (the Pesticides Advisory Committee) dismissed claims that pesticides were causing health damage, by defining the evidence of farm workers as subjective non-knowledge (Lash and Wynne 1992: 5). The point of this example is not to insinuate that there was some conspiracy on the part of toxicologists to conceal the harm that pesticides may cause. Rather the evidence produced by both the experts and farm workers (and the objective knowledge claims on which each was based) were contextualised in different ways. The experts' evidence was based on laboratory studies, whereas the farm workers' claims were based on use in practice. Knowledge can only be translated between contexts, and remain objective, if the assumptions on which it is based remain open (for example, that the conditions under which pesticides are deemed safe within a laboratory are reproducible under conditions of use in the field). Thus Law (1994) suggests that it may be better to withdraw from the objective/subjective duality by 'treating knowledge as a contexted product whose status depends upon its workability' (Law 1994: 29).

What is clear, however, is that knowledge claims based in 'science' still command an authority in policy discussions. Large science based organisations (such as government departments and commercial organisations) have the resources, expertise and privileges to make statements that are difficult to challenge and demystify. Science can be used to produce myths of authority and order. The discourse of risk assessment often claims such a scientific legitimacy for the knowledge it produces. Yet this knowledge is only available to a few individuals and experts, working in a few powerful institutions. They have the power to make what Haraway (Haraway and Darnorsky 1991) has described as 'stable statements'. But to make such a 'statement' requires enormous resources.

This is now, however, a totally one sided process. Experts do not always agree and, as has been pointed out by Giddens (1991), even the knowledge of experts appears to be becoming increasingly contested in late modern societies. For every expert employed by powerful concerns (such as the nuclear or pharmaceutical industries), we can also discern the voices of oppositional pressure groups (such as Greenpeace or the Terrence Higgins Trust). This may lead one to believe that the status of expert knowledge is becoming contestable. Yet this is often little more than debate, between the experts employed by different groups, over the divergent measures of danger arrived at by remarkably similar methods. The struggle, however, is not one between equals – some groups occupy strategic positions from which they can make durable statements that carry a considerable force.

What the 'expert' conceptualisation of risk often achieves is to define clearly particular boundaries while obscuring the connections between them. Boundaries are made public because they can often be used strategically by, for example, defining the experts' position as certain (and therefore safe) whereas particular groups are seen as a source of uncertainty and danger. One way to increase the democratic access to expertise would be to question the certainty of experts and the institutions that generate risk assessment. Risk assessment should be seen as a social process with an ingrained political dimension, rather than a physical entity discovered through hidden methods. As Wynne has observed, a systematic examination of the 'objective' measures of danger, arrived at by experts, will always remain essential, 'but the lingering tendency to start from this scientific vantage point and add social perceptions as qualifications to the objective physical picture must be completely reversed' (Wynne 1982: 138).

In addition, we have seen how the connections between risk boundaries are often obscured because, if revealed, they would diminish the power of those controlling them. Therefore, one progressive way forward may be to try and reverse this privileging of boundary over connection. Putting less stress on boundaries would lower the likelihood of particular groups (or localities) being used as a repository for danger and uncertainty. In addition, hazards, no longer separated by a rigid boundary, would be all the more readily identifiable as part of *our* problem. On the other hand, emphasising connection would serve to break down the dichotomies written into risk boundaries and the practices for managing them. Thus, the connection between expert and public may be exposed, and hence the institutional boundaries of control undermined. This exercise may not provide the illusory comfort of definitive expert statements because new, and overlooked, *fatal connections* will surely be revealed. But an examination of the nature of these *fatal connections* and their place in modernity is a much needed project.

Acknowledgements

My thanks to Mike Michael, Sally Macintrye and two anonymous referees who commented on earlier versions of this chapter.

Notes

1 Such as: Bayesian probabilities; probability density functions; discounted future probabilities; Monte Carlo techniques; stratum-specific attributable risks; and beta-binomial distributions.

2 The search of the *Excerpta Medica* database was carried out on May 24 1994 using the Bath Information Data Services. References were sought that either contained the word 'risk' in their title, abstract or keyword fields. Both English and non-English references were searched.

References

Abraham, J. (1993) Scientific standards and institutional interests – carcinogenic risk assessment of Benoxaprofen in the UK and United States, *Social Studies of Studies*, 23, 387–444.

Abraham, J. (1994) Bias in science and medical knowledge – the Opren controversy, *Sociology*, 28, 717–36.

Bauman, Z. (1993) *Postmodern Ethics*. Oxford: Blackwell.

Beck, U. (1992) *Risk Society: Towards a New Modernity*. London: Sage.

Crawford, R. (1977) You are dangerous to your health: the ideology and politics of victim blaming, *International Journal of Health Services*, 7, 663–80.

Crimp, D. (1991) How to have promiscuity in an epidemic. In Crimp, D. (ed) *AIDS: Cultural Analysis/Cultural Activism* (third ed). Cambridge, Mass: MIT Press, 237–72.

Dale, A. (1994) Scientific uncertainty in a world of risk – a review, *Futures*, 26, 862–867.

Davey, Smith, G., and Sheldon, T. (1993) Cholesterol and cholesterol lowering drugs in 1993, *Journal of the Irish Colleges of Physicians and Surgeons*, 22, 255–6.

Davey-Smith, G., Song, F., and Sheldon, T. (1993) Cholesterol lowering and mortality: the importance of considering initial level of risk, *British Medical Journal*, 306, 1367–73.

Davison, C., Davey-Smith, G., and Frankel, S. (1991) Lay epidemiology and the prevention paradox: the implications of coronary candidacy for health education, *Sociology of Health and Illness*, 13, 1–19.

Douglas, M. (1966) *Purity and Danger: An Analysis of Concepts of Pollution and Taboo*. London: Routledge and Kegan Paul.

Douglas, M. (1985) *Risk Acceptability According to the Social Sciences*. London: Routledge.

Douglas, M. (1990) Risk as a forensic resource, *Daedalus*, 119, 177–91.

Evans-Prichard, E. (1976) *Witchcraft Oracles and Magic among the Azande*. Oxford: Clarendon Press.

Fischhoff, B. (1977) Cost-benefit analysis and the art of motorcycle maintenance, *Policy Sciences*, 8, 177–202.

Forman, P. (1971) Weimar culture: causality and quantum physics, *Historical Studies in the Physical Sciences*, 3, 1–115.

Frankenberg, R. (1992) The other who is also the same – the relevance of epidemics in space and time for prevention of HIV-infection, *International Journal of Health Services*, 22, 73–88.

Gable, F., Aubrey, D., and Gentile, J. (1991) Global environmental change issues in the western Indian Ocean, *Geoforum*, 22, 401–19.

Gardner, M.J., Hall, J., and Downes, S. (1987) Follow-up study of the children born to mother resident in Seascale, West Cumbria, *British Medical Journal*, 295, 822–7.

Giddens, A. (1991) *Modernity and Self-Identity: Self and Society in the Late Modern Age*. Cambridge: Polity Press.

Hacking, I. (1975) *The Emergence of Probability*. Cambridge: Cambridge University Press.

Hacking, I. (1990) *The Taming of Chance*. Cambridge: Cambridge University Press.

Hall, S. (1986) Variants of liberalism. In Donald, J. and Hall, S. (eds) *Politics and Ideology*. Milton Keynes: Open University Press.

Hansson, S. (1989) Dimensions of risk, *Risk Analysis*, 9, 107–12.

Haraway, D., and Darnovsky, M. (1991) Overhauling the meaning machines: an interview with Donna Haraway, *Socialist Review*, 21, 65–84.

Hayes, M. V. (1992) On the epistemology of risk: language, logic and social science, *Social Science and Medicine*, 35, 401–7.

Jacobson, P. and Barnes, J. (1978) £66 million damages: the car that carried death in the boot, *Sunday Times*, 12 February, 4.

Kates, R.W. (1978) *Risk Assessment of Environmental Hazard*. New York: Wiley.

Kates, R., and Kasperson, J. (1983) Comparative risk analysis of technological hazards (a review), *Proceedings of the National Academy of Science*, 80, 7027–38.

Kolstad, C. (1994) George Bush versus Al Gore – irreversibilities in greenhouse-gas accumulation and emission control investment, *Energy Policy*, 22, 717–78.

Lash, S. and Wynne, B. (1992) Introduction to Beck, U. *Risk Society: Towards a New Modernity*. London: Sage.

Law, J. (1994) *Organizing Modernity*. Oxford: Blackwell.

Luhmann, N. (1993) Ecological communication – coping with the unknown, *System Practice*, 6, 527–39.

Lupton, D. (1993) Risk as moral danger: the social and political functions of risk discourse in public health, *International Journal of Health Services*, 23, 425–35.

Malinowski, B. (1922) *Argonauts of the Western Pacific*. London: Routledge and Kegan Paul.

Mandl, C., and Lathrop, J. (1981) Comparing risk assessments for liquefied energy gas terminals – some results. In Kunreuther, H. and Ley, E. (eds), *The Risk Analysis Controversy*, Berlin: Springer-Verlag, 41–60.

Massumi, B. (1992) Everywhere you want to be: introduction to fear, *Warwick Journal of Philosophy*, 4, 175–217.

Michael, M., and Still, A. (1992) A resource for resistance: power-knowledge and affordance, *Theory and Society*, 21, 869–88.

Moore, T. (1989) *Heart Failure: A Critical Inquiry into American Medicine and the Revolution in Heart Care*. New York: Simon and Schuster.

Norse, D. (1994) Multiple threats to regional food-production – environment, economy, population, *Food Policy*, 19, 133–48.

O'Kelly, R. (1989) Prescribing diseases: the Industrial Injuries Advisory Council. In Smith, R. and Wynne, B. (eds), *Expert Evidence: Interpreting Science in the Law*. London: Routledge, 131–51.

Otway, J.H., and Cohen, J.J. (1975) Revealed preferences: comments on the Starr benefit-risk relationship, *International Institute for Applied Systems Analysis*, 75–7.

Perrow, C. (1984) *Normal Accidents: Living with High Risk Technologies*. New York: Basic Books.

Pill, R., and Stott, N. (1982) Concepts of illness causation and responsibility: some preliminary data from a sample of working class mothers, *Social Science and Medicine*, 16, 43–52.

Posner, T. (1991) What's in a smear: cervical screening, medical signs and metaphors, *Science as Culture*, 2, 167–88.

Robinson, R. (1993) Cost-benefit analysis, *British Medical Journal*, 307, 924–6.

Sheldon, T., Song, F., Davey-Smith, G., Freemantle, N., Mason, J., and Long, A. (1993) Cholesterol screening and cholesterol lowering treatment, *Quality in Health Care*, 2, 134–7.

Slovic, P., Fischhoff, B., and Lichtenstein, S. (1978) Fault trees: sensitivity of estimated failure probabilities to problem representation, *Journal of Experimental Psychology: Human Perception and Performance*, 4, 330–44.

Slovic, P., Fischhoff, B., and Lichtenstein, S. (1918) Perceived risk: psychological factors and social implications, *Proceedings of the Royal Society of London*, 376, 17–34.

Taylor, P. (1984) *Smoke Ring: The Politics of Tobacco*. London: Bodley Head.

Treichler, P. (1991) Aids, homophobia, and biomedical discourse: an epidemic of signification. In Crimp, D. (ed) *AIDS: Cultural Analysis/Cultural Activism* (third ed). Cambridge, Mass: MIT Press, 31–71.

Wright, P. (1980) *On a Clear Day You Can See General Motors*. London: Sidgwick and Jackson.

Wynne, B. (1982) Institutional mythologies and dual societies in the management of risk. In Kunreuther, H. and Ley, E. (eds) *The Risk Analysis Controversy: An Institutional Perspective*. Berlin: Springer-Verlag, 127–45.

Wynne, B. (1989) Establishing the rules of laws: constructing expert authority. In Smith, R. and Wynne, B. (eds) *Expert Evidence: Interpreting Science in the Law*. London: Routledge.

Wynne, B. (1990) Sheepfarming after Chernobyl: a case study in communicating scientific information. In Bradby, H. (ed) *Dirty*. London: Earthscan Publications.

8. Prevention as a problem of modernity: the example of HIV and AIDS

Sue Scott and Richard Freeman

Introduction: modernity and the management of risk

Risk is a relatively modern concept, to the extent that it is a product of a particular set of understandings of free will and decision-making as well as the result of an increasingly manipulated environment. For Beck, for example, risk is integrally bound up with the development of modernity: '*Risk* may be defined as a *systematic way of dealing with hazards and insecurities induced and introduced by modernization itself*. Risks, as opposed to older dangers, are consequences which relate to the threatening force of modernization and to its globalization of doubt' (Beck 1992: 21, emphasis in original). More than this, however, it is the problem of risk which has come to constitute what might be described as modernity's paradox: while we seem to be less vulnerable to the vicissitudes of fate, we inhabit at the same time a culture which is increasingly sensitive to risk (Scott and Williams 1992).

Health, itself a modern construct, has become a prime focus of risk anxiety. As illness has become medicalised, something to be countered by expert and scientific intervention, so health has come to be understood as adequate, if not optimal, physical functioning which is to be maintained by care of the self and restored by medicine. If illness is no longer a matter of fate, then health equally becomes a matter of rational action; health is a norm to be achieved and from which deviance is an aberration. Health is therefore modern in the sense of being a product of post-Enlightenment conceptions of self and environment and the relationship between them. 'Threats come from everywhere – from the air that we breathe, the rays of the sun, the multinational petrochemical companies, the 'man' in the street, from our families, our sexual partners . . . even the cells of our bodies may turn against us' (Scott and Williams 1992: 3, Armstrong 1993). Sexuality, in turn, has come to be increasingly associated with health and risk. It is seen as integral to individual well-being and, at the same time, as a potential threat to it. Increasingly, too, it is a major constituent of personal identity. Risk, health and sexuality fuse in relation to HIV and AIDS.[1]

This means that AIDS discourse can be used as a prism through which to view the range of late twentieth century understandings of and

responses to risk. As Jeffrey Weeks puts it: 'A number of different histories intersect in and are condensed by AIDS discourse. What gives AIDS
a particular power is its ability to represent a host of fears, anxieties and
problems in our current, post-permissive society' (Weeks 1989: 2).
Meanwhile, risk and risk anxieties of this kind in relation to health have,
in late modernity[2], come to be managed through a discourse of prevention. Issues of risk are constructed as problems of prevention. This
applies to AIDS policy as much as to other preventive programmes such
as those relating to smoking, diet and cervical screening (Howson 1995).
This being the case, the argument which follows takes discourses of prevention in HIV and AIDS as expressive of more general problems of risk
management in late modernity.

AIDS embodies a set of risks managed in different social arenas: by
public policy, by medicine, and by individuals. The chapter considers
each of these in turn, but begins by setting out the ways in which HIV
and AIDS policy in developed countries has been locked within particular
modernist understandings. The next section sets out to articulate an
understanding of policy responses to AIDS which locates them within the
discourse of modernity.

Responding to AIDS

The level of social and political reaction AIDS has aroused may seem to
mark it as a 'special case'. Yet its modes of transmission are similar to
those of other viruses, such as hepatitis B.[3] Furthermore, the transmission
of the disease is related to certain specific sexual and drug-taking behaviours, which may be compared to pathogenic behaviours such as smoking
and the consumption of alcohol, for example, and to drug use more generally. Case management, too, is similar in many ways to that of other
chronic and incurable conditions. HIV and AIDS, then, have much in
common with general epidemiological patterns of the late twentieth century. The issues they raise may differ in their complications, but they are
not different in kind. AIDS provides, in microcosm, a demonstration of
broader contemporary issues in respect of prevention (Berridge and
Strong 1992, Rosenbrock 1986). The sociological significance of AIDS is
not peculiar to itself, but lies in its being representative of other social
and political anxieties (Weeks 1989).

An almost bewildering array of proposals and counter-proposals have
been formulated, and sometimes implemented, in the name of the prevention of HIV and AIDS.[4] Public policy debates have been conducted at
local as well as at national and international levels, often with seemingly
little connection between them. For all their variety, nevertheless, they
may be understood as conflicts between two ideal-type constructions, the

authoritarian and the liberal. As one comparative text puts it: 'Essentially the choice has lain between persuasion through education and obligation through law' (Misztal and Moss 1990: 13).[5] In this chapter, we understand these different sets of ideas in a Foucauldian sense not as distinct policy options but as points of emergence of competing, contradictory and sometimes congruent discourses.

The authoritarian response to AIDS is rooted in a tradition of municipal public health oriented around the 'control of disease'. It is characterised by the implementation of usually pre-existent regulations which permit the 'surveillance' of 'sources of infection'. Its attention is directed as much to potential as to actual behaviour; in consequence, it constructs individuals themselves as potential sources of infection. The effect of this is to translate the control of disease into the management of populations.[6] The discourse of authoritarian policy making includes restrictions on employment and residence and, potentially, extends to forcible testing and penal isolation. In its ultimate appeal to juridical norms it may be described as policing in the cause of prevention.[7] The liberal model of the prevention of AIDS identifies individual *behaviour* as the source of infection with HIV. In accordance with wider precepts of liberty, rationality and responsibility, it seeks to change individuals' behaviour by the provision of information, education and advice, supported by voluntary access to HIV testing. This has been the prevailing form of policy response to AIDS in western democracies (Pollak 1992).[8]

While the development of policy is often understood as a linear evolution from authoritarian to liberal modes, the patterns of policy making generated by these perspectives are rarely wholly distinct. They overlap; each contains elements of the other. Authoritarian prescriptions for the criminalisation of HIV transmission, for example, have been intended to supplement rather than supplant the provision of health education; they assume a majority of informed individuals changing their behaviour in what are prescribed as responsible ways. At the same time, purportedly liberal policy environments have preserved an ultimate recourse to law. In the UK, public health legislation allowing for the detention in hospital of people with infectious diseases was extended to cover AIDS in 1984; the criminalisation of HIV transmission was discussed by government ministers as recently as 1992.[9] The lingering presence of public health regulations such as these has contrived to make fierce disputes a continuing possibility. This erosion of boundaries between apparently distinct conceptualisations reflects their underlying fragility, the uncertainty with which each was developed. In the mid-1980s, both liberal and authoritarian approaches seemed experimental; each, in turn, functioned as something of a safety net for the other.

Prevailing AIDS prevention policies might best be understood as fateful attempts to cling on to conceptions of society rooted in progressivist understandings of modernity. This means that they are unresponsive to the shifting conditions which prevail in late modernity. They are intended as rational, extrinsic solutions to specific social problems and, as such, they lack reflexivity. As attempts at intervention which are legitimated by diktat and by education in turn, they exhibit many of the pervasive tensions of late modernity: tensions between the rights and responsibilities of individual and state, between individual autonomy and social order, between states and markets, between the national, the global and the local, between public and private.

At the same time, of course, they can be described as fateful. It is part of what has come to be understood as the crisis of modernity that the complex problems it produces are not amenable to simple solutions (Giddens 1990): policy 'solutions' posited at the level of the state are themselves constitutive of the 'problems' they are designed to address. Authoritarian prescriptions would have the state using methods more appropriate to the regulation of public space to monitor 'interior' subjectivity. Liberal discourse embodies ideas about individual behaviour and intent rather than social interaction, and fails to acknowledge the extent to which individual behaviours such as sex and drug use have become components of social identity. Both patterns are reliant on increasingly contested scientific and professional expertise.

Fundamentally, the choice is not between regulated and unregulated sexuality, between authoritarian, liberal and possibly liberatory discourses but between different kinds of disciplinary mechanism. The account of authoritarian discourse presented here parallels the Foucauldian conception of regulatory power, which describes the management of populations via categories of bodies. To describe liberal discourse, similarly, is to echo the idea of disciplinary power, which refers to the management or governance of the individual body, increasingly via self-surveillance (Foucault 1978). The point is that there is always governance, that governance is ever-present and inevitable, though its forms of expression may vary. Applied to sexuality, this means that just as, at the level of the individual body, there is no real sexuality, to be discovered under layers of repression (Foucault 1978, Weeks 1981), so, at the level of populations, there can be no unmanaged sexuality (Singer 1993). Part of the aim of this chapter is to describe and interpret processes of governance in relation to HIV and AIDS.

What is significant about AIDS is the ways in which it reveals the fragility of these pre-existing forms of governance and calls new ones, such as 'safer sex', into being. Some of these it has in common with other contemporary issues: the legitimacy of the nation state, the flawed nature of expert systems, and the breaching of the boundaries of the autonomous individual have each, and in combination, been called into question by other crises of modernity. These include the nuclear and other environmental threats; the sexual victimisation of women and gay men; industrial decline and the failures of the welfare state, and the globalisation of the economy at a more general level. AIDS exemplifies a process by which the incapacities of state and expert systems come to require the individual management of risk, the 'personalisation' of risk politics.[10] The following sections of the chapter discuss responses to this problem of risk at the levels of public policy, medicine and the individual in turn.

Public policies

AIDS has . . . provided important insights into the complexities of policy formation in pluralist societies (Weeks 1989: 13).

In many ways, AIDS politics and policy making display attempts to act through the state at a point where the locus of political and social activity has shifted to other arenas, both more global and more local and often non-public. In relation to AIDS, states have struggled with two kinds of problem, the first of competence, the second of scale. Ultimately, the state has deferred to alternative bases of authority, such as professional medicine, while the problem of AIDS remains much more a local and global rather than national one. This section sets out the processes which have resulted in a public policy focus on 'individual responsibility'.

The emergence of a new disease does not necessarily demand a health policy response by government. Ordinarily, the immediate challenge is to medicine, both as a science and a system of care (Canaris 1988, Rosenbrock 1986). Several different pressures, however, prompted government action on AIDS. These included the increased prevalence of HIV among marginalised populations other than gay men, such as injecting drug users, and its anticipated spread to the 'general' population; both of these implied an increasing burden of care for people with AIDS. There was also a perceived need for national guidance for policy making at the local level (Misztal and Moss 1990). The entry of the state into AIDS politics, nevertheless, tends to have been marked by conflict between the state and the gay community, and between the centre and regions or localities. There seems to have been a trajectory of AIDS policy making in which medical uncertainty opened a space for lay intervention, which was subsequently displaced by the intervention of the state (Misztal and Moss 1990).

Uncertainty about the nature of the problem, its extent and how to respond to it, both prompted and mitigated against radical proposals for public policy. In most Western countries, again, a pattern emerged in which available legislation was not to be applied in relation to AIDS. The use of law seemed more than likely to be counter-productive in political as much as in public health terms. While medicine cautioned against legalistic intervention, on the basis that HIV infection would be driven underground, such action would also have sustained the identity of the issue as a political problem. Governments opted for minimalist policy making: they made provision for health education and voluntary testing, the lowest common denominators of both liberal and authoritarian intervention.

The role of HIV testing in preventive policy making, meanwhile, is an ambivalent one (Strong and Berridge 1990). In different ways, the availability of the test underpinned both liberal and authoritarian constructions of the disease and consequent strategies of response. To some, it seemed to establish the extent of HIV infection among specific populations and to lead to a clearer understanding of the disease, making for greater precision in the quality of information available and in the ways in which it was distributed. It also led, however, to calls for forcible screening and the subsequent isolation of those found to be infected, and to the use of discriminatory testing in applications for employment and insurance. Testing was central to discourses of prevention, that is to the management of AIDS-related risk: some individuals, with appropriate counselling, would choose to test and, with continued support and the medical information derived from it, would choose to change their behaviour in responsible ways; others would have both the test and behavioural change forced upon them.

What remains important about HIV testing is its focus on the individual. It attends to individual behavioural change rather than change to social and sexual norms; even calls for the compulsory testing of population groups were predicated upon understandings of those groups as masses of individuals rather than as complex social networks without clear boundaries. The value of testing as a policy tool lay in its accordance with prevailing assumptions about the individualised, private nature of sexuality, with the requirements of the individual doctor-patient relationship, and with market interests in the new technology (Willis 1990). At the same time, the test represented a symbolic response to AIDS: it was, perhaps, a substitute for both prevention and cure (Rosenbrock 1986). In the absence of a pharmaceutical 'magic bullet', the test was a residual expression of medicine's technological fix (Willis 1992). For policy makers, it is perhaps best understood as a means of doing something without changing anything: 'the use of the test appears to function as some kind of magical control measure. In this context the test becomes a ritual, as have many other screening tests. Its administration reduces the anxiety generated by a perception of a disease out of control and masquerades as intervention' (McCombie 1986, cited in Willis 1990: 11).

State intervention in response to AIDS, even though it may have been necessitated as a result of medical uncertainty, was nevertheless based on medical professional authority. In formulating its strategies, the state sought to appropriate two alternative kinds of expertise. Initially, and in part, it used the insider experience of gay activists and information networks, but then increasingly came to rely on medicine for its legitimation.

A key political function of community-based AIDS Service Organisations (ASOs), in various fields, has been to act as mediators for state interests – specifically the production and distribution of preventive health education – while maintaining normative boundaries between the state and subcultures. The effect of government sponsorship of ASOs has been to remove policy from the publicly contested realm: the politics of prevention has been internalised among the communities of those affected. In common with other organisations dealing with other, equally intractable issues their symbolic role seems to have been to provide 'an institutional arrangement that enables complex societies to cope with social and political problems that cannot be solved' (Seibel 1989: 188).

In contrast, it has been argued that it is the greater 'power of professionalism' which has determined public policy responses to AIDS (Fox *et al.* 1989). This is taken as evidence of 'the authority that medical, scientific and public health professionals have acquired during this century' (Fox *et al.* 1989: 110). But this is to overplay the degree of expertise held by medical and scientific actors, and to ignore or even undermine the significant input into AIDS policy making made by those directly affected, particularly in the early stages of policy formation (Strong and Berridge 1990). The 'power of professionalism' lay not in its expertise, but in its status: the government deferred to medicine not for its problem-solving capacity but as a nominally legitimate means of regulating complex and threatening health issues. We turn to medicine in more detail in the next section.

Meanwhile, public policy was failing to address the local and global dimensions of the problem. Organised responses to AIDS began at the local level; whether in San Francisco, New York, Paris, Berlin, London or Edinburgh, AIDS politics continues to be based in those major urban centres with the largest and most powerful AIDS constituencies, both in terms of service demand (the numbers and organisation of those living with AIDS and HIV infection) and of service provision (clinical specialists and support workers). The impression of uniform national issues is illusory, being partly an effect of AIDS localities being metropolitan, if not capital cities. In fact, responses to AIDS began at the local level and extended worldwide, often via international networks of research scientists, clinical specialists, political activists and people with HIV and AIDS among others, whose work and interests cut across those of the nation state.

The global dimension of the AIDS problem has rarely been acknowledged by policy makers. Although it was the first disease to be considered specifically by the General Assembly of the UN (in October 1987) (Mann 1991), there has been, in practice, no institutional formum capable of providing health leadership at the supranational level. Until very recently the development of the European Community (now European Union), left policy responsibility for public health as well as for health care with the member states; this has meant that EC policy making in respect of AIDS has remained largely symbolic (Altenstetter 1993). National campaigns in the UK which have aimed condom advertising at travellers ('Don't go too far without one') reflect global trajectories but show little sense of the specific ways in which male sexual tourism, in regions of the world with high levels of HIV infection among sex workers, breaches the boundaries of the middle class family. Women who may be thousands of miles apart are linked through a shared risk which is itself the product of male expectations of heterosexual practice. As Giddens comments: 'In the modern era, the level of time-space distanciation is much higher than in any previous period . . . worldwide social relations which link distant localities (are intensified) in such a way that local happenings are shaped by events occurring many miles away and vice versa' (Giddens 1990: 64). Thus government attempts to maintain the boundaries of national communities by immigration control, for example, may be understood either as token gestures or as simplistic solutions which fail to embrace the complexities of the problem. In the context of global risk, AIDS is no more likely to be contained by national boundaries than is radiation.

Responses to AIDS have passed through successive phases of 'moral panic' (1982–1985) and 'crisis management' (1986–1987) (Weeks 1989). In turn, these have been seen to be succeeded by a period of 'normalisation' (Berridge and Strong 1992), which may be described as one of professional establishment and administration.[11] In periods of crisis and policy conflict, AIDS has broken the boundaries of health politics ordinarily set by the local administration of public health and health care; preventive policies were the means by which governments managed this crisis.

The policy 'solutions' produced in the period of crisis management addressed problems of accountability as much as of epidemiology. In response to what became essentially a political problem, government policy making everywhere can be characterised as having been hesitant and reluctant. It was important for policy makers to be seen to be acting, while in fact not doing (or risking) anything very much: HIV and AIDS education, it has been remarked, served public relations as much as public health (Kane 1992). To this extent, responses to AIDS may be deemed to have had as much to do with the negotiation of power and responsibility as with the practicalities of 'solving the problem'. Public policy making for prevention has been for the most part formalistic, seeking to redistribute responsibilities from the realm of government to that of the individual, from the national to the local, from the public to the private sphere (Freeman 1992).

Expert systems

Medicine is deeply involved in the relations of power – and hence the morals – of the culture in which it is embedded . . . Medicine is an essential element in the fight against AIDS, but it has also been a constituent agent in the formation of 'AIDS' as a social issue (Weeks 1989: 15).

AIDS has revealed the inadequacies of expert systems as much as of public policy. In the first place, it exposed a lack of useful knowledge, otherwise the very basis of professional identity and status. Scepticism about the knowledge of specialised elites is not new in historical terms, but it is a new experience for late twentieth century citizens raised on promises of scientific progress and trust in experts: 'The impact of AIDS is essentially linked with modernity – its virulence and relative untreatability lead us to question a cornerstone of faith in science, experts and progress' (Small 1988: 11). Medical science has shifted from a state of ignorance to one in which its knowledge is challenged. Medicine's continuing failure to produce either a cure for AIDS or a vaccine against HIV has raised questions about its ability to define and to intervene in disease as a linear, causal process. This is the context in which 'heresies' persist, both in relation to the link between HIV and AIDS and to the reality of heterosexual transmission.[12]

At the same time, some individuals with HIV and AIDS have become unusually well informed about the disease which affects them. Some have proved more expert than the experts: especially in the early 1980s informational networking rendered lay knowledge among gay men superior to that of some individual physicians, specialists as well as generalists (Berridge and Strong 1992). On balance, it can be argued that this has served to exacerbate a loss of faith in professional expertise more than to turn combatting the disease into a cooperative activity between doctor and patient.

Meanwhile, it is not merely the patient who holds medical knowledge, but the doctor who may also be at risk of becoming sick. This means that fundamental principles of the hallowed doctor-patient relationship are breached in important ways. First, media scares about HIV-infected health care workers imply a partial redefinition of the health care worker from healer to potential source of infection. Second, AIDS has generated a heightened awareness among health care workers of occupational hazard (see Grinyer, this volume). This has brought about the loss of a sense of invulnerability on the part of individual doctors (Bosk and Frader 1991), leading some, for example, to want to carry out pre-operative HIV testing without necessarily obtaining patient consent.[13]

Medical professional interests have become apparent in other ways, too. Medical influence, exerted at critical points in the formulation of AIDS policy, proved sufficient to ensure that strategies of prevention did not run counter to its interests. These were expressed, predictably, in terms of screening and treatment rather than primary prevention; public policy on HIV screening, for example, reflected the value system of the medical profession (Day and Klein 1989). Meanwhile, a changing conception of AIDS from epidemic disease to chronic illness (Fox 1990, Fee and Krieger 1993) has come about in part in order to make it more amenable to medical management. At the same time, the impact of AIDS has fostered a process of professional legitimation. The way in which the disease was adopted by the less prestigious specialisms of genito-urinary medicine and public health is not without significance. The more heroic opportunities it offered to research specialisms such as virology have been expressed more forcefully in well-documented intra-professional and international rivalries than in collaboration in the pursuit of public service goals (Connor and Kingman 1988). Both at the level of the individual doctor and of the profession as a whole, doctors have acted in ways which have revealed that their interests are not necessarily coincident either with those of individual patients or of the general population.

The impact of AIDS on relations between doctors and patients has heightened the tension between the loss of faith in expert systems characteristic of late modernity and the continuing need to trust in expert solutions. Paradoxically, scepticism about the prospect of expert solutions may co-exist alongside persistent hope. It is possible to reject biomedicine both intellectually and politically while at the same time making difficult, personal choices about using AZT. This dilemma can be understood as part of a developing pattern of reflexive modernisation (Beck 1994): perhaps more precisely, it shows how risk issues in late modernity call for a 'recognition of ambivalence' (Bauman 1991, cited in Beck 1994: 10). This is further instanced by the way in which AIDS activism has generated demands for more medicine, not less, and for drugs to be made available at earlier stages in the process of research and development.

We can draw analogies between AIDS discourse and discussions of the breakdown of trust in experts as a result of incidents such as Chernobyl (Beck 1992). Experts can do little more in the context of HIV and AIDS than define areas of risk; they cannot, in the end, reduce or remove it. For medicine, this has meant seeking to maintain its cultural authority while attempting to manage a failure of technical capacity; this it has done in part by stressing the primacy of individual responsibility. This, in turn, produces an individual experience of responsibility without autonomy and a need to manage anxiety. These issues are considered in the next section.

The individualisation of risk management

As has already been shown, public policy and professional medicine, both separately and together, have structured a process of the individualisation of risk management in response to HIV and AIDS. Apart from testing, health education has been the principal conduit of this process of individualisation. In late modernity, health education has become one of the major ways in which responsibility for health has passed from the level of the social to that of the individual: the governance of health continues through practices of self-surveillance. The focus of health education has shifted from disease process to personal behaviour (Aggleton and Homans 1987), as evidenced by the dominance of 'lifestyle' in discussions of prevention (Blaxter 1990). Here, the point is that AIDS was simply a late addition to the growing portfolio of risks which individuals are expected to manage in their everyday worlds.

It is worth remembering, too, that in the specific context of heterosexual AIDS there were few, if any, alternative and communal bases of social action. First, the idea of a 'heterosexual community' is virtually meaningless: its sense is undermined by divisions between women and men.[14] Second, ideas of community conjured up by understandings of AIDS as a threat to 'normality' have been exclusive rather than inclusive, symbolic rather than real. While its modes of transmission are individualised, the talismen to which we have recourse for protection from AIDS bear the mark of communal constructions of deviance and normality, self and other: 'I'm clean', 'I'm straight', 'I don't sleep around'.[15]

In response to AIDS, the twofold task of health education has been taken to be to dispel ignorance and to stress the necessity for personal risk avoidance. Its principal message has been to promote 'safer sex', the core elements of which are negotiation and condom use. Importantly, safer sex is predicated upon what might be described as a process of sexual reskilling. Modernist sexuality can be seen as Fordist sexuality, as something to be worked at and improved upon and as acceptable if done by the right people at the right time, in the right places and in the right way. Further, it can be seen as Taylorised in that the way to the finished product (male orgasm) is held to be by means of linear progression through a series of simple operations. While the introduction of condoms might be taken as part of this process of Taylorisation (Bardeleben *et al.* 1989), for the post-Pill generation and for gay men condoms are, on the contrary, a disruption of the process of linear progression. Significant reskilling is required for them to be successfully incorporated into sexual activity. In this way, safer sex can be understood as post-Fordist sex, requiring new skills and more flexibly managed bodies. Though the emergence of AIDS met with a hope that it might provide a context in which a longstanding feminist call for a re-interpretation of heterosexuality might be realised (Coward 1987), change in sexual behaviour among heterosexuals has not, in general, taken place (Ford and Bowie 1988, Holland *et al.* 1990, Blaxter 1991). Safer sex is premissed on an awareness and acceptance of risk and, in turn, on the production of trust. In this context, trust may be understood as the solution to a specific problem of risk (Luhmann 1986). In turn, this raises the question of the relationship between risk awareness and risk avoidance.

While bio-medical experts can provide risk assessments relating to the trajectory of AIDS in general epidemiological terms, and even relating to the likelihood of infection with HIV as a result of engaging in specific risk practices with an infected partner, they can offer little or no useful assessment of the risk attached to any given partner. Of necessity, then, individuals must become their own experts in risk assessment. To do so, they must construct an informational basis of risk assessment for themselves. The requisite knowledge has to be built up via the exchange of information: in the context of HIV and AIDS education, 'talk' is often suggested as a route to risk reduction. The assumption here is that sexual histories are exchanged and safer sex negotiated in appropriate ways.

Knowledge of a partner, however, is unlikely ever to be complete. Imperfect understanding, failures of memory, the deliberate withholding of information and active deception make for two kinds of problem. First, in so far as the effect of successful talk – the exchange of intimate information – is to generate interpersonal trust rather than increased knowledge, it may lead to increased rather than diminished risk taking. Talk may well deal with the problem of anxiety, but it may also increase potentially risky practices. As sharing sexual histories can tell us little about a person's network of sexual contacts, no matter how 'truthful' we are, then the production of trust may itself be understood as a high risk activity.

The second kind of problem has to do with the likely results of failed talk. Sexual negotiation implies a degree of autonomy which may not be readily available. In such circumstances, trust may well be posited as a solution. Research suggests that for many young women, for example, trust may have fatalistic overtones which can be summed up by the phrase 'you have to trust somebody sometime' (Holland *et al.* 1992). Here, the need to trust has its roots in romantic, feminine discourse and is likely to result in an understanding of love as prophylactic. In this context, trust becomes a functional substitute for knowledge.

Meanwhile, the linear association between risk awareness and risk avoidance is liable to be disrupted by the complexities of the relationship between sex and identity. In respect of risk management in relation to HIV and AIDS, readily available heterosexual, masculine discourse may produce a strong element of fatalism: 'it won't happen to me', 'straight men don't get AIDS', or even 'real men take risks' (Wight 1993). Trust in this context is not built up via the exchange of information; it is rooted neither in a relationship nor in a rational process of risk assessment, but in cultural understandings of sexuality and in gendered sexual scripts (Gagnon and Simon 1973, Jackson 1978). At the same time, safer sex may be experienced as a reduction of sexual expression. It represents a prescriptive sexuality which may threaten 'liberated' sexual identities, both heterosexual and homosexual. In the extreme, hard-won sexual freedoms may be defended by rejecting the precepts of safer sex, and by asserting the right to a risk-taking identity (Douglas and Calvez 1990).

In summary, the management of risk in relation to HIV and AIDS is predicated on a reconsideration not necessarily of heterosexual practice, but of sexual identity. What is seen to matter is not what you do, but who you are or seem to be, or even simply want to be. To a large extent this is because, at best, safer sex can protect only from HIV, not from the expanded symbolic meanings of AIDS (Treichler 1987, cited in Weeks 1989).

Commentary: risk and difference

In this chapter we have set out the process of the individualisation of risk management in relation to HIV and AIDS, and tried to show how it is representative of the more general motor of modernity. Almost inexorably, the processing of the issue through public policy and expert systems has served merely to identify the individual as ultimately responsible for the awareness, assessment and avoidance of risk:

All these and all the other experts dump their conflicts and contradictions at the feet of the individual and leave him or her with the well intentioned invitation to judge all of this critically on the basis of his or her own notions (Beck 1992: 137).

Individuals' search for safety continues in other ways. In the context of intimate relations, trust has become a symbolic solution to the risk of HIV infection; trust implies not the rational assessment of risk, but an engagement with fatalism. One of the reasons why it is so difficult to translate anxiety about HIV and AIDS into rational dialogue is precisely because it calls trust and intimacy, the insecure bases of fragile sexual identities, into question.

For the most part, sociological understandings of AIDS have been built up from the previously separate domains of the sociology of health and illness and of sexuality. The sociology of AIDS has been more empirical than theoretical, driven both by an overwhelming lack of available data and by a sense of urgency in responding to crisis. To this extent, it can be argued that sociology has been co-opted into supporting both medicine and social and public policy, that it has been expected to legislate rather than to interpret (Bauman 1992). The cumulative effect is a somewhat fragmented, undertheorised understanding of HIV and AIDS.

In part, this chapter represents a search for an intellectual framework which allows us to consider a number of different dimensions of the issue in a coherent way. We have wanted to account not only for individual practices, but for a whole range of attempts to manage AIDS as well as wider questions of risk in modern society. Implicitly, we assume that different aspects of these issues are interrelated and interdependent, that we are unlikely to be able to understand one element in isolation from others. It might be possible to draw new insight from theories of the state, the professions and of social movements. However, it is in recent attempts to theorise late modernity that we have seen the greatest potential for the development of an understanding capable of dealing with the order of complexity that this issue raises.

In our view, what was needed was a theory capable of locating risk anxieties historically but which might also allow for the specific nexus of responses to HIV and AIDS in the late twentieth century. We also wanted to account for the heterogenous nature of AIDS itself as well as for the diversity of those affected by it. Foucauldian ideas focused our analysis on the discourses around AIDS, but we wanted also to consider their intersubjective dimensions. From here, we go on to show the need for a more complex understanding of the increasingly reflexive awareness of individual actors in responding to AIDS.

In a general way, this chapter set out to show that current theories of the risk society (Beck 1992) can offer useful accounts of the process of individualisation and of the management of risk anxiety at a number of levels in the late twentieth century. In this instance, however, in relation to HIV and AIDS, the problem is that writers such as Beck and Giddens deal primarily with the management of risk anxiety produced by external threats in the public realm. Although Giddens discusses the development of trust in the context of intimate relations as, in part, a response to external risk anxiety and lack of trust in expert systems (Giddens 1991, 1992), he fails to offer an analysis of how to manage the emergence of risk within the sphere of the intimate itself. In this context, the significance of AIDS lies in having revealed a lack of understanding of the processes of risk management in personal and sexual relationships.

Giddens' recent writings (1990, 1991, 1992) lead to the view that the narrative construction and reflexive reconstruction of the self in the context of the 'pure relationship' is a central feature of what he describes as 'high' modernity. He describes a process whereby identity is constituted via the reflexive ordering of narratives, defining this as the reflexive project of the self (Giddens 1991). He goes on to argue that sexuality is central in this process and is doubly constituted both as a medium of self realisation and as a means by which to create and express intimacy (Giddens 1992). For him, concepts such as fate and destiny no longer have genuine currency in contemporary public life, but belong to belief systems which see the future as beyond human control. Fatalism continues to have a role only as a refusal of modernity, a rejection of the possibility of acting to alter the course of events (Giddens 1991).

However, while the idea of the reflexive project of the self may be a powerful analytical tool it has, as yet, limited currency. It asserts, more or less implicitly, a generality, a commonality of experience which is no longer valid; the inclination to cling to the generalising tendency of modern social theory has limited application. As yet, theorists of late modernity have failed to deal satisfactorily with difference and structural location. The sociology of AIDS reveals a need to understand the ways in which differently positioned individuals respond differently to risks which, though their effects may be the same, are in many cases differently perceived.

Giddens appears to assume that the 'pure relationship' based on choice, dialogue and negotiation is attainable in practice, and is not merely an ideal construction (Giddens 1992). The problem, however, is that the 'reflexive project of the self' which might lead to engagement in pure relationships is not a universally available and ungendered choice. As one critique has it: 'In the absence of an analysis of power the framework of the "pure relationship" . . . decomposes into a version of voluntarism which stresses personal decisions, subjective motivations and private actions' (Hay et al. 1994, p. 461). The problem is with 'Giddens' assertion that the transformation of intimacy epitomises the relationship between the global and the local . . . What is missing in this formulation is any recognition of just who is doing the transformation and how they are doing it' (Hay et al. 1994: 463).

Where difference is discussed is in postmodernist accounts, with their focus on fragmentation and local sites of global transformation (Lyotard 1984, Kroker and Kroker 1987). However, while opening up to analysis the complexities of social life in the late twentieth century, postmodernist positions too readily let go of the threads of modernity which, in our view, continue to tie individual actions into social relations based on gender, race, status and sexual orientation. Neither Giddens' ideal-typical 'pure relationship' nor postmodernism's customised sexual identities have much salience for the majority of people left to negotiate sexual encounters in the context of HIV and AIDS. What is needed is a theory of late modernity which can successfully incorporate feminist and other critical understandings of sexuality. Feminist work on the gendered nature of power and of sexual interaction (Jackson 1978, Holland *et al.* 1991), for example, has generated significant modifications to theoretical conceptions of the private realm. It might also provide the basis for a more nuanced and stratified understanding of the experience of risk than can be derived from the more general focus of Giddens and Beck alone.

For now the point is that, in respect of prevention, the risk represented by AIDS is necessarily different for different individuals in different places, even though there may be some connection between them. To return to our earlier example, the actual experience of being HIV positive will be very different for sex workers in the East and middle class women in the West. More fundamentally, the diversity of modes of transmission and of illness experience undermine the idea of AIDS as a single entity. AIDS has not established a commonality of interest or of identity among those affected by it. It will only be through developing ways of understanding the meanings which attach both to the risk and to the reality of AIDS at specific sites and through placing these in a global context that a sociology of AIDS might move beyond the confines of modernist understandings of the disease toward more reflexive interpretation.

Notes

1 Sex and disease have been associated at least since the emergence of syphilis in the fifteenth century. Their brief separation in the mid twentieth century has made their reconnection in the 1980s seem the more stark. In conjunction with new constructions of sexuality and of identity, this process of reassociation has become intrinsically linked to questions of personal choice and the individualisation of risk.
2 We understand modernity to be characterised by attempts at rational intervention in social life. Society is regulated by the bureaucratic apparatus of the state and by professional expertise. A core aim is to 'colonise the future', an idea adopted by Giddens (1991) but previously used by Sandberg (1977; see also Glennerster 1981). Among the distinguishing features of late modernity is a heightened sense of insecurity, fragility and risk. This calls modernity's precepts into question but also demands that they be applied more intensively.
3 Exploration of comparable issues such as these belongs to what has been described as the 'pre-history' of AIDS (Berridge and Strong 1992); for a discussion of Hepatitis B in the light of responses to AIDS, see Muraskin (1993).
4 The global range of policies is well documented in Misztal and Moss (1990) and Blaxter (1991).
5 Pollak draws a similar distinction between 'liberal' and 'coercive' policies (Pollak 1992). This dichotomy is not specific to AIDS, but is typical of historical responses to sexually transmitted diseases (see, for example, Weindling 1993).

6 Some groups represent greater risk than others, in accordance with a moralistic conception of guilt imputed in the transmission of HIV. Where gay men, prostitutes and drug users have been discriminated against, haemophiliacs have been compensated.

7 It is perhaps important to note that authoritarian prescriptions of this kind need not necessarily be understood as a form of state activity. Industrial and commercial organisations, both large and small, can be bureaucratic (and repressive) in their restrictions on employment, for example. Exclusion from housing and from access to health and life insurance, similarly, may take place in the private as much as the public sector.

8 Here, too, the market assumes a role, for example in the provision of condoms and in the dissemination of health education messages by sophisticated media, both public and commercial.

9 The discussion took place in response to media coverage of the case of a West Midlands man accused of deliberately infecting four women with the virus (*Guardian*, 16 December 1992).

10 Gerd Göckenjan notes that, in contrast to other grand social anxieties of the 1980s such as nuclear proliferation and the environment, concern about AIDS might be dissolved by personal behavioural change (Göckenjan 1987).

11 The notion of a linear trajectory may oversimplify a complex history. As Mildred Blaxter points out, 'Many countries' reaction has been cyclical, with periods of action and reaction, waves of concern followed by periods when the problem is down-played' (Blaxter 1991: 31).

12 For detail, see Street (1993); for a review of recent debate on the extent of heterosexual transmission, see Christie (1992).

13 Following a special debate at its annual meeting in July 1987, for example, the British Medical Association felt it to be within the bounds of ethical conduct for physicians, at their own discretion, to test for HIV without their patients' consent. The decision was reversed the following year as a result of the opposition to it expressed by leading members of the profession such as Michael Adler, specialist in genito-urinary medicine at the University College and Middlesex School of Medicine, and Donald Acheson, the Chief Medical Officer.

14 Communitarian responses to AIDS tend to have been limited to pre-existing groups with a strong sense of identity, such as gay men.

15 In an interesting parallel, Ronald Frankenberg discusses the regulation by adults of what is seen as uncontrolled adolescent sexuality and its relation to the prevention of HIV infection (Frankenberg 1992).

References

Aggleton, P. and Homans, H. (1987) *Educating about AIDS*. Bristol: National Health Service Training Authority.

Altenstetter, C. (1993) The whys and ways of European Community-wide responses to AIDS. Paper delivered to the Third Biennial International Conference of the European Community Studies Association, Washington, 27–29 May.

168   Sue Scott and Richard Freeman

Armstrong, D. (1993) Public health spaces and the fabrication of identity, *Sociology*, 27, 393–410.

Bardeleben, H., Reimann, B.W. and Schmidt, P. (1989) AIDS und das Problem der Prävention – Fakten und Fiktionen, *Journal für Sozialforschung*, 29, 97–128.

Bauman, Z. (1992) *Intimations of Postmodernity*. London: Routledge.

Beck, U. (1992) *Risk Society. Towards a New Modernity*. London: Sage.

Beck, U. (1994) The reinvention of politics: towards a theory of reflexive modernization. In Beck, U., Giddens, A. and Lash, S. *Reflexive Modernization. Politics, Tradition and Aesthetics in the Modern Social Order*. Cambridge: Polity.

Berridge, V. and Strong, P. (1992) AIDS policies in the United Kingdom: a preliminary analysis. In Fee, E. and Fox, D. (eds) *AIDS: The Making of a Chronic Disease*. Berkeley: University of California Press.

Blaxter, M. (1990) *Health and Lifestyles*. London: Tavistock/Routledge.

Blaxter, M. (1991) *AIDS: Worldwide Policies and Problems*. London: Office of Health Economics.

Bosk, C.L. and Frader, J. E. (1991) AIDS and its impact on medical work. The culture and politics of the shop floor. In Nelkin, D., Willis, D.P. and Parris, S.V. (eds) *A Disease of Society. Cultural and Institutional Responses to AIDS*. Cambridge: Cambridge University Press.

Canaris, U. (1988) Gesundheitspolitische Aspekte im Zusammenhang mit AIDS. In Korporal, J. and Malouschek, H. (eds) *Leben mit AIDS – mit AIDS leben*. Hamburg: ebv.

Christie, A. (1992) Shooting straight: ignorance and injustice, *Digest of Organizational Responses to HIV and AIDS*, 1, 8–11.

Connor, S. and Kingman, S. (1988) *The Search for the Virus: The Scientific Discovery of AIDS and the Quest for a Cure*. London: Penguin.

Coward, R. (1987) Sex after AIDS, *New Internationalist*, March, 8.

Day, P. and Klein, R. (1989) Interpreting the unexpected: the case of AIDS policy making in Britain, *Journal of Public Policy*, 9, 337–53.

Douglas, M. and Calvez, M. (1990) The self as risk-taker: a cultural theory of contagion in relation to AIDS, *Sociological Review*, 38, 445–64.

Fee, E. and Krieger, N. (1993) Thinking and rethinking AIDS: implications for health policy, *International Journal of Health Services*, 23, 323–46.

Ford, N. and Bowie, C. (1988) Sexually-related behaviour and AIDS education, *Education and Health*, 6, 86–8.

Foucault, M. (1978) *The History of Sexuality. Volume 1. An Introduction*. New York: Pantheon.

Fox, D.M. (1990) Chronic disease and disadvantage: the new politics of HIV infection, *Journal of Health Policy, Politics and Law*, 15, 341–55.

Fox, D.M., Day, P. and Klein, R. (1989) The power of professionalism: AIDS in Britain, Sweden and the United States, *Daedalus*, 118, 93–112.

Frankenberg, R. (1992) The other who is also the same: the relevance of epidemics in space and time for prevention of HIV infection, *International Journal of Health Services*, 22, 73–88.

Freeman, R. (1992) The idea of prevention: a critical review. In Scott, S., Williams, G., Platt, S. and Thomas, H. (eds) *Private Risks and Public Dangers*. Aldershot: Avebury.

Gagnon, J.H. and Simon, W. (1973) *Sexual Conduct*. London: Hutchinson.

Giddens, A.(1990) *The Consequences of Modernity*. Cambridge: Polity.

Giddens, A. (1991) *Modernity and Self Identity*. Cambridge: Polity.

Giddens, A. (1992) *The Transformation of Intimacy*. Cambridge: Polity.

Glennerster, H. (1981) From containment to conflict? Social planning in the seventies, *Journal of Social Policy*, 10, 31–52.

Göckenjan, G. (1987) AIDS-Politik. Von der Metapher zur Normalität, *Medizin, Mensch, Gesellschaft*, 12, 194–200.

Hay, C., O'Brien, M. and Penna, S. (1994) Giddens, modernity and self identity – the 'hollowing out' of social theory, *Arena*, New Series, 2, 45–75.

Holland, J., Ramazanoglu, C., Scott, S., Sharpe, S. and Thomson, R. (1990) *'Don't Die of Ignorance' – I Nearly Died of Embarrassment: Condoms in Context*. WRAP paper 2. London: Tufnell Press.

Holland, J., Ramazanoglu, C., Scott, S., Sharpe, S. and Thomson, R. (1991) *Pressure, Resistance, Empowerment: Young Women and the Negotiation of Safer Sex*. WRAP paper 6. London: Tufnell Press.

Holland, J., Ramazanoglu, C., Scott, S., Sharpe, S. and Thomson, R. (1992) Risk, power and the possibility of pleasure, *AIDS Care*, 4, 273–83.

Howson, A. (1995) *The Social Construction of the Cervix. Gender, Health and Citizenship*. Unpublished MS. University of Edinburgh, Department of Sociology.

Jackson, S. (1978) *The Social Construction of Female Sexuality*. London: Women's Research and Resource Centre.

Kane, S. (1992) The structure of AIDS intervention: a critique of categorical distinctions from national and transnational perspectives. Paper delivered to the sixth conference on Social Aspects of AIDS, South Bank Polytechnic, London, 9 May.

Kroker, A. and Kroker, M. (1987) *Body Invaders: Panic Sex in America*. Montreal: New World Perspectives.

Luhmann, N. (1986) *Love as Passion*. Cambridge: Polity.

Lyotard, J.F. (1984) *The Postmodern Condition: A Report on Knowledge*. Minneapolis: University of Minnesota Press.

Mann, J.M. (1991) Global AIDS: critical issues for prevention in the 1990s, *International Journal of Health Services*, 21, 553–9.

Misztal, B.A. and Moss, D. (eds) (1990) *Action on AIDS: National Policies in Comparative Perspective*. New York: Greenwood.

Muraskin, W. (1993) Hepatitis B as a model (and anti-model) for AIDS. In Berridge, V. and Strong, P. (eds) *AIDS and Contemporary History*. Cambridge: Cambridge University Press.

Pollak, M. (1992) Organizing the fight against AIDS. In Pollak, M., with Paicheler, G. and Pierret, J. (1992) *AIDS: A Problem for Sociological Research*. London: Sage.

Rosenbrock, R. (1986) *AIDS kann schneller besiegt werden. Gesundheitspolitik am Beispiel einer Infektionskrankheit*. Hamburg: VSA.

Sandberg, A. (1977) *The Limits to Democratic Planning*. Stockholm: Liberforlag.

Scott, S. and Williams, G. (1992) Introduction. In Scott, S., Williams, G., Platt, S. and Thomas, H. (eds) *Private Risks and Publilc Dangers*. Aldershot: Avebury.

170   Sue Scott and Richard Freeman

Seibel, W. (1989) The function of mellow weakness: nonprofit organizations as problem nonsolvers in Germany. In James, E. (ed) *The Nonprofit Sector in International Perspective. Studies in Comparative Culture and Policy.* New York: Oxford University Press.

Singer, L. (1993) *Erotic Welfare. Sexual Theory and Politics in the Age of Epidemic.* London: Routledge.

Small, N. (1988) Aids and social policy, *Critical Social Policy*, 7, 9–29.

Street, J. (1993) A fall in interest? British AIDS policy, 1986–1990. In Berridge, V. and Strong, P. (eds) *AIDS and Contemporary History.* Cambridge: Cambridge University Press.

Strong, P. and Berridge, V. (1990) No one knew anything: some issues in British AIDS policy. In Aggleton, P., Davies, P. and Hart, G. (eds) *AIDS: Individual, Cultural and Policy Dimensions.* Brighton: Falmer.

Weeks, J. (1981) *Sex, Politics and Society.* London: Longman.

Weeks, J. (1989) AIDS: the intellectual agenda. In Aggleton, P., Hart, G. and Davies, P. (eds) *AIDS: Social Representatioins, Social Practices.* Lewes: Falmer.

Weindling, P. (1993) The politics of international co-ordination to combat sexually transmitted diseases, 1900–1980s. In Berridge, V. and Strong, P. (eds) *AIDS and Contemporary History.* Cambridge; Cambridge University Press.

Wight, D. (1993) Constraints or cognition: factors affecting young men's practice of safer heterosexual sex. In Aggleton, P., Davies, P. and Hart, G. (eds) *AIDS: The Second Decade.* London: Falmer.

Willis, E. (1990) Does policy drive technology or technology drive policy? The politics of HIV testing. Paper delivered to the fifth conference on Social Aspects of AIDS, South Bank Polytechnic, London, March.

Willis, E. (1992) The social relations of HIV testing technology. In Scott, S., Williams, G., Platt, S. and Thomas, H. (eds) *Private Risks and Public Dangers.* Aldershot: Avebury.

Notes on Contributors

Paul Bissell is Research Associate in the Department of Pharmacy, University of Manchester. He is currently researching social aspects of the provision of pharmaceutical services.

Michael Bloor is Director of the Social Research Unit and is a Reader in the School of Social and Administrative Studies, University of Wales Cardiff. He was previously a Senior Research Scientist at the Medical Research Council's Medical Sociology Unit in Glasgow.

Phil Brown is Professor of Sociology at Brown University. His research interests are community responses to toxic wastes, race and class biases in the burden of environmental hazards, social movements in health and the environment, physician involvement in identifying environmentally caused disease, diagnostic issues in psychiatry, interaction in mental health settings, and theoretical models of the social construction of health and illness.

Simon Carter is a researcher at the MRC Medical Sociology Unit at the University of Glasgow. His research interests are in the areas of the sociology of risk and science, and social and health aspects of travel and tourism.

Richard Freeman is a Lecturer in European Politics at the University of Edinburgh. His doctoral research on the role of prevention in health policy and on policy responses to HIV and AIDS was done in Manchester and Cologne. His research interests lie in European social policy and in comparative health policy and politics.

Jonathan Gabe is a Senior Research Fellow at Royal Holloway, University of London. He has published widely in the areas of mental health, health care professions, health policy and the mass media and health. He is a co-editor of the journal *Sociology of Health and Illness*.

Anne Grinyer is a Tutorial Fellow in the School of Independent Studies at Lancaster University, where she obtained her PhD on science, policy and the public and the construction of risk around AIDS/HIV. Her academic interests include the sociology of scientific knowledge, medical sociology, and the public understanding of science.

Karen Lane is a mother of two. She was awarded her PhD from Adelaide University, South Australia. She has lived and taught in Germany, Holland and England and more recently returned to

Australia to Deakin University, Geelong. She lectures in the media and popular culture as well as health sociology.

David Pilgrim is currently Senior Research Fellow at the Health and Community Care Research Centre, School of Health Sciences, University of Liverpool. His main research interests are in the areas of mental health, community care and the sociology of professions.

Jennie Popay is Professor of Community Health and Director of the Public Health Research and Resource Centre, University of Salford. Her research interests include gender and social class, inequalities in health, the relationships between lay and professional knowledge, and the links between research, policy and practice.

Anne Rogers is Senior Research Fellow at the National Primary Care Research and Development Centre, University of Salford. Her current research interests are in lay knowledge and health services utilisation in the areas of mental health and population demand for primary health care services.

Sue Scott is a Senior Lecturer in Sociology in the Department of Applied Social Science at the University of Stirling. She was a member of the Women Risk and AIDS research team 1987–1993 and is now a member of a research team to investigate the processes and outcomes pertaining to sex education in Scottish schools. Her main research interests are in the sociology of sexuality and the body and in the methodology of social research.

Gareth Williams is Reader in Sociology at the Institute for Social Research and Assistant Director of the Public Health Research and Resource Centre, University of Salford. His research interests encompass the organisation and development of health services, lay perspectives on health, illness and health care, and chronic illness and disability.

Index